Arms and Ethnic Conflict

Arms and Ethnic Conflict

John Sislin and Frederic S. Pearson

ROWMAN & LITTLEFIELD PUBLISHERS, INC.
Lanham • Boulder • New York • Oxford

ROWMAN & LITTLEFIELD PUBLISHERS, INC.

Published in the United States of America
by Rowman & Littlefield Publishers, Inc.
4720 Boston Way, Lanham, Maryland 20706
www.rowmanlittlefield.com

12 Hid's Copse Road, Cumnor Hill, Oxford OX2 9JJ, England

British Library Cataloguing in Publication Information Available

Library of Congress Cataloging-in-Publication Data

Sislin, John, 1965-
    Arms and ethnic conflict / John Sislin and Frederic S. Pearson.
        p. cm.
    Includes bibliographical references and index.
    ISBN 0-8476-8854-2 (alk. paper) — ISBN 0-8476-8855-0 (pbk. : alk. paper)
        1. Defense industries—Political aspects. 2. Arms transfers—Political aspects.
    3. Ethnic conflict—Political aspects. 4. Security, International. 5. World politics—
    1989- I. Pearson, Frederic S. II. Title.

HD9743.A2 S57 2001
338.4'7355—dc21

                                                                        2001019019

Printed in the United States of America

♾ ™ The paper used in this publication meets the minimum requirements of American
National Standard for Information Sciences—Permanence of Paper for Printed Library
Materials, ANSI/NISO Z39.48–1992.

Contents

Figures

Tables

Preface

The harrowing scenes of carnage in Israel and the Palestinian territories in 2000 and 2001 represent a fundamental rationale for this book. To what extent do arms accumulations advance or retard the prospect for reasonable accommodation among conflicting ethnic communities? In the Middle East, a definitive peace agreement appeared tantalizingly within reach; indeed, in 1995 the basic outline of a detailed peace protocol, including supposedly intractable issues such as rights of refugees and control of Jerusalem, was reached. Unfortunately, though, Israeli Prime Minister Itzhak Rabin had not reviewed the draft when he was gunned down. Thus the peace process fell victim to the gun, in 1995 and again in 2000–2001, symbolically.

The importance of ethnic conflict has become unmistakable in the post–Cold War setting. It is perhaps the primary political challenge of our time. Thankfully it is receiving significant scholarly attention, but the aspect of armament in these conflicts often has been neglected. Perhaps that is because arms access in civil disputes is devilishly difficult to measure, elusive often by design as parties try to hide or camouflage their arsenals and sources. However, we felt that measurement and empirical analysis of this question deserved a concerted initial attempt. We hope at least to tease out the nuances of possible effects and consequences of arms acquisitions, leaving definitive studies of our suggestive findings to a later date when better data might be available or discovered through more exhaustive search routines.

In this analysis we proceed with open minds. While we instinctively deplore killing and destruction, and suspect arms levels as one primary contributor to those total casualties, we also realize that armed self-defense is a time-honored concept in law and politics. We want to see in practice whether situations are improved or worsened by arms acquisitions and under what circumstances one could expect one result or the other.

Generally we proceed from existing conflict theory, deriving logical expectations and then testing them to the extent possible. We try to be explicit about our assumptions, expectations, and measurement criteria so that others might assess the validity of our findings and conclusions. Our policy recommendations are guided by our analysis but guarded by the limitations of our data. We also adopt the classic research design model of Most and Starr (1989) in which they argue that one must ask both what causes something to happen and what accounts for its not happening. Therefore, in regard to ethnic violence, we look at outbreak, nonoccurrence, escalation, de-escalation, settlement failure, and settlement success. The reader might quarrel with our classifications, but he or she should be able to deduce our methods.

We wish to thank those who have helped and advised us in this difficult endeavor. Among them are Paul Beaver, D. Scott Bennett, David Carment, Joel Glassman, Ted Robert Gurr, Robert Harkavy, Patrick James, Michael Klare, David Kinsella, Edward Laurance, Roy Licklider, Lora Lumpe, Michael McGinnis, Marie Olson, Patrick O'Neil, Abdulahi Osman, Philip Schrodt, Joseph Smaldone, and Joseph Tenkorang. We also are extremely grateful to Jennifer Knerr and her fine staff and editors at Rowman & Littlefield for lending expertise to "make this read like a book." All these friends helped foster the study, but of course they are not responsible for our assertions or conclusions.

We also wish to thank our families, who endured the stresses of hurried writing schedules and calmed our nerves whenever possible. The "endgame" of writing a book can be as hectic and harried as the endgame of conflict settlement, and behavior in either case is not always as reasonable as it should be. They have our love and admiration.

Chapter One

Arms and Ethnic Conflict

In a November 1998 speech, U.S. Secretary of State Madeleine Albright pointed to a major emerging global policy problem: "The world is awash in cheap and deadly arms," she said. "The result of this is greater risk that minor incidents will produce not only bloody noses, but dead bodies, and that regional arms races will feed cycles of escalating conflict." She then alluded to the civil chaos in Albania that resulted in 1997 "when armory doors were thrown open and weapons spread like a rampaging disease throughout the country. The surge in crime, vigilante justice, and outright warfare brought Albania to the brink of collapse" (Albright 1999). She might also have warned that arms from Albania would find their way into nearby regional disputes as well, as they subsequently did in the Kosovo uprisings in Serbia.

The "rampaging disease" she mentioned in some measure threatens peace and stability in several regions of the world, and threatens to involve major powers both diplomatically and militarily, as seen in the NATO and Russian confrontation over Kosovo. Secretary Albright herself cited the human and economic costs of such an epidemic:

> This is a market that is bullish on death and bearish on the building blocks of a decent life. Consider that the warring parties in Afghanistan recently spent $200 million on weapons over a three-year period. For the same money, they could have built 400 rural hospitals to give health care to families who have never had it; or educated 200,000 Afghan young people from kindergarten through high school.
>
> In Angola over the past four years, enough money has been spent on bullets to kill every man, woman, and child ten times. But somehow, no one can find the resources to provide food for the young or medicine for the ill." (Albright, quoted in Lumpe 1999, 30)

The secretary went on to note changes in U.S. policy regarding the export of lethal "small arms" that do so much damage in ethnic conflict. She called for global standards and restraint on the supply of such weapons.

1

The United States indeed has long been the world's leading arms exporter, both at large and to developing states in particular. While U.S. exports have often consisted of "major" costly weapons for which profit margins are great, large supplies of smaller, more portable but lethal arms have been shipped as well. Since 1995, these have included 158,000 M-16A1 assault rifles to Bosnia, Israel, and the Philippines; 124,815 M-14 rifles primarily to the Baltic republics and Taiwan; 26,780 pistols to countries like Chile, Morocco, Bahrain, and the Philippines; 1,740 machine guns largely to Morocco and Bosnia; and 10,570 grenade launchers to, among others, Bahrain, Egypt, Greece, Israel, and Morocco (Lumpe 1999, 28). Many of these countries have been involved in internal or regional wars and disputes, and some can cite pressing security and self-defense needs. However, the overall effect of this armament remains largely unknown. Where do the arms end up, and with what impact on future violence or peace negotiations?

Clearly, Washington is not the only arms supplier to strife-ridden regions. Indeed, the so-called weapon of choice in ethnic disturbances from Liberia to Chechnya has been the simple, cheap, and ubiquitous AK-47 Kalashnikov assault rifle. Cash-starved former members of the East bloc have exported and reexported these rifles in abundance, allowing bands of roving youthful fighters in various countries to wreak devastation, sometimes of even genocidal proportions, on civilians and military alike. Similarly, Belgian Fabrique Nationale FN MAG machine guns are used in seventy-four countries; German Heckler & Koch HK21 machine guns in fourteen countries; Israeli Uzi and German HK MP5 submachine guns in forty-seven and forty-two countries, respectively; Belgian FN-FAL, German G-3, Israeli Galil, and Austrian AUG assault rifles in more than a dozen countries each; and Belgian FN35 and Italian Beretta M92/M34 pistols in thirty-five and fifteen countries, respectively (Renner 1999, 25).

It is easy to assume that such weaponry makes wars more likely to begin and worsen once under way. Yet there are contrary opinions about the effect of modern weaponry, ranging from assumptions that such equipment is inevitably destabilizing, to assumptions that it can protect the oppressed and stabilize politically charged situations (Brzoska and Pearson, 1994). The latter assumption revolves around versions of balance of power or deterrence thinking, familiar in international strategic studies, predicting that parties will be less likely to launch into violence if they face significantly armed opponents. It is, therefore, crucial to understand more precisely the likely effects of armament, particularly in the plethora of internal and ethnic wars that have sprung up globally since the end of the Cold War.

Military spending, strategic thought, and peacemaking efforts have long focused on international disputes and threats played out across state boundaries. The emergence or reemergence of domestic fighting in many countries after 1990 seemed to catch observers by surprise. While some expected a more peaceful era and budgetary "peace dividends" in the "New World Order" of diminished superpower rivalries, the world instead witnessed the outbreak of deadly civil wars, often infused with heavy ethnic hatred, fears, and resentments. Defense budgets leveled off or diminished for a time, but new "peacekeeping" or potential "war-fighting" responsibilities, as well as major power political and economic interests pointed toward a revival of military spending at least in the United States by 1999. Bosnia, Chechnya, and Rwanda—not the Persian Gulf War—became the proto-typical conflicts of the immediate post–Cold War era, although as the new century dawned, there were signs that the outbreak of new ethnic fighting might have peaked and begun to decline (Gurr, 2000a). Violence erupted for many reasons, including the breakup of larger states such as the Soviet Union and Yugoslavia, as well as the relaxation of limits that the two Cold War superpowers, in their mutual global competition, had placed on regional disputes. Most important, though, were the underlying grievances and discrimination perceived by various ethnic and political communities and factions, ranging from Angolans to Afghans.

Today's civil wars and domestic conflicts involve military preparations of various sorts. Although we occasionally hear of missiles, tanks, planes, and artillery being used in civil wars, small arms remain the prevalent weapons, acquired—sometimes illicitly or through government and private channels—by various warring groups or governing authorities. Indeed, one analyst finds that largely because of their low cost and widespread availability, "light weapons were the only arms used in 46 of 49 conflicts" since 1990 (Klare 1999a, 21). The variety of political and military effects associated with various levels of armament is apparent even in the following few examples:

- On January 4, 1997, the tension on Cyprus between Greek Cypriots and Turkish Cypriots grew when the Greek side announced that it was planning to acquire $426 million worth of Russian S-300 antiaircraft missiles.[1] Turkey responded that it would use military force if the missiles were deployed (Bohlen 1997, 2). Moreover, there was some concern that Turkey would not wait until deployment, and might consider carrying out a preemptive attack before the missiles could be made operational. On both sides, although the arms plans may have reflected underlying policy difficulties and frustrations at the slow pace of conflict settlement on Cyprus, they seemed to spark the potential for a new round of fighting on that volatile island, with the potential to draw in other NATO partners.

- In Angola during the mid- to late-1970s, U.S.-backed covert operations were designed to keep perceived Soviet allies from winning a too-easy victory. Thus, a destructive sequence unfolded. Forces of the dissident groups, National Union for the Total Independence of Angola (UNITA) and the National Front for the Liberation of Angola (FNLA), received just enough U.S. equipment from neighboring Zaire to harass the forces of the Popular Movement for the Liberation of Angola (MPLA), but not enough to allow a resounding victory. It was enough, however, to stimulate a counter-Soviet arms supply to MPLA, which included *kytusha* rockets that proved decisive in routing the Western- and South African-backed forces (Stockwell, 1978).

- The unwillingness of the Irish Republican Army (IRA) and certain Ulster Unionist groups to disarm and foreswear violence was a major obstacle delaying the advancement of the Northern Irish peace process. A central issue in the efforts to bring peace to Northern Ireland became the relationship of peace negotiations to disarmament talks. In the mid-1990s, it seemed as if the British government's position was that both talks had to occur in parallel, while Sinn Fein, the political arm of the IRA, for example, wanted the two issues separated. The whole question of what disarmament meant, what it symbolized, how—and the best time—to talk about it, ended up threatening the duration and stability of cease-fires and peace negotiations and caused the suspension of the new unified Northern Irish Assembly.

- In Bosnia, arms flows were treated as one useful policy option to bring the various parties to the peace table. Arms and training supplied to Muslim forces, after agonizing deliberation, may have facilitated a stalemate and contributed to a peace settlement, although the Serbs and Croats also may have achieved enough satisfactory territorial gains by that time to allow for a cease-fire. The United Nations had enacted an arms embargo on Yugoslavia as it crumbled on September 25, 1991—before Bosnia even declared its independence. The embargo worked to favor the Serbs, however, since they had access to former Yugoslav armed forces' equipment (Doherty, 1995). Finally allowing the Bosnians to obtain weapons in spite of the embargo strengthened them and made a negotiated settlement feasible, since the Serbs stood potentially to lose territory already acquired.

Thus, the effects of arms supplies during internal wars are complicated, evidently mixing with other political and psychological factors to determine the outbreak, the course, and the outcome of fighting. The mere flow or presence of arms in a country does not mean that ethnopolitical violence is necessarily imminent. Sometimes fighting might erupt without new arms infusions, and sometimes such infusions might not spark immediate violence. Arms acquisitions have been thought to affect the escalation of or result in a decisive turn in a conflict, as in the Angolan example, but also to facilitate de-escalation through forced negotiation, as in Bosnia. The Irish case also demonstrates that arms accumulation can create problems and is one key negotiating point for parties interested in bringing a conflict to an end.

Our overall thesis is that arms, by themselves, are neither necessary nor sufficient to start, escalate, de-escalate, or resolve a conflict. However, it is crucial to know which of these actions is most likely under certain political, economic, cultural, and military circumstances. Policy makers contemplating strategies such as those tried in Bosnia or Northern Ireland require better "data" than mere hunches and hopes before dispatching weapons or invoking disarmament or embargo schemes. Increasingly, there is an evident policy distinction to be made between short-term and long-term consequences, as in the effects of U.S. arms supplies to the Afghan "freedom fighters" in the 1980s. Though this aid assisted in defeating Soviet forces, reverberations are still being felt in Afghanistan's lingering civil war, in the reported reexport of arms to regional powers such as Iran, in the supposed terrorist role of former Afghan fighters such as Osama bin Laden, and in Russia's own domestic turmoil. Thus, it is imperative to develop better-informed policies on what to expect from arms shipments and sanctions in the midst of domestic turmoil, and the types of factors and strategies most likely to bring about certain desired or undesired outcomes.

We mainly confine our discussion in this volume to a subcategory of domestic fighting involving "ethnopolitical" warfare of the type so dramatically prevalent in the 1990s. Partly this is because of the unresolved nature of ethnic group claims to territory and status in many parts of the world, a fact hanging over, remarkably, since the end of the nineteenth century. The resolution of these claims represents a primary preoccupation for those interested in world order and justice in the early twenty-first century. Certainly the outraged reaction of Kurds to the arrest of their leader, Abdullah Ocalan, by Turkey in 1999, their attacks on European and African embassies implicated in his arrest, their acts of self-immolation and protest, and their leader's subsequent seeming cooperation with Turkish authorities surprised many who did not realize the multinational implications and political complications of ethnic struggle.

In addition, while many generalizations about armament apply both to civil wars in general and ethnopolitical wars in particular, the latter have been characterized by relatively well-developed theoretical and explanatory frameworks. These frameworks allow us to examine the relative impact of arms against a set of other causative factors. In general, the literature suggests that such wars are the outgrowth of persistent ethnically defined grievances seized upon by heroic, opportunistic, or ruthless leaders.

> In almost every case, unscrupulous and ambitious demagogues have sought power and/or wealth by arousing the ethnic prejudices of their kinfolk, forming militias and paramilitary bands, and conducting attacks on civilian targets—usually neighborhoods or villages inhabited by members of a different ethnic group. Although the fighters may espouse a particular ideology or religious dogma, ethnic hostility, poverty, and a craving for booty usually fuel these conflicts. (Klare 1999a, 19)

From the perspective of the fighters, of course, justice and liberation from the tyranny of ethnic oppressors require armed struggle. In this sense, today's ethnopolitical warfare is an extension of the process of nationalist liberation struggles begun and legitimized in the early nineteenth century, which then peaked in the 1960s and 1970s. This raises the perplexing question of when it is justified, as well as expedient, to arm such "oppressed peoples" and invoke some version of international law's "inherent right of self-defense." Repeatedly, groups rising in rebellion consider their demands just, while the governments they condemn consider them illegitimate and their tactics terrorist. The debate also centers on the role of state sovereignty in the evolving international system, that is, outside powers' entitlement to aid so-called oppressed minorities, and besieged governments sending troops to chase rebels into foreign sanctuaries. Turkish leaders, for example, refer to Kurds as "mountain Turks," and their warriors as terrorists; Turkish troops have pursued Kurdish warriors into neighboring Iraq, where ironically, as a result of the Gulf War of 1991, a protective zone for Kurds was enforced by Turkey's allies, the United States and the United Kingdom. Serbs use similar descriptions for the Kosovo Liberation Army (KLA), which received supplies from neighboring Albania. In such disputes, what happens to principles of sovereignty so fundamental to the state system we have known since the seventeenth century in which governments are presumed to have a local monopoly on political armament? What happens if the oppressed victims in turn perpetrate atrocities on their enemies, as seen repeatedly in the long and brutal histories of Rwanda and Burundi and in the Balkans? These and related compelling questions will be dealt with during the discussion of the impact of armament on the origin, course, and outcomes of ethnic wars.

ETHNOPOLITICAL CONFLICT DEFINED

An ethnic group is "a named human population with a myth of common ancestry, shared memories, and cultural elements; a link with a historic territory or homeland; and a measure of solidarity" (Smith 1993, 28–29). An "ethnopolitical group" is a politically active ethnic group (Gurr, 1993). However, when the press reports an attack by Kurds on a Turkish military outpost or a Basque bombing of Spanish facilities, presuming that the attack really took place, it does not necessarily mean all Kurds or Basques took part in or backed the action. The entire ethnic community need not be politically active; many ethnopolitical struggles involve only a fraction of the people belonging to a particular group. At times, subgroups or factions organize under particular platforms, agendas, or titles; hence, the Irish Republican Army (IRA), the Palestine Liberation Organization (PLO), and others have been known to splinter or spawn offshoots or rivals with different tactical and strategic perspectives and objectives. An extreme example of splintering occurred in Iraq where two main Kurdish groups arose during the 1990s: the Patriotic Union of Kurdistan (PUK) and the Kurdish Democratic Party (KDP), which at times have warred with each other and occasionally collaborated piecemeal with the central Iraqi authorities, rather than unite firmly against Baghdad.

Ethnic group grievances, often longstanding and perhaps covered over by years of relative social tolerance or repression, tend to rise to the surface given certain environmental conditions, and produce interethnic tensions. These tensions can in turn spawn specific disputes if the groups become politicized and take action to redress feelings of discrimination and deprivation. Fundamentally, ethnic conflict is about ethnic identity as it relates to nationality, power, or security, and can take

political form as a struggle for autonomy, legal reform, security guarant
nomic remedies, territory, or independence.

Among the environmental factors thought to drive ethnic tension, disputes, and eventually violence, are: (1) economic downturns, pitting one group against another in the job market; (2) the removal of outside controls (as when the Soviet Union disintegrated) or empires collapse; (3) migration or other changes in the relative population balance in a particular locale; and (4) political reforms such as changes in nationality laws, educational opportunities, or security guarantees (Van Evera, 1994). The validation of group identity is central to the psychology of the participants, as they may feel deprived of rights, status, and material benefits in comparison to other reference groups. Thus, ethnic groups fight for autonomy, political power, resources, self-determination, and cultural uniqueness. Identity lies at the heart of these conflicts (Rothman 1997).

The mere fact of a state's cultural heterogeneity, of course, need not imply violence. Social tensions might be funneled into legitimate political conflict and competition. Quebec is an example of a situation that has, in various phases, featured sporadic violence, but ultimately relies on political processes such as referenda and negotiations. However, sometimes ethnopolitical groups and/or governments do opt for systematic, organized rebellion and violence (Weede and Muller 1998).

Three forms of violent ethnopolitical conflict exist. Rebellion, a first type, entails political tension between the state and "ethno-national" groups living in a specific territory that seek to maintain their unique identity and are concerned about discrimination. In rebellion, such groups turn to violence to redress grievances or gain autonomy or independence. In a second form of confrontation, governments also can prompt or initiate fighting. Fearing ethnic groups' mobilization or simply seeking to maintain or consolidate the current power distribution, states might turn to military repression, among other tactics, to contain potential disruption and supposed threats to the status quo. Thus, in cases such as Tibet in China, the Baha'i in Iran, or the Shiites in Iraq, much of the violence is meted upon the ethnic group by the state, rather than the reverse. Finally, in the third type of conflict, when two or more ethnic groups view the political landscape within a state in zero-sum terms (where one side can only gain when the other loses), and when at least one of these groups has ambitions to advance its resources or power, *intergroup* violence might also erupt. Adding complexity to these factors is the role of outsiders, acting to aid some faction in the fighting, to contain the violence, or to take political advantage of the situation.

Although it sometimes seems to be a new phenomenon, ethnopolitical conflict has been a consistent facet of the world system in the twentieth century. Over the past fifty years, such conflicts generally have grown both in frequency and violence. While many of the world's ethnic groups possess a sense of security and live peacefully, ethnopolitical violence, where it occurs, is usually premised on perceived threats to group identity and produces significant death and disruption (Fearon and Laitin 1996).

During the early 1990s, ethnopolitical conflict seemed to occur with greater frequency than in the Cold War period from 1945 to 1989, as figure 1.1 shows (though we also note a downturn in warfare as the 1990s ended). One explanation for this upsurge was the Cold War's end. While the U.S.-Soviet competition brought great tension, it also brought a sense of predictability and stability to international affairs. The two superpowers engaged in both conflict instigation and conflict management, attempting to make sure that disputes did not get out of hand. Many smaller tensions among peoples were subordinated to or managed within the larger superpower context, although some ethnic conflicts, as in Vietnam, Azerbaijan, and Nicaragua, were exacerbated by superpower manipulation.

army Subrdin Subrding or managed

A second reason for the apparent rise in both the frequency of, and the interest in, ethnopolitical conflict lies in the concomitant decline of international war, particularly in the initial post–Cold War era of the 1990s. Only six international wars were fought in the early to mid-1990s, of which the most notable were the Iraq-Kuwait war in August 1990, the subsequent Gulf War between Iraq and a coalition of states during 1990–91, and a brief border war between Ecuador and Peru in 1995.[2] Conversely, over the same period, ninety-five internal wars were fought, many over issues of ethnicity and nationalism. These included the catastrophic violence in Afghanistan, Bosnia-Herzegovina, Chechnya, Peru, Rwanda, Somalia, Sri Lanka, Liberia, and Sudan. In the latter half of the 1990s, one major international war would be added:

Figure 1.1   Armed Conflicts for Self-Determination, 1956–2000

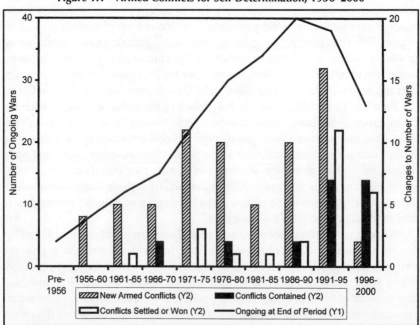

Source: From Table 2, "Armed Conflicts for Self-Determination and their Outcomes, 1956–2000," in Ted Robert Gurr, Monty G. Marshall, and Deepa Khosla, *Peace and Conflict 2001: A Global Survey of Armed Conflicts, Self-Determination Movements, and Democracy* (College Park, Md.: Center for International Development and Conflict Management, University of Maryland, 2000), 16. Reprinted with permission.

Ethiopia and Eritrea, and there was additionally low-intensity, but still quite fighting between India and Pakistan. Meanwhile, the peace process in Angol\ ᴗ.ᴜκe down by 1998 and fighting resumed. Fighting also erupted in the Democratic Republic of the Congo (formerly Zaire) (Sollenberg, Wallensteen, and Jato, 1999).

The decline of international warfare, which may or may not be long lasting, is generally explained as the result of one or more critical factors. According to Mueller (1989), war between the major powers of the Western world, such as the United States, Japan, Germany, Britain, and France, is becoming obsolescent. (See also the critique of this view by Ray [1989].) This supposedly is largely because the idea of warfare is fading in the developed world, much as dueling and slavery have largely faded from human history (indications are that slavery merely has taken on new forms). Nevertheless, like the "end of history" (Fukuyama 1992), which supposedly accompanied the end of the Cold War, this conclusion seems premature, especially in light of continued border tensions in some regions—Ethiopia and Eritrea, and India and Pakistan, for example—and various states' regional ambitions and arms races.

A more specific explanation for the recent lack of international fighting is that "democratic" states, while quite war-prone vis-à-vis authoritarian states, seldom if ever fight *each other* (Doyle 1995; Brown, Lynn-Jones, and Miller 1996). This is supposedly due to the presence of strong international and domestic norms as well as important international institutions and interdependencies, all of which operate to make democracies turn to other forms of politics, aside from war, to achieve their mutual goals and resolve their mutual disputes. As more and more states in the world move toward democracy, violent forms of conflict should recede, unless, of course, the democratic peace was mainly a statistical anomaly, subject to erosion as more combinations of hostile democracies become possible (McLaughlin Mitchell, Gates, and Hegre 1999).

One interesting offshoot of the democratic peace thesis is the possibility of its application to domestic and civil wars. One might argue that democracies such as Canada are better equipped to solve their internal ethnic tensions through political and legal channels than on the battlefield. Of course, pluralistic democracy did not preclude a bloody ethnically related civil war in nineteenth-century America, nor continued unrest in Spain, Britain, and Israel during the 1990s. Indeed, one branch of theory argues that democracies are likely to see more open political conflict because of a tolerance for protest and group interest articulation. This leads to the hypothesis of an inverted "U-shaped" relationship, in which undemocratic and fully democratic countries see the least violence, since the former represses it and the latter offers positive grounds for resolving tensions. It is "intermediate" democracies or "semi-democracies" that are thought to be the most violence-prone (Ellingsen 2000, 237, 243).

Finally, economics also might play a role in the decline of both international and domestic warfare (McMillan 1997; Ellingsen 2000). In an increasingly global economy, warfare is so disruptive that any outbreak of major fighting brings on economic costs to the participants (even to the winner) that outweigh benefits to be gained through acts of war. Again though, with history as a guide, highly interdependent trading states have fought brutal wars with each other, for example, Russia and Germany in World War I, and the United States and Japan in World War II. Likewise, while hate crimes and acts of sporadic terrorism and ethnopolitical skirmishes occur in advanced economies such as Spain, France, or Britain, they seem less prevalent or sustained in such states than in the developing world, particularly during times of prosperity. "In fact, the risk of incidence of domestic conflict in a country with a low socioeconomic level is 85 times higher than that of a country with a high socioeconomic level" (Ellingsen 2000, 243).

Whatever the explanation, as a result of the general decline of international war, internal conflict, much of it ethnopolitical in nature, has taken on more prominence, albeit with some signs that trends toward global democratization and economic interdependence might have dampened such disputes as well. Taken together, such conflicts have produced millions of casualties—by some estimates, between 3.5 and 4.3 million people from the time of the upswing in the 1980s through 1993 (Gurr 1994). Those figures continue to rise. In Sudan alone, fighting between government forces and southern ethnic factions over the past seventeen years has resulted in nearly two million deaths (Associated Press 2000). Millions of refugees, about 25 or 28 million according to some estimates (Gurr 1994), have fled ethnopolitical fighting. According to *Refworld,* the Web site of the United Nations High Commissioner for Refugees, the UNHCR was concerned about 21.5 million people as of January 1, 1999, including refugees, asylum seekers, returned refugees, and internally displaced persons, among others. This figure represents about 1 out of every 280 people on earth. As the situation in Rwanda and Zaire/Democratic Republic of the Congo demonstrated, not only do these people face the dangers of war but refugees can also put incredible economic and political strains on neighboring or host countries. The most deadly conflicts of the mid-1990s are listed in table 1.1.

Table 1.1   The Ten Deadliest Ethnic Conflicts Since 1970[a]

	Conflict	Casualties	Current Hostilities Began
1/2.	Afghanistan	1,200,000	1978
	Sudan	1,200,000	1983
3.	Rwanda	800,000	1990
4/5.	Angola	600,000[b]	1975/92[c]
	Iraq	600,000	1980
6.	Somalia	400,000	1990
7.	Burundi	200,000	1972/93[c]
8.	Bosnia-Herzegovina	195,000[b]	1992
9.	Indonesia	170,000[b]	1975/84[c]
10.	Liberia	150,000	1989

Source: Brown (1996, 4–7).
[a]Brown presents a list of all types of internal conflicts. We only consider ethnopolitical conflicts drawn from that list.
[b]Brown presents a range of casualties; we present the average number here.
[c]Different years indicate breaks in the conflict, as in Angola and Burundi, or different ethnic groups involved, as in Indonesia.

By the end of the decade, Sudan would surge ahead with, as noted above, almost two million deaths. Jongman (1999/2000) suggests that subsequent fighting would keep Afghanistan in second place with a death toll of 1.5 million; casualties in Rwanda also have risen to between 825,000 and 1 million. Jongman estimates that both Burundi and Indonesia have seen more than 200,000 killed—in the case of Burundi, just since 1993. Unfortunately, some of these figures will continue to rise. Some of these states had vast arms imports (Afghanistan and Indonesia, for example), while others (Rwanda and Burundi, for example), though receiving weapons, had far lower import levels.

Additionally, economic disruption caused by such fighting is substantial. As noted by Secretary Albright, government military spending can undermine economic development by taking resources that could otherwise be used to support investment or welfare programs. In Sri Lanka for example, lost output between 1983 and 1988 from the war between the government and ethnic Tamils was estimated to be at least $1.5 billion, equivalent to about one-fifth of the Sri Lankan gross domestic product (GDP) (Grobar and Gnanaselvam 1993). A recent estimate by the Institute of Policy Studies in Colombo put the economic cost of the war at 170 percent of Sri Lanka's 1996 GDP (Sri Lanka 1999). Likewise, by 1986, the conflict between the Angolan government and UNITA, which began in 1975, had cost that government about $15 billion (Meldrum 1987). Articles in the Russian press detailed the costs of the Chechen conflict for the Russian government, which totaled trillions of rubles at the most economically inopportune time imaginable. Subsequent efforts to rebuild Chechnya also were thought to be in the trillions. Former Russian Vice President Oleg Davydov blamed the war for delaying Russia's entry into the Council of Europe and for a loss of $1.5 billion. Russia's government pension fund, a shaky social security safety net, would prove insufficient as well, after funds were diverted from it to cover the costs of the war (Illarionov 1996).

Ethnopolitical conflicts can foster political instability both within a country and among countries that have an interest in the conflict or are dragged into it. Violence can bring down governments and strain foreign relations, as it did among the NATO allies over what to do (and who should do it) regarding places such as Bosnia and Kosovo. Finally, ethnopolitical conflicts wreak environmental havoc, for example, with land mines that continue to kill and injure as a final legacy of the violence, and with fighting that prevents land from being reclaimed for agricultural uses and destroys natural resources and habitat. Famine has been one product of the Sudanese civil war, raging since 1983. Fighting produces refugees who flee rather than cultivate land; the result is starvation, compounded when fighting prevents aid from reaching those who need it (McKinley 1998). The Lebanese civil war of the 1980s also led to a corrupt, drug-based economy with a heavy emphasis on smuggling.

Clearly not all of this damage is a function of armament per se; in Rwanda it was clear that hateful and fearful people could be conditioned and coerced (with guns and grenades, see Boutwell and Klare 2000, 48) into mass killing armed with only the most primitive implements—spears and machetes, for example. Yet

...dvanced armaments facilitate faster killing with potentially greater ...for the spread of violence. It is much easier to kill defenseless civil-...... e with primitive implements such as machetes than to kill professional or paraprofessional soldiers and militia that way. For ultimate political victory, substantial arms caches are generally thought necessary. This brings us to the question of the role of arms in fueling ethnic fighting.

ARMS AND CONFLICT

As evident from the previous section, ethnopolitical conflict is part of a larger process. Underlying the conflict process are intercommunal tensions over issues of identity, which can lead to violence in one form or another. The onset of violence, or initial escalation, is the first of three phases through which ethnopolitical wars develop. Once initiated, violence might further escalate or de-escalate, or oscillate through a series of discreet escalations or de-escalations. Finally, wars eventually come to an end, and when the violence stops, either through one-sided victories, interim cease-fires, exhaustion, or final agreements, the underlying grievances might or might not have been resolved. Hence, renewed violence remains a possibility in many instances (Licklider 1995).

Existing theories of ethnopolitical violence often focus on these distinct dispute phases. As noted by Gurr and Harff (1994, 77–78), "there is no comprehensive and widely accepted theory of the causes and consequences of ethnopolitical conflict. Rather, there are approaches and hypotheses that seek to explain particular aspects." If, for example, one suspects that arms transfers to a violence-prone region might be an early warning indicator of war, then one should focus on arms transfers to countries that have yet to experience the outbreak of violence to assess the role of arms as a catalyst for violence. Every dispute has a beginning, middle, and end, difficult as they might be to designate with precision; it is easiest to see the effect of arms (or other causative factors) by looking at each major stage of conflict separately, recognizing of course that one phase affects the next.

Initiation of violence or rebellion often involves the realization by some group that it is systematically disadvantaged relative to others in society, and that there is little likelihood of an institutional remedy on the horizon. Persistent deprivation can lead to a formal articulation of grievances, and generally, since authorities or other groups are expected to resist these at least initially, an additional discrepancy arises: between demands and reform. Reform often is a step or two behind and when satisfaction is not achieved, violence can be somewhat of a last resort (Gurr 1993 and 2000b). The amazing aspect of this process is how people with bitter historical experiences at each other's hands often coexist for long periods in relative tranquility, even intermarrying and establishing commercial ties, and then suddenly turn on each other or on the government. Governmental authorities can be influential in bringing about such outbursts either through direct instigation of groups for political gain, through slow or aborted reforms, or through harsh and repressive tactics pitting groups against each other. Many of the recent cases of "ethnic cleansing" or "ethnocide" in places such as the Balkans, central Africa, the former Soviet Union, and Indonesia, for example, have featured rampaging ethnically based "militia" armed or encouraged by certain governmental authorities. Economic downturns, nationalistic political campaigns, foreign interference, scapegoating, propaganda campaigns, and discriminatory legislation can be the catalysts of violence, particularly when ambitious or unscrupulous leaders manipulate perceived fears, placing the blame for an ethnic group's disadvantages on another group or on government policy (Brown 1996; Kaufman 1996; Van Evera 1994). Both governments and ethnopolitical leaders can be looking for scapegoats.

The course of the conflict once it crystallizes into a violent dispute over specific grievances depends on a variety of factors. The dispute might escalate or expand in some way in terms of violence intensity (casualties or rate of killing), geographic scope, or internationalization (involvement of outside parties). It might continue at a relatively constant pace, or it might de-escalate and find solution in reform, agreement, or enforced settlement (by a victor or outside intervention). A combination of factors can determine this course, including outcomes of fighting, the pace of political negotiations for a settlement, outside pressure (sanctions and incentives), exhaustion, or institutional reform.

One key factor in both violence outbreak and escalation is the amount of "fuel" provided for fighting, in terms of available manpower, resources, and weaponry (including spare parts). For example, in Morocco's war in the former Western Sahara, Polisario guerrillas started out with battlefield victories until the Moroccan government, with U.S. support, in desperation built huge sand walls and enclosed fortifications that effectively shut down the Polisario's quick-hitting use of mobile firepower. In Burma, successful negotiations between the more than one dozen rebel armies and the Burmese government, mostly in the 1990s, followed by the disbanding of those armies, seemed to put to rest the decades-long civil war, even as discontent and arms availability persisted. American pressure and Anglo-Irish talks played a key role in bringing about Northern Irish peace accords in the 1990s; these outside pressures were especially significant in that resources for arms reputedly had long come from outside sources. On the other hand, Serb, Croat, and Bosnian arms acquisition, both from domestic capture and foreign suppliers, and the Talibaan's capture of arms in Afghanistan, appeared to allow the initiation and expansion of fighting in these countries. Ultimately, then, there is a propensity within each conflict to expand or contract in relation both to developing political, economic, and social circumstances and to the availability of key resources such as arms (Craft 1999).

The final phase of war, termination of violence, depends in part on the continued provision of fuel, in the form of personnel, funding, arms, ammunition, and spare parts, but is not conditioned solely by access to weapons or the exhaustion of the combatants. Perhaps more than in other forms of warfare, national and physical survival itself is perceived to be at stake in ethnic violence, as in the Chechen struggle against Russia. Attendant emotional and patriotic appeals can be greater with ethnic conflict than even in the case of cross-border fighting, as fear of attack, or even of genocide, along with accumulated grievances mount. This increases the chances of resistance or escalation of extremist terrorist acts, even in the face of overwhelming odds, severe deprivation, or arms deficiencies, and of prolonged resistance to settlements deemed unreliable or unstable. Even the combined weight of the NATO powers could not immediately deliver a Kosovo peace agreement according to a predetermined timetable in February 1999.

As noted previously, some ethnic conflict is characterized by large-scale fighting involving heavy weapons, on the order of the Bosnian war, while most disputes are fought on a smaller, though potentially quite brutal scale. The scope of the international arms market and indigenous production capabilities in the developing world all but assure governments' access to a range of weapons. Ethnic groups also can and do acquire arms from varied sources both distant (often major powers or regional neighbors) and proximate (acquisition on the spot from raids on armories or battlefield capture) (Karp 1993; Neuman 1995; Wood and Peleman, 1999). In one bizarre twist in 1997, for example, the Zairian government evidently armed exiled Hutus in Zaire to fight on behalf of the corrupt Zairian army against largely ethnic Tutsi rebels in Zaire's border provinces. In 1998, the new leader of the newly named Democratic Republic of the Congo, Laurent Kabila, found himself engaged in battle with the very people whom he had armed a year earlier.

One example of the resourcefulness of groups in conflict involves the Liberation Tigers of Tamil Eelam (LTTE) in Sri Lanka, also called the Tamil Tigers, who have been quite adept at acquiring arms to prolong their multiyear independence struggle. They have bought weapons from dealers in Hong Kong, Singapore, Lebanon, and Cyprus, from corrupt military officers in Thailand and Burma, and directly from governments, including those of Ukraine, Bulgaria, and North Korea (Bonner 1998a). Reportedly, they obtained money for these purchases in part from donations by Tamils living abroad, in Canada and the United Kingdom. Group ties also can be forged with organized criminal groups. Supposedly, the LTTE might even have managed to obtain a few of the American-made Stinger missiles shipped by Washington to mujahedin rebels in Afghanistan during the 1980s.

In the Rwandan conflict, arms also were acquired in a variety of ways, involving more than a dozen supplier states (Goose and Smyth 1994; Boutwell and Klare 2000). The Rwandan government received arms from Egypt, France, South Africa, and the United States. The Tutsi-dominated Rwandan Patriotic Front (RPF) acquired light but lethal weapons from Uganda, China, and defeated government troops, and apparently made purchases funded by Rwandan exiles from independent arms dealers in Africa and Western Europe (Human Rights Watch, 1994a). What ethnopolitical groups cannot steal or purchase from private dealers, often they can buy on the open market from any number of states (provided funds are available), or they can acquire arms with the aid of friendly factions or gov-

ernments (and their intelligence services) abroad, or simply pick the
battlefield.

As mentioned earlier, there is a political controversy about whether s
arms to ethnic disputants inevitably destabilizes, or can be used to stabilize   conflict situation and promote peace settlements. This debate came to the fore most
vividly as the American government tried to decide what to do about the Bosnian
miasma. Should an arms embargo apply to all parties to the fighting and to their
nearby ethnic kin in neighboring states, or should arms be supplied selectively to
one side or another in order to promote strategic balance and even stalemate that
might lead to fruitful negotiations? The notion of stalemate is particularly pertinent, since some conflict studies specialists have argued that "ripeness" for settlement is a key to the success of mediation and negotiation attempts (Kleiboer 1994;
Zartman 1995a). Presumably ripeness means readiness, and readiness to negotiate
can be due to factors such as exhaustion and need satisfaction, as well as to rational
readings that battlefield prospects have dimmed. One way to make dimming
prospects clear is to change the balance of forces to the detriment of the party or
parties resisting a settlement. In choosing to arm one side to redress military imbal-
ances and promote stalemate, of course, one does not know the precise mix or
proper balance to insure that the weaker side, now strengthened, does not gain so
much confidence that it is no longer ready, or "ripe" to negotiate. These uncertainties represent key policy and analytical puzzles about the actual, and about the
rightful, effects of arms supplies before and during violent episodes.

During the Cold War period, a large literature was generated on the relationship
between arms and war. It dealt with such issues as interstate arms races and power
balances, and the political and economic relationship between the arms supplier
and arms recipient (see Brzoska and Pearson 1994). Such perspectives make good
sense in the context of an international arms market where *states* are the sellers
and the buyers, and the fighting occurs among them. This state-centric focus was
reinforced by the annual publication of yearbooks containing officially reported or
estimated arms imports and exports, agreements and deliveries, as published by
American, British, and Swedish sources, as well as most recently by the United
Nations.[3] However, these data compilations, themselves sometimes confined only
to reports of major or heavy weapons transfers, largely ignore the vital role of arms
traffic affecting internal wars. Only recently have researchers begun to analyze
closely the role of "light" or "small" arms in such contexts (See Boutwell, Klare,
and Reed 1995; Boutwell and Klare 1999; Karp 1993; Klare and Andersen 1996;
and Singh 1995).

Unfortunately, prior to domestic violence breaking out, researchers seldom map
arms flows to ethnic groups or regions of tension. Thus, there are few reports of
potentially destabilizing arms accumulations. Once the conflict is under way, there
are numerous obstacles to identifying patterns in arms acquisitions—obstacles
such as battlefield access, group hostility, and government reticence. Local media,
foreign correspondents, and academic researchers often are censored regarding

conflict, and local sources can be biased either in favor of the ethnic group or the government.

Finally, compounding such matters is the fact that many arms are shipped on the black or gray markets, involving smuggling or falsified documents that make tracking shipments purposefully difficult (Klare and Anderson 1996; Naylor 1995). Frequent stops and surreptitious routes can be utilized to throw off customs inspectors and avoid hostile territories and ports. It is thus difficult to count weapons acquired illegally. Of course, small arms, particularly rifles or ammunition, are plentifully available and can be exceedingly difficult to track or account for no matter how they are shipped.

In part, because of such data problems, the role of arms in ethnic conflict has remained relatively unclear, as researchers have been restricted in both the breadth and the depth of their analyses across time. Thus, it has been difficult to reconcile seemingly contradictory trends. Sometimes, for example, as we have noted, ethnopolitical violence has occurred without much sophisticated weaponry. For example, in Mexico's Chiapas state, the rebels of the Zapatista National Liberation Army (EZLN), in their ambitious effort to advance the rights of indigenous and poverty-stricken peoples, reportedly had so few weapons to use initially that they resorted to toy guns (*Keesings* 1994, 39809). Despite their reputedly formidable weapon stocks, on the other hand, most of the damage caused by the IRA in Northern Ireland and Britain and by the Basque separatist organization, ETA (Euskadi Ta Askatasuna), in Spain has featured just a few weapons (mainly homemade bombs). The results were sporadic (though causing heavy property damage) and relatively limited, but shocking in terms of casualties.

The lesson suggested by these examples is that the role of arms varies and can be quite complex and situational. A systematic review of cases of various sorts, that is, war and no war, with and without arms, is necessary to improve the predictive power of explanations and the success of conflict resolution strategies. The general lack of understanding of the role of various types and levels of armament has impeded positive, consistent policy reform on management of ethnopolitical conflict. States, groups, and dealers transfer arms often with little thought of their impact on long-term events and arms agglomerations either in the state in question or in the surrounding region, which explains in part how U.S. forces ended up facing American-made weapons in Somalia and the Persian Gulf (Hartung 1995b).

Seldom are there serious calls or timely steps to stop guns flowing into a regional ethnic conflict, despite the lip service paid to arms control or the imposition of arms embargoes. A major power arms embargo of the Ethiopian-Eritrean war did not come until the year 2000, after two years of combat. A peace agreement was arranged shortly thereafter. Certainly the perceived urgency of measures to stem both covert and overt flows of small arms is nowhere comparable to that expressed about "weapons of mass destruction," despite the fact that most casualties worldwide come from rifles, small artillery, and mines, and not from nerve gas, anthrax, or nuclear weapons. Indeed, according to Michael Renner, senior researcher at the Worldwatch Institute, small arms are responsible for "as much as 90 percent of the casualties in current regional conflicts and civil wars" (Erwin 1998, 32).[4] Embargoes are enacted, then conspicuously ignored, as in Bosnia and Rwanda. More than $2 million worth of arms were sent to Bosnia during the "embargo" period (Klare 1996). Arms were allowed to flow from the Middle East and other sources to Bosnian Muslims toward the end of that war, even as Congress debated a formal or partial end of the embargo.

This leaves us with several central questions about the role of armament in ethnopolitical disputes.

1. What arms do ethnic groups possess and where do they obtain them?

In news photographs and in video clips on television news programs, fighters in civil wars brandish rifles, fire artillery, and are even seen driving captured tanks or military vehicles. Before we attempt to understand and assess the impact of arms on ethnopolitical wars, taking stock of the arms held by fighting or conflicting groups is necessary. While government arms inventories can be reconstructed from public information compiled in annual yearbooks such as the U.S. *World Military Expenditures and Arms Transfers* compilations, a systematic presentation of the weapons acquired and used by ethnic groups is lacking, as is an estimate of that portion of governmental arms devoted to domestic conflict. Because of the clandestine and obscure nature of such arms shipments, the data-gathering task is extremely challenging and difficult.

2. Under what circumstances do arms produce or contribute to the *initiation* of ethnic conflict?

It has long been argued that arms acquired by one actor can bring on violence either because the actor becomes emboldened or because other actors fear the buildup and take preemptive military action. This line of reasoning also might hold in cases of internal conflicts. In particular, one wonders whether inflow of arms is a reliable predictor or "early warning indicator" of impending violence and rebellion. This is not a foregone conclusion, since groups might act out of frustration rather than force calculations, or already possess stockpiled or hidden arms caches acquired much earlier.

3. In what ways might arms fuel *ongoing* violence?

Can an infusion of arms to one side, or lack of weapons or related supplies lead directly to escalation or de-escalation of fighting? Once a domestic war is under way, further arms acquisitions might produce positive or negative effects on the conflict's development. In 1987, the Indian army intervened in Sri Lanka in an effort to manage the dispute between the Sri Lankan government and the Tamil Tigers. The war's expansion by the Tamils, facilitated by growing access to arms in part channeled by or through sections of India, seemed to heighten concerns in New Delhi, leading to a futile Indian intervention and thus causing a further critical expansion of fighting. In this sense, arms transfers might be an early indicator of subsequent outside military intervention in a domestic dispute.

In addition, arms infusions to the Sri Lankan government permitted major attacks on LTTE outposts and allowed the war to continue for years despite military setbacks, as new weapons compensated for battlefield losses.

On the other hand, the decisive Cuban intervention in Angola, as well as South Africa's failed intervention there, influenced the ways in which arms were used and to what effect, and had major regional consequences, such as the fall of South Africa's apartheid regime. In some instances arms flows also appear to *follow* combat escalations, to replace weapons destroyed or lost in the fighting.

4. Do arms flows facilitate or hinder efforts to *resolve* ethnopolitical violence and conflict?

Adding arms to a war, in the appropriate circumstances, might end it. For example, arms acquired by one side, especially by a superior side in an asymmetrical relationship, could produce an expansion of the fighting as that side gains victory. The war might end, although differently, if arms are given to the weaker side, creating a balance or stalemate. On the other hand, adding arms to a conflict might inflame the situation, causing one or both sides to continue fighting and to resist what they see as untenable settlements.

5. What is the effect of arms infusions on the likelihood and success of *third-party* efforts to resolve the conflict?

Peacekeeping and peacemaking operations by international organizations such as the United Nations, and regional institutions such as the Organization of American States (OAS), Economic Community of West African States (ECOWAS), the Organization of Security and Cooperation in Europe (OSCE), and NATO are becoming more imperative yet remain expensive (though not as expensive as intractable wars) and politically tense. Controversies abound about political mandates and contributions of personnel and material to such endeavors. The costs of unilateral state intervention, particularly with military force, also frequently are quite high. If arms transfers raise the costs and dangers of third-party intervention, for example by empowering local groups to fight the intervenors, then multilateral peacekeeping itself becomes less feasible, either because fewer parties will join in or because success becomes more problematic.

6. Finally, what steps can be taken vis-à-vis arms *policies* and arms control to prevent, mitigate, or resolve ethnopolitical conflict?

Leaving aside the problems of improving ethnic relations and reducing tensions causing ethnic conflict, there are a number of possible steps that could remove arms from the conflict equation. One approach is arms control. For example, in countries experiencing civil war, arms sometimes flow through porous borders. Strengthening border controls could slow such flows, but represents a massive logistical and political challenge. A second approach is disarmament. Incentives or sanctions that remove guns from the combatants' hands might de-escalate conflicts or prevent further bloodshed, as well as reassure the parties about their security from attack. However, sanctions are notoriously leaky, and questions of "justice in war" also arise when parties are denied the potential of "self-defense" or when sovereignty is breached. Nevertheless, calls for greater "transparency" of arms flows in order to expose dangers and facilitate early warning could be another important form of conflict management in civil wars.

BENEFITS OF EXAMINING
ARMAMENT EFFECTS

Two advances can be realized by examining the role of arms in ethnopolitical conflict and more rigorously determining the consequences of arms flows for such fighting. The first benefit is that it helps policy makers to be more effective in dealing with or managing disputes. A second benefit is that students and observers come to know more about the prospect and the course of ethnopolitical conflicts.

As ethnic and identity conflict has become a larger concern of the international community, theorists and political leaders have grappled with the possible positive (deterrence or self-defense) and negative (escalation or regional spread) effects of arms shipments, particularly for groups suffering human rights violations. In places as disparate as the Congo and Indonesia, the United Nations and other organizations also have discovered that they are not fully prepared to confront the challenges brought on by armed ethnic fighting. This is evident when one examines the issue of arms control for light weapons.

In the early 1990s, former UN Secretary-General Boutros Boutros-Gali came up with the concept of "micro-disarmament," that is, disarmament of groups in conflict. Efforts to disarm ethnic groups are not new—the Indians tried to disarm the Tamil Tigers in 1987—but the approach, which sounds good in theory, can be difficult to apply in practice. Gun buy-back programs, more rigorous customs enforcement, technology transfer restrictions, Interpol cross-border law enforcement, border blockades, and embargoes are further strategies proposed or applied in various cases. Many of these depend on favorable logistical circumstances (such as easily accessed borders) and consensus among potential suppliers and bordering states. Efforts at small-arms control or micro-disarmament have met with a range of outcomes: in cases such as Kosovo and Northern Ireland, the ethnopolitical group would not readily hand over arms—skillful diplomacy had to devise inventive alternatives with only partial indications of success. Other attempts have found groups turning in outdated weapons for money to buy better ones. However, in some cases, as in Bangladesh, where ethnopolitical groups in the Chittagong Hill Tracts, evidently more trusting of the government, did disarm, the approach has been more feasible. The intermittent success of arms control and disarmament measures reflects the fact that policy makers are only just beginning to understand the dynamics of ethnic conflict and the impact of guns.

Some leaders in the international community are interested in selling arms, or in providing them for purposes of defense, while others strive to control arms flows to ethnopolitical conflicts. States have taken mixed and complicated approaches to arms policy making. Washington, Moscow, Paris, Bonn, or Beijing might be interested in stemming arms transfers to a particular crisis zone at one time, and equally interested in dispatching arms at another time—they are, after all, the world's leading arms exporters. Shortly after the Ethiopian-Eritrean peace settlement in 2000, voices were heard in Washington advocating the lifting of embargo and resumption of weapon sales to these impoverished lands. The probability of gaining full unanimity for sanctions is usually remote, but full coverage might not be necessary to choke off the fighting in particular wars. We need to know much more about which suppliers, close at hand or at a distance, are crucial for the fueling of a war.

While ethnopolitical groups acquire arms in a variety of ways, states remain a primary and critical source of weapons; the most secure form of resupply is via states, and the main guarantee of sophisticated arms and spare parts is from states. Indeed, governmental arms supplies might be needed if ethnopolitical groups are to have a chance of drawing out a conflict long enough to force the local government to offer concessions.

Just as arms suppliers, such as the Americans, British, French, Chinese, and Russians, have reasons for transferring arms to governments, so too do suppliers— both states and private dealers—have a series of rationales for transferring weapons to substate actors. One such reason is economic: to make money. In many East European countries and in some of the former Soviet republics, particularly Russia, Belarus, and the Ukraine, defense exports are a valued export commodity that can fetch significant profits for cash-strapped governments and industries. A second reason to transfer arms can be political–military in nature and focuses on one of several related security calculations. One reason to supply relates to ethnic kinship. Armenians have tended to support kinship groups living in the Nagorno-Karabakh region of Azerbaijan, and, of course, the mosaic can become even more complex as expatriate Armenians living in the United States, for example, enter into the fray. Tamils in India have supported Tamil rebels in Sri Lanka. Sometimes money is supplied, which in turn finances arms purchases in international channels; sometimes arms are sent directly. The goal is to promote the security of the ethnic or kinship community.

A related political reason for a state to supply arms is that it is trying to undermine the stability of another state and thereby increase its own felt security. Pakistan's support of various ethnic groups in India and particularly Kashmir, and India's support of rebels in the Bangladesh independence war are examples of this rationale. Sometimes neighboring states attempt simultaneously to destabilize each other. In this event, the situation can very much resemble Cold War proxy wars supported by the United States and the Soviet Union (as seen in the reversal of patron roles in Ethiopia and Somalia during the 1970s and 1980s). For example, Uganda armed the Sudan Peoples Liberation Army (SPLA) guerrillas in Sudan, and the Sudanese government turned around and armed rebels fighting in the northern part of Uganda. Likewise, Iran and Iraq armed Kurdish groups fighting for autonomy in each other's territory. One variation on this theme involves arming the foes of international opponents, as seen, for example, when Libya supplied the IRA and rebels in West Africa, presumably to weaken the West's global and regional influence while strengthening its own regional footing.

A final political reason to supply arms to internal wars is to acquire various forms of influence. Iranian arms to Bosnian Muslims in the mid-1990s apparently were designed in part to provide political inroads for Tehran. All in all, arms might be used to shape the nature of the fighting or its outcome, but are also used in a larger sense to affect politics in states and regions undergoing conflict.

For many years, researchers have been studying the international arms trade, but that trade and its consequences are changing today. Thus, we must reorient our examination of the arms trade, not to stop studying sales of arms between governments, but to extend research toward trade and traffic in small arms and among subnational actors, such as organized ethnic groups. While multiple factors influence the course of conflicts, leaving arms out of the equation gives an inadequate picture of the ethnic conflict process.

CONCLUSION

In the following chapter, we examine the prevalence and pattern of armament in ethnic disputes. Arms are very easy for ethnic groups and governments alike to acquire; indeed, they represent in themselves a prevalent and persistent form of currency and barter in the international political economy (Pearson 1994). We discuss the types of arms each side might acquire and the sources for those arms, and we address important data problems and approaches as well. In chapters 3 through 5, we examine the impact of arms on each phase of ethnopolitical violence (to answer the second through fifth questions listed above). In each case, we believe that arms interact with other factors to push a conflict in one direction or another. Among the methodologies used to answer these questions are both case studies and aggregate compilations of data over many cases during the Cold War and post–Cold War periods. It is our contention that though there are always estimation problems in acquiring quantitative data on arms transfers (see Krause 1992; Brzoska and Olson 1987; Brzoska and Pearson 1994; Pearson 1994), and even more problems when dealing with nonstate actors' arms acquisitions, innovative approaches and cross-references can produce reasonable estimates and suggestive initial patterns and findings. These are then supplemented by more in-depth analyses of specific illustrative cases in which arms acquisitions or denials have played a telling role.

Finally, in the last chapter, we offer a series of policy recommendations to address the negative consequences of arms flows, including increased violence potential. These recommendations are designed to improve the efficacy of arms control and disarmament measures by suggesting when such efforts are appropriate, and what appropriate efforts would look like. Policy makers are confronted by a growing array of internal war scenarios in which peacekeeping or peacemaking depends at least in part on disarmament and controlling arms traffic. We are at the infant stage in devising means for doing so, but the framework of alternatives and possible policy approaches is coming clear. Since arms play an integral role in all aspects of ethnic conflict, our understanding can only be enhanced by focusing first on arms as they affect the outbreak, then the escalation, and finally, the management of violent disputes.

NOTES

1. All dollar amounts in this text are U.S. currency unless otherwise specified.

2. The six international wars conducted during the period from 1989 to 1996 were Iraq-Kuwait (1990–91); India-Pakistan (an intermediate and intermittent armed clash during the 1990s); Cameroon-Nigeria (a territorial dispute during 1996); Mauritania-Senegal (a territorial dispute during 1989–90); Ecuador-Peru (a territorial dispute during 1995); and the 1989 U.S. military intervention in Panama. Of these, only the Iraq-Kuwait dispute would meet the widely used quantitative requirement to be classed as a "war": the occurrence of at least 1,000 battle-related deaths per year (Wallensteen and Sollenberg 1997).

3. See publications of the U.S. Congressional Research Service and the Arms Control and Disarmament Agency, such as *World Military Expenditures and Arms Trade*; Britain's International Institute for Strategic Studies (IISS), which publishes, for example, *The World Military Balance*; the Stockholm International Peace Research Institute, such as the annual *SIPRI Yearbook*; and the *UN Register of Conventional Arms*. American publications use U.S. government data, Swedish and British sources generate their own information through case analysis, and the United Nations presents country self-reports of exports and imports.

4. For an excellent study of the effect of arms on the role of civilians in conflict, see ICRC (International Committee of the Red Cross) (1999).

Chapter Two

The Diffusion of Arms

In 1993, the United Nations initiated a process reminiscent of one begun by the League of Nations decades earlier. In an effort to prevent "destabilizing" arms accumulations, it began publishing an annual register of global arms transfers, the *UN Register of Conventional Arms,* based on voluntary reports by supplying and receiving states.[1] The *Register* was an attempt to institutionalize the principle of "transparency" in arms reporting, on the theory that publishing records would help diminish perceived threats by providing "early" or timely warning of dangerous buildups. In the process, of course, questions were raised about the adequacy of the count (some states—albeit fewer than first feared—refused to report) and its comprehensiveness (only certain classes of armament were included). While the UN register improved overall awareness of arms movements, it raised new questions about what arms are crucial to war making and about reexports and "opaque" (less than transparent) transactions (Laurance, Wezeman, and Wulf 1993). In this chapter, we look more specifically at the various classes and combinations of weapons thought crucial to ethnopolitical warfare.

The notion of arms distribution is, of course, a very broad concept, referring to a variety of weapons and related or potentially useful military equipment, supplies, and even training. Arms "transfers" generally can refer to sales, gifts, aid, loans, or logistical support from government or private (companies, groups) suppliers. Transfers can be measured either in terms of number of weapons shipped or in monetary value, and can be counted according to when the *agreement* takes place or when the *shipment* actually arrives (the latter being a more difficult measurement task).

Obviously also, there can be much confusion over what is meant by "arms" themselves. One of the most comprehensive definitions of the term is found in the annual compilations of military data, the *World Military Expenditures and Arms*

Transfers yearbooks, released by the U.S. Arms Control and Disarmament Agency (ACDA), which defines arms subject to transfer as:

> military equipment, usually referred to as "conventional," including weapons of war, parts thereof, ammunition, support equipment, and other commodities designed for military use. Among the items included are tactical guided missiles and rockets, military aircraft, naval vessels, armored and nonarmored military vehicles, communications and electronic equipment, artillery, infantry weapons, small arms, ammunition, other ordnance, parachutes, and uniforms. Dual use equipment, which can have application in both military and civilian sectors, is included when its primary mission is identified as military. (ACDA 1996, 183)

Since pickup trucks have been militarily useful in several civil wars, one may quibble with the stipulation in the last sentence, but the basic definition is sound.

All of these types of weapons and equipment can find their way into ethnopolitical conflict. Cases such as Rwanda might give the false impression that the larger conventional arms, such as tanks and combat aircraft are used solely by governments, while ethnopolitical groups only rely on small arms. Though this picture is accurate in many such wars, in a significant number of cases, major conventional arms are employed on both sides. The Chechens used captured Russian tanks against the Russians, and the Polisario of Western Sahara used tanks against the Moroccan government. The mujahedin in Afghanistan used heavy artillery. Aircraft is generally the one category in which governments have the presumptive monopoly, as pilots are scarce even for governments in many developing countries, and advanced aircraft often scarcer. Few members of an opposition or rebel group would be able to fly combat aircraft, unless employing mercenaries, but several ethnopolitical groups have obtained and used surface-to-air missiles, as for example in Serbia and Sri Lanka, to counter the state's advantage in air power.

Much of the literature on the arms trade has focused on "major" conventional weapons—a rather well-defined category of armament including artillery and infantry equipment, aircraft and missiles, and naval boats and ships. These weapons generally are the easiest to track and are the focus of established arms databases, such as the UN *Register* (see, for example, Gerner 1983; Catrina 1994). However, Karp (1995) argues that the focus on major armaments is now outdated and ill suited to the study of civil and internal wars because of changes in the international arms trade and in the type of fighting witnessed today.

THE ARMS TRADE TODAY

Several key changes since the end of the Cold War seem to be affecting domestic conflict and ethnopolitical wars. In the twentieth century, the arms trade has undergone three phases, interspersed with two transformations: World War II and the end of the Cold War.[2] The first half of the twentieth century saw the "Merchants of Death" era, when, generally, surplus arms were sold by governments, while, more sensationally, relatively advanced equipment was offered by private and often colorful arms dealers (see Pearson 1994). Unregulated arms sales were considered of sufficient menace as to warrant an international arms-trade register under the auspices of the League of Nations.

After World War II, the nature of the market began to change. The primary arms suppliers and primary purchasers became governments. The dominant suppliers were the United States and the Soviet Union whose greatest exports were to the countries of NATO and the Warsaw Pact. Aside from these two main alliances, most arms were imported by the emerging nations in the developing world, which were searching for security while also becoming proxies in the superpower struggle. The principal arms-importing region was the Middle East, partly for reasons of regional international warfare and partly because of petroleum trade revenues. The scope of the market grew dramatically to a high point in 1987. Klare (1995) terms this period the "proliferation model," in which increasingly sophisticated arms were developed in the advanced industrial countries and then transferred in often lucrative deals (with highly polished government marketing efforts), or for less money in the interest of Cold War competition, to the Third World. Over time, some less-developed countries began making weapons or weapon components as well, sometimes as the result of major power arms embargoes (as in the United Kingdom-United States embargo during the initial Arab-Israeli dispute, and subsequently in South Africa, India, and Chile).

The end of the Cold War again changed the nature of the arms market, although there is some uncertainty still about the extent and direction of the changes, especially since major powers like the United States and Russia are still prime arms distributors (Hartung 1995a; Khripunov 1999; Lumpe 1999). Overall, the market has contracted somewhat, declining from 1987 through 1994. In 1995, however, it began to rebound possibly as a result of the Persian Gulf War, concerns about the future of ethnic conflicts and peacekeeping requirements, export pressure in the former East bloc, and, ultimately, NATO expansion. Judging from the most current data available, global arms imports seem to be leveling off to around $22 billion to $23 billion per year (see figure 2.1). Most arms exports continue to go to the Middle East and Asia. It is indicative of the importance of *small arms* that Africa, which imports the least amount of *major* conventional arms, has the largest number of regional violent conflicts. Mergers of defense industries in the West, combined with the at least temporary eclipse of some "second-tier suppliers" in the developing world, have reduced the number of exporting companies. However, the Soviet and Czech breakups also have added new export sources, such as the independent Ukraine, Belarus, and Slovakia, as well as other former Soviet allies free to sell on their own (Castle and Musah 1998).[3]

**Figure 2.1   Imports of Major Conventional Arms during the 1990s,
in Constant 1990 $U.S. Million**

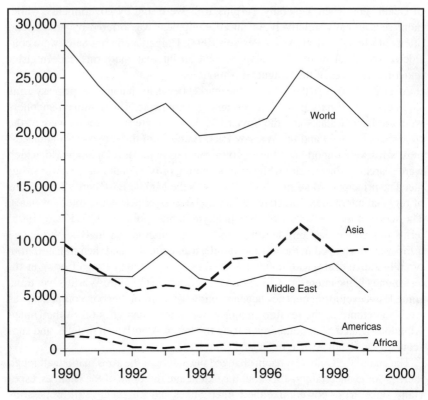

Source: Based on data from SIPRI (2000), Appendix 7B.1.

   The motives for selling or transferring arms have changed somewhat as well.
Ideological incentives, if they were ever primary over power calculations, are all
but gone, replaced by mainly economic incentives, including the urgent need for
revenue of many former "Second World" states', and conditioned by ethnic and
regional power balancing. The NATO bloc, along with the Chinese and Russians,
still maintain certain strategic concerns. The United States continues to assert a
global police role along with an oft expressed concern about arms getting into the
"wrong hands," and treats arms transfers as part of the strategy of power balancing and supposed economic liberalization and political democratization. Apart
from economic incentives, states such as China still appear willing to ship arms
abroad to undermine the dominance of other major powers such as the United
States. While there is concern about arming and subsequently disarming ethnopolitical rivals in destabilizing situations, many barriers to international weapons
traffic have been lifted.

Opposing the trend toward liberalized arms traffic is the fact
superpower would previously dispatch arms to a country facing
other superpower, such symmetry no longer need occur. There a
term guaranteed "supplier-patron" commitments. The United State ⎯⎯
other major powers also have become more concerned with the emerging supply
of potentially destabilizing equipment and weapons in the hands of terrorists and
"rogue states." The list of sensitive items ranges from the chemical-bacteriological-
nuclear domain to more advanced missiles and weapon delivery systems, and to
advanced conventional technology. Revenue-starved and nominally revolutionary regimes such as North Korea and Iran are suspected of developing proto-high
technology weapons for export. They sometimes used foreign-bought components, as from the USSR or China. This added horizontal (spread) and vertical
(sophistication) weapon proliferation potential, combined with a revitalized economic rationale pushing sales, produced something of a buyer's market for arms,
although governments of less-developed states are hard pressed to afford cash
purchases.

One other potential market change concerns so-called inhumane weapons and
the campaign by nongovernmental organizations (NGO) and some medium-sized
states to eradicate them. Thus, land mines have come under a partial global-man-
ufacture-and-use ban; key major (e.g., the United States) and regional (e.g., Israel)
powers have refrained for military reasons from signing the treaty even as they
pledge to restrict reliance and access to these weapons.

Finally, as noted in chapter 1, the nature of warfare also has changed. In the
post–Cold War era, heavy arms may be somewhat less relevant than light weapons
to the types of internal conflicts that have emerged. Although there are plenty of
suppliers for major equipment, and countries continue to purchase major conventional weapons, as seen in large U.S. sales to Egypt and Gulf states in 1999, much
of the weaponry used today is of the smaller variety.

MEASURING ARMS IN CONFLICT

At this point, we define two basic types of armament, which might be employed
by ethnic groups and states militarily. First, we define "major conventional
weapons." This definition is most often associated with the analysis and research
produced by SIPRI, which tracks such items as aircraft, armored vehicles,
artillery, guidance and radar systems, missiles, and warships, and has been using
this definition of major conventional arms to compile one of the main standard
sources of arms trade data. A newer, alternative definition, which is in many ways
similar to SIPRI's approach, is the politically generated definition of major arms
used in the *UN Register of Conventional Arms*. Codified by a group of experts in
1991, and sensitive to what would be politically acceptable, the *Register* divides
major conventional weapons into seven basic categories, as seen in table 2.1.

Table 2.1   Major Conventional Arms as Defined by the United Nations

1. Battle Tanks: Tracked or wheeled self-propelled armoured fighting vehicles with high cross-country mobility and a high level of self-protection, weighing at least 16.5 metric tonnes unladen weight, with a high muzzle velocity direct fire main gun of at least 75 millimetres calibre.
2. Armoured Combat Vehicles: Tracked, semi-tracked or wheeled self-propelled vehicles, with armoured protection and cross-country capability, either: (a) designed and equipped to transport a squad of four or more infantrymen, or (b) armed with an integral or ogranic weapons of at least 12.5 millimetres calibre or a missile launcher.
3. Large Calibre Artillery Systems: Guns, howitzers, artillery pieces, combining the characteristics of a gun or a howitzer, mortars or mulitple-launch rocket systems, capable of engaging surface targets by delivering primarily indirect fire, with a calibre of 100 millimetres and above.
4. Combat Aircraft: Fixed-wing or variable-geometry wing aircraft designed, equipped or modified to engage targets by employing guided missiles, unguided rockets, bombs, guns, cannons, or other weapons of destruction, including versions of these aircraft which perform specialized electronic warfare, suppression of air defence or reconnaissance missions. The term "combat aircraft" does not include primarily trainer aircraft, unless designed, equipped or modified as described above.
5. Attack Helicopters: Rotary-wing aircraft designed, equipped or modified to engage targets by employing guided or unguided anti-armour, air-to-surface, or air-to-air weapons and equipped with an integrated fire control and aiming system for these weapons, including versions of these aircraft which perform specialized reconnaissance or electronic warfare missions.
6. Warships: Vessels or submarines armed and equipped for military use with a standard displacement of 750 metric tonnes or above, and those with a standard displacement of less than 750 metric tonnes, equipped for launching missiles with a range of at least 25 kilometers or torpedoes with similar range.
7. Missiles and Missile Launchers: Guided or unguided rockets, ballistic or cruise missiles capable of delivering a warhead or weapon of destruction to a range of at least 25 kilometers, and means designed or modified specifically for launching such missiles or rockets, if not covered by categories I through VI. For the purpose of the Register, this category:
   a. Also includes remotely-piloted vehicles with the characteristics for missiles as defined above;
   b. Does not include ground-to-air missiles.

Source: United Nations General Assembly (1992).

Governments have access to the range of major arms and normally acquire some weapons from each of the United Nation's seven categories. Ethnic groups also come into possession of some of this equipment from time to time, particularly battle tanks, armored combat vehicles, and artillery. As we will see below, however, while a group obtains major weapons to use against a government or perhaps another ethnopolitical faction, a state normally acquires arms for a variety of reasons, including both internal and external threat perception, considerations of prestige, alliance relations, and "bureaucratic politics." This fact complicates the assessment of motive in arms acquisitions, since some of those acquisitions may not be salient to internal ethnic tensions.

As noted, "light arms" have become an emerging focus of the arms trade literature, particularly as applied to domestic warfare, though a commonly accepted definition of the term is only just recently coming into being. A definition of such weapons may be grounded in political sensibilities, military–technical specifications, or even guided by data availability. Years ago, the United States Army defined "small arms" as comprising anything up to 60 caliber. Subsequently, equipment such as recoilless rifles and mobile rocket launchers joined the ranks (Howe 1981, 16). Karp (1995) has suggested alternative definitions, based on three different foundations. First, small arms might be defined by elimination—that is, for example, they are weapons *excluded* from the existing SIPRI data sets or the *UN Register,* which focus only on *major* weapons.[4] Second, conceptually small arms might be those lethal items, such as pistols and grenades, which can be *carried* by a soldier; this might be called the "portability" definition of light arms. The third definition builds on the second by including weapons that can be carried in a light vehicle. This definition blurs the distinction somewhat between light and heavy arms, but in Karp's view, it is more accurate "from a military and political perspective" (Karp 1995).

Beginning with a very broad definition that takes into account such implements as machetes, the United Nations has defined small arms as "any means of lethality other than the sheer use of physical force. In this sense, small arms need not be manufactured and may not even be seen as weapons until so used e.g. sticks, stones, fire, water" (Rana 1995, 2). Most definitions and studies, however, tend to focus on manufactured weapons. According to the United Nation's definition, manufactured small arms, also known as light weapons, are conventional arms that can be carried by an individual or on a light vehicle. Small arms thus include: revolvers and self-loading pistols, submachine guns, rifles, machine guns, grenades, fuel air explosives, mines, and antitank weapons. This definition corresponds to Karp's third definition, which is the one we employ in our analysis.

The distinction between the so-called major conventional arms on the one hand, and small arms, portable arms, or light weapons on the other, remains important for at least two reasons.[5] First, different types of weapons may produce different consequences. For example, light arms and heavy weapons might give rise to different intensities of violence and related physical damage. While conflicts generally limited to small arms can produce significant casualties, heavy arms have the potential for substantial killing and collateral damage over wider areas in less time. Heavier weapons also might allow a warring party to "win" a war decisively, while reliance on small arms might only lead to prolonged fighting (Karp 1993 and 1995). Second, data on different types of weapons vary in terms of coverage and quality. As noted above, data on heavy weapons imports by governments tend to be plentiful, if not always totally reliable (sources still tend to disagree); heavy weapons acquired by ethnic groups are much easier to spot than small-arms acquisitions.

In order to test propositions about the varied effects of armament on internal war, we have generated a sample of ethnic conflicts under way in the mid-1990s, looking at the type of armament acquired and employed in various circumstances. This allows us to be more systematic in identifying the effects of armament than heretofore possible using only case study approaches, though we also supplement our analyses with case studies to make up for deficiencies in the data themselves. Clearly, data collection requires some decisions about the way to measure the flow of arms and their impact, and those decisions bear some preliminary explanation and discussion.

The two primary dimensions of arms acquisition by ethnic groups concern the types of arms they acquire and the methods used to acquire them. In examining the patterns, various characteristics of arms transfers can be studied (Sherwin and Laurance 1979). Quantitative analyses of arms acquisitions at the state level have often used the monetary value of imported or exported arms as an operational definition of an "arms acquisition" or an "arms transfer." This is partly the result of the availability of precisely this type of data, as collected by the ACDA, SIPRI, or the International Institute of Strategic Studies (IISS). However, this measure is not applicable at the intrastate level, because for most ethnic conflicts, the value of the arms acquired cannot be determined. Affixing a price to an arms shipment is difficult when the source or quantity of arms is unknown or when the quality (for example, new versus secondhand) is uncertain. A review of the literature reveals only scattered statements of value concerning the conflicts we examined. In one case, UNITA rebels in Angola were thought to have acquired an estimated $250 million in arms from the United States between 1986 and 1991 and $80 million in arms annually from South Africa during 1986–92, while exchanging an estimated $200 million in diamonds for arms with Zaire in 1993 (Beaver 1994; Hartung 1995b; Mathiak 1995). Additionally, ethnic militia in Bosnia were thought to be spending $1 billion annually during their conflict (Klare 1995). It might be possible to track a government's shipments to recipients in another state, but without official records and the status of the arms, valuations would be mainly guesswork. Thus, the shipment would be at best an indication of the supplier's policy priorities (see Hartung 1995).

Therefore, we focus our attention on two more discernible characteristics of arms: type of arms acquired (hopefully but problematically including the number of weapons) and methods and circumstances of acquisition. The first basic dimension of arms is whether they are light or heavy weapons. Anecdotal evidence from prior studies (Karp 1993) suggests that many, perhaps the majority, of ethnic conflicts are fought with only light arms. A second dimension focuses on the *sources* of arms. We suggest three broad distinctions: *domestic procurement, indigenous production, and importation.* Domestic procurement differs from indigenous production in that in the former case, arms are present in finished form (often acquired or stolen from government armories or on the battlefield), while in the latter, they are manufactured, modified, or remanufactured.

In terms of importation, one could hypothesize that ethnic groups are more likely to have multiple suppliers than are governments. While we could use the state where the arms originated as a shorthand marker for arms' origin, the actual supplier is often a defense firm or some other nonstate actor, including terrorist or political groups, secondhand dealers, or smugglers. Indeed, the Pakistani government reportedly privatized arms shipments to Kashmir in order to conceal its role in the uprisings there over the years (Neuman 1995).

A further hypothesis concerning importation considers the geographic distance between the original suppliers and the recipients. Once the suppliers are identified, it is straightforward to determine if they are contiguous, regional, or extraregional actors relative to the state undergoing the conflict. One might predict that the difficulty of arms acquisition at great distances would mean that most arms are procured just across or near the borders themselves. However, groups and suppliers also might try to cover their arms transfer tracks by arranging a large number of transshipment points between the original supplier and the final destination. This could involve many states at quite a distance.

Data

A variety of sources were searched to identify information on types and methods of arms acquisitions. Clearly, data on arms acquisition are much more developed and complete for states than for armed groups, but we delve into the arms traffic for both. For states, we use four main compilations of arms information, those of ACDA, SIPRI, IISS, and the United Nations. ACDA's *World Military Expenditures and Arms Transfers* covers both developed and developing countries beginning in 1963, with data generally ending about three years before the publication date. Annual imports and exports of arms are presented in millions of U.S. dollars. As noted above, ACDA uses a very broad definition of arms, including small arms. Unfortunately, there is no way to specify a dollar figure just for the small-arms component. Therefore, while we can determine the annual imports for a country like Peru, we do not know how much of Peru's arms imports were devoted to small arms and how much went for heavy weapons.[6]

Overall, ACDA data on arms transfers to governments are well accepted and often used in quantitative analyses by arms trade scholars, but two problems persist. One is that computing the value of non-American arms (particularly Soviet/Russian arms) can be difficult, and politically influenced. A second problem concerns concatenation of the data. Since each volume covers about ten years, to identify arms imports for a country for the entire period of coverage, for example, from 1963–95, means using data from several volumes. Sometimes the estimates for imports vary from volume to volume. The standard approach in constructing long-time series of data using ACDA as a source is to start with the most recent volume and then fill in with the next most recent volume(s).

In SIPRI's *World Armaments and Disarmament,* much of the data on conventional arms focuses on Third World countries, with coverage dating to 1951. SIPRI's data on conventional arms are different from ACDA's in two important respects: first, SIPRI collects information on *major* conventional weapons and thus has a more restricted operational definition of arms; second, SIPRI identifies agreements and deliveries of actual pieces of equipment, not just the value of that equipment.

The IISS annual yearbook, *The Military Balance,* identifies the organization, quantity, and types of weapons, both heavy and light, in a country's military arsenal. As with ACDA, almost all countries in the world are covered, but the compilation only dates to about 1970. It allows conclusions about the weapons present, but not necessarily about each shipment.

Members of the United Nations created the *Register* to promote confidence building and perhaps encourage restraint among the member states, in addition to providing early warning of destabilizing and excessive arms buildups. Each year since that time, an average number of about eighty-five states submits some information to the *Register* concerning their major arms imports and exports. These figures include the major arms exporters and capture much of the international arms trade, although only approximately half of United Nations members participate. The inclusion of both export and import reports allows verification of reported shipments. The *Register's* coverage is not as broad as the other three sources, there are as yet only a few years of annual reports.

Like SIPRI, and as noted in table 2.1, the *Register* focuses on actual deliveries of seven specific classes of heavy weapons in the prior year. Thus, the data are very up-to-date. However, the specificity of reports varies. For example, in the spring of 1997, the U.S. submission included a note that it had exported seven combat aircraft to Finland in 1996. However, American submissions are notorious for not giving more detail than merely the category of weapon. In this case, the type of aircraft was not specified, and it was left to Finland to report that it had received nine, not seven F-18 fighter jets.[7]

In our government arms data compilations, we mainly relied on ACDA and SIPRI reports, using the other sources for substantiation. We pose two major caveats at the outset, however. First, as noted already, states acquire arms for many reasons, only one of which is for use in domestic conflict. Hypothetically, Israel might import $500 million in arms in a year, of which a small amount represents arms primarily for "internal security." Conversely, Angola might import only a few million dollars in arms, with almost all of it devoted to domestic security. Thus, relying solely on dollar values or even numbers of weapons, without taking into account various uses for arms and the scale of government military involvement at home and abroad, can produce misleading results. SIPRI's data can be helpful in this regard. By selecting a type of weapon often used in internal conflict, such as armored personnel carriers or combat helicopters, the data on government arms might be refined a bit. However, this is an imprecise estimation procedure at best. Ultimately, all sources of governmental arms data are a bit coarser than scholars would like.

A second problem concerns the correlation or relatio.
sitions and arms use. A key assumption in much of the
warfare is that government arms acquisitions either spark o.
The problem here is that most governments acquire arms acr.
eral armament might increase governmental confidence in its n
in fighting against an ethnic rebellion, authorities might use w
years or even decades before. It is difficult to argue a direct ca.   .ction
between arms and warfare in such cases. We might find an instance   .ere a government buys arms for several years in a row, then does not do so for a few years,
while the ethnopolitical violence occurs in the interim. The relation between government arms acquisitions and holdings and rebel group strategies also needs careful exploration. Thus, timing and time lags need to be considered throughout the
analysis.

When delving into minority group armaments, we used additional supplementary sources. *Keesing's Record of World Events, Jane's Defence Weekly,* and *Military and Arms Trade News* (a newsletter and on-line service that extracts articles
from a variety of global military sources and news wires) were searched for the
mid-1990s. If these sources did not yield a substantial amount of information about
a specific conflict, we examined a mix of scholarly and news articles. Two points
must be stressed regarding this effort. First, the search was meant to be representative of only one type of available information sources on arms possessed by ethnic groups, that is, open-source media reports. Second, many of the reports come
from a relatively small set of overseas correspondents and official statements by
the local press or government. This means that caution must be taken so that precision is not mistaken for accuracy: ten reports each indicating that Pakistan is
arming Kashmiris could all stem from a single source, which might or might not
be correct. While we believe our limited search is more comprehensive than previous accounts, and will produce robust results, a broader data search is likely to
add more information to the overall picture of arms flows into and out of civil wars.

Our sample of ethnic conflicts is drawn from existing data on violent ethnopolitical disputes going on in the 1990s. Identifying ethnic conflicts is complicated, for example, by the mix of motives involved in some wars where territory
or independence is the primary issue but ethnic division is reflected as well. A single authoritative list of disputes, similar to the list of interstate wars compiled by
the Correlates of War project, initiated at the University of Michigan in the 1960s,
is not yet fully established.

Our starting point is the data set of Gurr and Harff (1994) that presents sixty-
three cases of serious and emerging ethnic conflicts in 1993. We adopt this set
because of its authoritative nature and the fact that it deals with conflicts alive in
the 1990s. This increases the feasibility of gathering data on arms flows to groups
and governments, though we note that there are other important unresolved ethnic
tensions in the world that might not be represented in the list. It includes mainly
cases of rebellion and uprising against established governmental authorities,

ı in some cases there was group versus group violence. Sometimes governments are representative mainly of one ethnic community, which is usually the majority. In some cases, such as Syria, for example, a minority controls the government. It is not always possible to distinguish group against government from group against group violence, but pure cases of the latter are relatively rare in the data. Thus, we gain some but not a great deal of information about intergroup fighting, even though intergroup conflict is potentially influenced by and in turn influences armament patterns, especially if one supposes that intergroup arms races take place. Ultimately it will be important to test this possibility, but for now we confine our analysis largely to cases of group versus government fighting.

One characteristic of these cases concerns the type of dispute: armed major conflict, low-intensity conflict with significant violence, serious dispute with little violence, and serious conflict in which most violence is a consequence of state repression. We discarded sixteen cases classified as serious disputes with little violence, since in these cases—such as the attacks on immigrants in Germany and France (group versus group)—we did not expect to see an organized effort to obtain arms by the victimized ethnic group. Including cases classified as mostly one-sided affairs involving state repression of ethnic groups was also a difficult decision. Some of these cases, such as Chinese repression of Tibetans and Bhutan repression of Nepalese, do not seem to evidence significant arms acquisition by groups, but others, such as fighting between Indonesia and East Timor, do. We decided to leave all the state repression cases in our sample, although some of them will not factor into our tests, as we are concerned with arms acquisition patterns and not the question, albeit important, of whether essentially unarmed ethnic groups are victimized.

Gurr (1994) also presents an updated and revised list of serious and emerging ethnic conflicts in 1993–94, with some differences from the earlier data set. He somewhat altered his typology of conflicts, which muddles the comparability of cases, but we nevertheless added the cases to our list that were not included in the earlier data set. Additionally, because of updating, we added the cases of Chechnya and Ghana, although they do not appear on either of the preceding data sets. As a result, we are able to identify a sample of forty-nine ethnic conflicts, which form the foundation for our analysis. The cases are presented by region in table 2.2.

Since many of the states in our sample were the locus of several conflicts, we differentiate, where possible, between multiple ethnic groups fighting in the same location. India, for example, as noted above, was the site of four separate major ethnic disputes involving Hindu nationalists, Kashmiris, Sikhs, and a variety of groups in the northeast region. However, in this case and several others, it is not always possible to differentiate clearly information about arms acquisitions among various ethnic combatants within a single state. This requires some caution in reading our analysis, since some of the totals encompassing multiple ethnic communities may not apply to all the groups. Differences among the ethnic conflicts, including date of initiation, duration, casualties, and geographic location, should, however, be sufficient to highlight patterns in the effect of arms on violence if any exist.

Table 2.2 Sample Cases of Ethnopolitical Conflict Active in the 1990s by Region

Conflict	*Group*
Americas	
Guatemala	Indigenous Peoples
Mexico	Zapoteks, Mayans, and other Indigenous Peoples
Peru	Indigenous Peoples
Europe (West and East)	
Northern Ireland	Irish Nationalists/Unionists
Spain	Basques
Turkey	Kurds
Bosnia-Herzegovina	Serbs, Croats, Bosnians
Croatia	Serbs
Serbia	Kosovar Albanians
Azerbaijan	Armenians, Azeri
Georgia	Abkhazians, Ossetians
Moldova	Slavs
Russia	Chechens, Ossetians
Middle East	
Israel	Palestinians
Iran	Kurds, Baha'i
Iraq	Kurds, Shiites
Asia (Central, South, East)	
Afghanistan	Hazaris, Pashtuns, Tajiks, Uzbeks
Bangladesh	Chittagong Hill Tribes
Bhutan	Nepalese
Burma	Chin, Shan, Karen, Kachin, Mon, Wa
Cambodia	Vietnamese
China	Tibetans
Fiji	East Indians
India	Hindu, Sikhs, Kashmiris, Nagas and Northeast tribes
Indonesia	East Timorese
	West Papuans
	Aceh in North Sumatra
Papua New Guinea	Bougainvillians
Philippines	Moro
Sri Lanka	Tamils
Africa	
Angola	Mbundu, Ovimbundu
Burundi	Hutu, Tutsi
Chad	Bideyet
Djibouti	Afars
Ethiopia	Oromo
Ghana	Konkomba, Namumba
Kenya	Kalenjin, Rift Valley Peoples
Liberia	Gios, Krahns, Mandingoes
Mali/Niger	Taureg

Table 2.2 *Continued*

Conflict	Group
Africa	
Morocco	Polisario
Nigeria	Ibo, Ogani, Yoruba
Rwanda	Hutu, Tutsi
Senegal	Diolas in Casamance Province
Somalia	Rival clans
South Africa	African National Congress/Zulu *Inkata* Freedom Party
Sudan	Southerners
Uganda	Acholi, Baganda
Zaire[a]	Kasaian

Source: Data based on Gurr (1993, 347–77), with supplementary information by authors.
[a]In 1997, Zaire became the Democratic Republic of the Congo. We are focusing on the earlier conflict in Zaire.

INITIAL FINDINGS

Our review of the literature turned up some evidence of arms acquisitions by groups in forty of the forty-nine cases of ethnopolitical violence. In three of the cases where no information was uncovered—Nepalese in Bhutan, Tibetans in China, and Kasaians in Zaire—it is likely that the ethnic population in question was on the receiving end of state repression in those years and did not fight back.[8] In another five cases, it is not clear if ethnic groups acquired arms. Cases with the most information included violence in Afghanistan, Angola, Bosnia and Herzegovina, Chechnya, India, Rwanda, and Sri Lanka. Biases in media coverage are reflected in the data, but we have tried to supplement media accounts with scholarly sources to increase validity.

Types of Arms

Ethnic groups were expected to employ mainly light weapons in combat. In our sample of conflicts under way in the mid-1990s, most of the time this expectation was correct (table 2.3). In twenty-six cases, evidence revealed only small/light arms. Two cases were noteworthy in that they showed some ambiguities of the small-arms definition. In Sri Lanka, the LTTE possessed heavier, sophisticated, as well as light, armament; they even had small naval vessels (although these would not be included in the United Nation's definition of major arms). However, the LTTE's use of these boats was rather idiosyncratic and did not correspond to what might be expected in standard warfare; group members tended to pack them full of explosives and run suicide missions against larger government ships. In Somalia, the government had acquired heavy arms from the United States, which may

Table 2.3 Patterns in Types of Arms Acquired by Ethnic Groups in the 1990s

Evidence of Heavy Arms	Evidence of Heavy and Light Arms	Evidence of Light Arms
Georgia (Abkhazia)	Afghanistan	Bangladesh
	Angola	Burma
	Azerbaijan	Djibouti
	Bosnia-Herzegovinia	Ethiopia
	Burundi	Ghana
	Croatia	India
	Iraq	Indonesia (E.Timor)
	Moldova	Indonesia (W. Papua)
	Morocco	Indonesia (N. Sumatra)
	Russia (Chechnya)	Kenya
		Mali/Niger
		Mexico
		Northern Ireland
		Papua New Guinea
		Peru
		Philippines
		Rwanda
		Senegal
		Serbia (Kosovo)
		Somalia
		South Africa
		Spain
		Sri Lanka
		Sudan
		Turkey
		West Bank/Gaza

have ended up in the hands of various clans, but there was no evidence that they were used. The use of the so-called technicals, that is, jeeps armed by clans with machine guns, suggests that the heavier land equipment was largely inoperable.

Groups are more likely to acquire and use light arms than heavy weapons for several reasons. First, they are unlikely to receive or make effective use of sophisticated advanced and heavy weapons systems that are costly, require concealment, require advanced training, and impede mobility. Sophistication renders heavy weapons difficult to deploy in battlefield settings as well as difficult to maintain, and skilled operating personnel may be lacking. Relative economic costs also help dictate the limited variety of arms seen in domestic combat. The AK-47—the standard Soviet combat rifle and the weapon of choice for many ethnic combatants—is available almost worldwide at prices as low as a few dollars. In South Africa, the black market price for one is $20, but a better deal can be had in Mozambique at $6 (Hey, Anybody Want a Gun? 1998). Even rather sophisticated small arms, such as infrared night vision equipment, have hit global markets at discount prices in recent years, especially with the breakup of the Soviet bloc. As financial costs decrease, the probability of successful arms acquisition rises, especially for groups able to generate a fairly regular income, as in Angola and Sierra Leone where rebels have been adept at capturing and using portions of the diamond and resource trade. Light arms and primitive implements generally are more readily at hand and subject to less government control than heavy weapons. Light arms are difficult to count and track and can be transferred, smuggled, concealed, moved, and stored with little notice.

While we expect light weapons to be the norm in domestic warfare, there is one major exception to this general pattern. Heavy weapons are likely to be acquired when states break down. The collapse of a state—manifest in the reduction in governance and order—also can throw open its arsenals. Under this condition, or when government troops abandon equipment, many of the obstacles noted above do not apply. When a state collapses, former soldiers—with substantial military training—frequently wind up among ethnic combatants, bringing their weapons and training with them, as in Chechnya, for example. The cost of acquiring and transporting heavy arms diminishes. Finally, controls over these weapons fall away. As a result, since any combatant fighting against heavy equipment appropriately used is at a strategic disadvantage, heavy weapons are likely to pervade fighting within or on the borders of the collapsed state.

Heavy armament was involved in eleven of the sampled cases during the 1990s (table 2.3). In two of these—Bosnia-Herzegovina and Croatia—the combatants acquired such weapons as a result of Yugoslavia's breakup, and in five cases— Azerbaijan, Chechnya, the Georgian conflicts involving Abkhazians and Ossetians, and Moldova—from the breakup of the Soviet Union. The heavy weapons acquired by the Kurds in Iraq apparently resulted from Baghdad's loss of control over its forces during the Gulf War. The heavy equipment used in Afghanistan in the 1990s resulted from almost total state breakdown as well as outside assistance. Such weapons also were used in Rwanda, although in this case they were mainly limited to use by the Hutu forces that took over the government. UNITA rebel forces in Angola have had some heavy weapons, such as T-54/55 tanks and armored personnel carriers, although the majority of UNITA's forces seem to have retained light arms (Human Rights Watch, 1994a). Thus, where states broke down, both light and heavy weapons were used in subsequent internal warfare, and in some isolated cases, ethnic fighters have been able to gain access to heavy equipment while confronting weakened or especially corrupt governmental authorities.

What sorts of arms do governments employ in dealing with internal, ethnically based fighting? Governments usually possess both heavy and light weapons, but not all states are prepared to give their military forces carte blanche to use the full arsenal. In some cases, governments do not use heavy weapons at all, even though they have them. On the other hand, states often respond to violence directed against the state with more, even disproportionately more force than was used by the rebel or opposition group.

Several factors affect states' willingness to employ major arms. First, it appears that democratic regimes are less likely to confront severe domestic ethnic warfare or to use major force against their own minority populations, except as a last resort. That is not to say, of course, that local police or military commanders will not unleash unusually heavy bombardments, as they did in Philadelphia, with disastrous results, against the MOVE urban militant group during the 1970s. However, the more concerned a government is about its image in the international community, the more likely it will refrain from using heavy arms, which may seem out of proportion when compared with opponents' force levels and which may generate civilian atrocities. Israeli reaction to Palestinian demonstrations and violence in 2000 and 2001 may have been an exception to this expectation. In some circumstances a hard-pressed government, even a "democratic" one, might, as in the Philippines in 2000, attempt a major offensive against rebels, using high-powered weaponry to get the war over with quickly before a stalemate or involvement by the international community occurs.

In addition to the success or failure of previous negotiations, social geography, therefore, can be an important factor influencing governments' employment of arms, entailing such considerations as the dispersal of ethnic fighters among the general population, the potential for collateral damage to innocent civilians, and distances that must be traversed to reach rebel sanctuaries. The Turks unleashed major attacks on the Kurdish minority, for example, when the Kurds fled from Turkey and sought sanctuary in neighboring Iraq. Turkish forces have on occasion followed the Kurds deep into Iraqi territory. In Sri Lanka, the concentration of Tamils in the northern part of the country has had a similar targeting effect, despite the potential for killing civilians in major attacks. Finally, more portable and lighter weapons can be most appropriate for the type of hit-and-run counterinsurgency warfare encountered in many situations of ethnic rebellion. Certainly mobility is a key consideration, and one would expect that helicopters, armored personnel carriers, or fast patrol boats might be at a premium in ethnic warfare.

Sources of Arms

Both ethnopolitical groups and governments appear to use multiple sources of arms, both internal and external, and multiple means of acquisition outlined earlier. Several types of external actors have been known to provide weapons to armed fighters; these include governments, commercial or private arms dealers, other ethnic groups, and criminal syndicates. Thus, for example, Bulgarian arms manufacturers such as Arsenal have sent weapons to rebel groups in the Congo, Angola, Eritrea, Sri Lanka, and Rwanda during the 1990s (Bonner 1998c, 3). Such supplies might arrive either through legal routes or covertly and through black markets. Overt or open sales are conducted through normal commercial channels. Black market sales involve the transfer of arms:

in knowing violation of the supplying and/or receiving country's laws and regulations, and normally mean some risk of punishment for those caught engaging in such activities. By definition, black market transactions are conducted in secret and typically involve falsified records and weapons that have been stolen or improperly obtained from government arsenals or legitimate dealers. (Klare and Andersen 1996, 57)

Often, black market transfers are worked out with private dealers and arms manufacturers (Lock 1999; Lumpe 2000; Rahman 1997). Bonner (1998b, 3) describes one such circuitous illicit arms transfer to groups in India: Peter von Kalikstein-Bleach, a British arms dealer, was hired by Kim Davy, an alias for Niels Christian Nielsen, a Danish client, to purchase weapons. Mr. Bleach engaged Border Technology, a British arms trading firm, to acquire the weapons. Border Technology obtained the weapons from Arsenal, the Bulgarian arms manufacturer. Mr. Bleach bought a Russian cargo plane in Latvia, which was flown to Bulgaria, where it was loaded with weapons. The plane then flew to India, where the cargo of arms was parachuted to a militant Hindu nationalist group near Calcutta. Unfortunately for Mr. Bleach, the plane, which was flying on to Bombay, was grounded by the Indians. They arrested Mr. Bleach, while Mr. Davy escaped. In this example, neither Bleach nor Border Technology appear to have broken any British laws, since the weapons were not British, nor in Britain. Clearly, however, though the end-user certificate—a document indicating to whom the weapons were to be shipped—appeared genuine, specifying the Bangladesh Defense Ministry, in reality, it was a fraud.[9]

Two other points about the black market are worth mentioning. First, since the 1980s, the black market has become a more prominent source for both light and heavy arms, though light arms tend to predominate. However, arms on the black market can be expensive, depending on the desperation of the source, and risky. Much of the cost of such equipment is involved in moving the shipments secretly to their final destination and in lining the pockets of entrepreneurs and smugglers; these costs can make black market supplies too expensive for some warring groups (see Naylor in Boutwell et al.1995, 44–57).

Aside from private dealers, governments also engage in covert operations to arm ethnic groups, although sometimes the term "covert" can be a bit of a misnomer. Iran's arms shipments to the Bosnian Muslims in the mid-1990s would be considered illicit, since the United Nations had established an arms embargo to prevent countries from providing arms to fuel the conflict. It has since turned out that Washington knew of the Iranian transfers and turned a blind eye; the transfers appeared to further the then-American goals of strengthening the Bosnians vis-à-vis the Serbs in order to make negotiations more feasible and balanced.

Just as states have several motivations in selling weapons to other states (see Kemp 1971; Pierre 1982; Pearson 1994; Clinton 1995), various external arms suppliers might perceive advantages in transferring arms to ethnopolitical fighters. As indicated in chapter 1, the reasons can be categorized as economic (profit), political (influence), and military (security), or a mix thereof. Profit appears to be the main economic reason to supply ethnopolitical groups, but one cannot discount the other factors, depending upon the situation. Unlike states, groups are not in a position to require "offsets" (i.e., compensatory economic concessions to the arms buyer to offset the heavy cost of modern weapons) or to take advantage of coproduction or licensing arrangements (i.e., agreements to provide access to newer arms technologies and provide production jobs in the purchasing state). Technology transfer is effectively prohibited, and what remains are pure moneymaking opportunities, even if the group's economic resources are limited. Some governments and firms have seen transfers to substate actors as a means of shoring up an eroding arms market in the early post–Cold War era.

Turning to the political reasons to sell weapons, external suppliers sometimes seek to gain influence with a particular ethnopolitical community, thinking of the future if that group comes to power. Conversely, the struggle might be to prevent a group's coming to power, as in the Afghan conflicts of the 1990s where the Russians ironically armed some of the same mujahedin groups they fought against from 1979–89 because these groups came to oppose the militant Talibaan, an organization Moscow did not wish to see make any more gains. Thus, arms transfers can be seen as an investment against the success of the most feared group or government. Of course, the wisdom of the investment could later be called into question.

In chapter 1, we reviewed the supply of arms to defend a favored ethnic or kinship group across a border. Thus, we can see political motivations in the support networks ethnic groups build to raise money for arms and other material. Such networks have been created by the Irish outside of Ireland to aid the IRA, by Tamils living outside of Sri Lanka to aid the LTTE, and by many other groups. Arms also might be sent as a form of rescue to aid an ethnic community because it is a "minority at risk" (Gurr 1993; Stavenhagen 1993). In this case, support might come from groups or states without an ethnic stake, but which, for humanitarian reasons, do not wish to see an embattled ethnopolitical faction lose any more ground.

In the previous chapter, we also saw that some external actors try to stir up political instability and insecurity and create dependencies in an enemy state by throwing "gasoline on the fire." This seems to have happened as Liberia's neighbors aided various fighting groups, some of which were ethnically based, in the long, tragic Liberian civil war of the 1980s and 1990s (Stedman 1996). India and Pakistan, Iran and Iraq also have a long history of such machinations. These strategies can relate to hopes of beneficial territorial and border adjustments.

There is also the idea of transferring arms to substitute for or preclude the need for direct military intervention, or to influence the development of a conflict, regional power balance, and ultimately, the way conflict is brought to an end. In a sense, this focuses on arms provided once fighting is under way in an effort to steer the conflict toward a resolution more favorable to the arms supplier. Bosnia is a good example of Washington's intricate efforts, including training and logistical support to Bosnian forces in the midst of a supposed arms embargo, to "rebalance" power and generate a stalemate to promote a negotiated outcome. The complications of such balancing acts often can be underestimated, however, as arms provided can crop up unexpectedly in subsequent conflict outbreaks. Suppliers might be disappointed in their lack of overall influence and control over recipients and ultimate negotiations, at least without substantial further commitments of funding or personnel. And clearly, Bosnian rearmament policies did not preclude the need for, and in fact might have spurred the interest in subsequent direct Western and Russian military intervention.

From the recipient's perspective, there are several constraints for an ethnic group seeking arms from external sponsors. First, available equipment is likely to vary among suppliers and over time. Ethnic group imports differ from government acquisitions in several respects. For example, we have seen that it might become necessary to arrange arms deals via long and complex paths, particularly when the shipments are covert. Arms presumably destined for Burundi were loaded in India and shipped to Tanzania in 1995; their origin was unclear, perhaps by intent (*Military and Arms Trade News,* July 17, 1995). Furthermore, normally in such arrangements there are no contractual assurances of resupply, parts availability, technical advice, warranties, or ammunition, all of which are commonly part of intergovernmental arms arrangements. A supplier might be willing to transfer arms at one point and unwilling or unable to do so later. Thus, multiple suppliers often become necessary, though not necessarily very feasible. It is difficult to sustain a supply network, particularly with reliance on one primary "brand" of arms (i.e., American, French, Russian) and the chances of information leaking out increase with the number of participants (of course, in some cases suppliers or recipients might not object to being identified).

A second problem for arms recipients, as we have noted, is developing sufficient resources to meet payments. Groups have applied some of the same methods as states to try to raise funds for arms, and some groups have acquired resources to trade. In addition to diamonds in places such as Angola and Sierra Leone, this includes reported drug trafficking by West Irian Papuans, *Sendero Luminoso* (Shining Path) in Peru, the Burmese and Lebanese militia, and the LTTE in Sri Lanka. In addition, ethnic groups sometimes collect revenue, both within a country and from external sources. Some groups in India and the Sri Lankan LTTE reportedly have extorted funds from local businesses. Ethnic militia in Burma have taxed businesses and conducted trade. We have seen that many groups have supporters, including relatives living abroad, who provide financial assistance. During the disarmament debates in the Northern Ireland peace agreement of 1998, it was revealed that large American-smuggled arms caches, consisting of many types of guns usually hidden in the Irish Republic, had in some cases never even been uncrated. Naturally, the cultivation and development of fund sources can take much time and effort and require that fighting groups have political emissaries able to conduct effective negotiations.

For ethnopolitical groups in combat, domestic sources of arms can be more convenient and sometimes even decisive. These include battlefield capture or raids on government police or military facilities. Sometimes groups simply take up arms readily at hand. In many countries, small arms, such as hunting rifles and shotguns or pistols are common, to some extent legal, and might, initially, satisfy group needs. In the January 1994 Chiapas state rebellion in Mexico, for example, members of EZLN reportedly employed rifles that were common among Mexican farmers. They also turned to smuggling guns from the United States, purchasing them on the black market in nearby El Salvador and Nicaragua, and buying guns from corrupt officials in the Mexican army, police, and private militia (Klare and Anderson 1996; *Keesing's* 1994, 39809). Afghanistan, and to a lesser extent Pakistan, represent countries seemingly awash in arms, due in large part to foreign infusions particularly during the 1970s and 1980s (*Jane's Defence Weekly* 1994, 22). As an extreme of leftover supplies, some of the weapons used in the late 1990s in Indonesia by the Revolutionary Front for an Independent East Timor (FRETILIN) appeared to date to the Portuguese colonial administration.

We have noted that indigenous arms production in these contexts includes the manufacture, remanufacture, or adaptation of arms, as for example, in modifying ordnance, devising weapons-launch platforms, or assembling explosives. While a number of governments have production capabilities, at least for small arms, this method should not be exaggerated as an option for groups. Most ethnic communities cannot manufacture their arms from scratch. Rather, several groups have modified equipment or assembled certain types of bombs, mines, and other explosive devices. Some have used small factories or shops to modify hunting rifles to take standard military ammunition, and a few have assembled crude missiles or otherwise modified weapons. Examples include the Serb manufacture of a rocket in Bosnia and the Bougainville Revolutionary Army's (BRA) efforts at making explosives from leftover World War II ordnance on Papua New Guinea. Such efforts often require significant ingenuity and skill as well as safe havens from which to attempt production.

ACQUISITION CALCULATIONS

Groups in Conflict

Ethnopolitical groups are for the most part opportunists. Those that can take advantage of all three types of arms acquisition (import, capture, and manufacture) do so, as in Sri Lanka. However, for a variety of reasons, not all groups have access to the three modes. In addition to the constraints we have noted and the Internet notwithstanding, groups are likely to have limited information concerning possible arms suppliers, the quantities and quality of the equipment, and the likelihood of successful delivery or resupply. Governments also are apt to crack down on illicit arms shipments when they become excessive.

Simply transferring the logic or motives of a state's arms acquisition patterns to the group level can be misleading (Bell 1978). For example, states may seek armaments to gain international prestige or technological advancement, as well as for security per se. Ethnic fighters, on the other hand, are more likely to focus strictly on tactical needs, although there may be some residual symbolic value for them in being well armed. The question ultimately comes down to what groups have to do to meet their goals, goals that are likely to involve concessions (e.g., recognition, territorial awards, political autonomy, economic opportunities) from either the government or other ethnic communities. For groups perhaps more than for governments, a total military victory might not be necessary to wring fundamental concessions from other actors in the dispute. The level of violence required for a group to "succeed" can vary widely. In some cases political authorities might negotiate with them relatively quickly if not wholeheartedly (e.g., Mexico), while others find negotiation long delayed and then merely occasions for short lulls in ongoing civil wars (e.g., Sri Lanka). Even a rumor or threat of arms acquisition can lead to opponents' threatened preemptive attacks or to heightened international concern and resumed negotiations (as seen variously in Cyprus).

We can only begin at this point to think about how a group might seek to acquire arms given its perception of where the government's concession threshold lies. Resourceful organizational leaders might, for example, pursue a combined strategy of fighting and moves to gain international attention, offsetting some of the need for armaments as such. The KLA was able to focus enough attention to bring NATO threats of military intervention to bear against Serbia.

Group strategic calculations, therefore, fundamentally hinge on whether the expected utility of attempting to acquire arms in general or certain types of weapons in particular is greater than the expected utility of not making the attempt, given potential political and military gains versus anticipated costs and obstacles. By eschewing armed struggle, a group presumably continues to live under whatever conditions or disadvantages it currently experiences. It might have prospects of nonviolent remedies, through resistance or electoral and negotiation processes. We proceed from the point where the expected utility (E_U) of attempting to acquire arms is greater than the value of not doing so. The political challenge, therefore, becomes how to maximize the value of attempting to acquire arms, given the group's operational environment, including what arms are available and on what terms, the group's goals and resources, and the goals, resources, and staying power of potential adversaries or allies.

On the one hand, an ethnic community that is facing discrimination of some form or has grievances against the government can choose not to acquire arms. In this case, the status quo will likely continue. The E_U of acquiring a particular type of weapon should be viewed as equal to the probability of successfully obtaining such arms multiplied by the value of possessing them (pSV). The latter term relates both to political and military benefits of having the weapons, and the operational capability to use them.

Moreover, we suggest that the probability of acquiring arms is a function of several elements among which are: *resources, availability, and delivery, plus capability and situational amenability.* If an ethnic group or a government has no *resources* or funds, no reasonable prospect that sufficient arms are *available* either domestically or abroad, and no prospect of *safe shipment,* it cannot hope to trade for or purchase arms and there is little use in seeking them. Likewise, if the group has no battlefield prospects or no personnel able to operate tanks and planes, then having such items is not useful, and there is little reason to seek these categories of equipment. And if there is little perceived political payoff in resorting to arms, or if massive government counterattack is likely, there is little incentive to arm.

On the other hand, in extremis, a group might have reached such a height of threat perception and desperation that armed struggle seems the only available option, that is, the perceived need for arms far outweighs considerations of feasibility (as in the Warsaw ghetto uprisings of World War II). The E_U of possession is thus related to the net estimated combat impact (I), less the likelihood of gaining political concessions (pC) without using arms (E_U = I-pC).

The pC estimation might depend on governmental responsiveness or needs and potential outside support for either the group or the government. The probability of successfully employing the weapons (I) is thus a function of such factors as the ability to operate the equipment, maintain the arms in working order, and find a safe haven in which to store the equipment.

Thus, an ethnic group considering sustained military struggle, as opposed to sporadic acts of defiance, has several basic considerations. One is whether or not its resources are adequate; another has to do with whether arms or intervention from outside the country are likely. The availability of arms in relation to the stability and strength of the government and the likelihood of successful weapon deployment are further considerations, and the impact of having or using the weapons weighs in as well (see table 2.4).

Table 2.4 Opportunities and Constraints of Three Modes of Arms Acquisition

	Arms Acquisition Methods		
Critical Factors	*Importation*	*Domestic Procurement*	*Indigenous Production*
Availability	Can obtain sophisticated arms	Generally limited to small arms, except in cases of state breakdown	Generally limited to small arms
	Spare parts may be an issue	Sufficient quantity may be an issue	Sufficient quantity may be an issue
Resources Required	High, but money can be raised from foreign contributions or local resources	Low	Low
Shipment Safety	Arms may be seized prior to delivery	Generally not salient; storage considerations	Generally not salient; storage considerations

To understand how groups are likely to arm, we need to look beyond the various constraints frequently mentioned and also consider group needs and preferences. Specific groups are likely to have different specific needs. It is possible to make two general assumptions about groups' arms-seeking behavior. The first assumption is that ethnic groups have preferences and that they are able to put these preferences for types and sources of their weapons in some order. Second, we assume that the group leaders try to maximize the value they receive in attempting to acquire arms. Together, for analytical purposes, these assumptions cast ethnic groups as rational value maximizers. Other things being equal, they prefer to spend fewer resources on arms than more, choosing safer acquisition methods over more risky (less reliable) ones, and obtaining more rather than fewer arms (at least up to a point of saturation).

A given group's most preferred method of arms acquisitions is not a priori clear. Karp (1993) has suggested that state sponsorship is necessary for ethnic groups seeking to win conflicts (that is, a military victory), and so a plausible argument can be made that groups tend to opt for importation in general over other methods. Within the importation category they might prefer to obtain arms from states rather than private dealers or on the black market. States can stand behind or guarantee the quality of weapons deemed technologically decisive for equalizing or gaining advantage vis-à-vis adversaries, whether the local government or rival groups. This can be particularly important in less-developed countries where technology levels are relatively low and a select new weapons system could prove decisive. States as suppliers also might validate the ethnic fighters' cause by symbolic political support.

However, few conflicts, especially in the post–Cold War period, appear to attract the extent of foreign interest necessary to assure highly potent governmental arms shipments. Indeed, some might attract state interest in stemming the flow of weapons. Since foreign weapons of relatively good quality might be available locally or nearby through battlefield capture, raids, or illicit purchases, the group might prefer to rely on its own cunning for local acquisition. Nevertheless, a combination of acquisition channels might be necessary for sustained fighting by any particular group, especially as resupply becomes imperative and opponents move to shut off arms channels by intercepting shipments, for example.

We can better understand a group's likely calculations and value rankings by examining the impact of different acquisition strategies on the expected utility calculation suggested above. The mode of acquisition directly affects the three facets of the expected utility calculation. Domestic procurement, for example, generally would appear to require less financial resources and entail greater certainty of delivery than importation, so that the probability that an ethnic group might prefer this means of acquisition is high. This correctly focuses attention on the quantity and type of arms available in the local environment and whether the ethnic group considers this quantity and quality sufficient and appropriate to its needs. Finally, locally available arms—excluding cases of state breakdown—are likely to consist of light weapons, artillery, or munitions components, which present few difficulties for storage and use, suggesting that the probability of employing them successfully is also quite high.

Indigenous production, or the manufacture or remanufacture of arms, has some of the advantages of domestic procurement in that it may not be very expensive to acquire and process (adapt) materials and parts. Additionally, safety concerns are limited to protection of arms manufacturing complexes, prevention of accidental explosions or toxic spills, and securing transport. Since explosives can be quietly manufactured almost anywhere, for example, costs would be very low. Generally, however, indigenous production will be quite limited because the required skill level in making sufficient supplies of small arms, such as pistols or rifles, is high enough that the effort would be considered impractical by many political groups. Reliance on indigenous production can depend on the strategy to be employed; explosives are useful in urban uprisings with terrorist overtones; crude mines might be useful in keeping larger government forces at bay; modified launch platforms allow mobility for quick hit-and-run strikes. Indigenous production, therefore, can be a mainstay for small-scale and guerrilla operations, but might be only one, and indeed a minor one, of a combination of methods used in more massive and sustained military operations.

Importation of arms from black market sources, private dealers, or foreign states seems the most costly and least reliable option, but one that can bring weapons and resupply commitments, such as antiaircraft equipment, unavailable by other means. Funding and logistics become important considerations, although at times friendly foreign states might subsidize the shipments. Safety of transport and weapon stock availability in the cases of private dealers and the black market are also concerns (Karp 1993). The probabilities of an ethnic group having sufficient resources to purchase weapons abroad and successfully receive the arms, and the probability that the weapons sought will be available are perhaps lower than is the case for the other two modes of acquisition. Reliance on ethnic kin or close neighbors abroad can diminish some of these concerns.

Looking to data on ethnopolitical wars in table 2.5, despite the apparent advantages compared to other methods, it does not seem that domestic acquisition is the most common form of group arms acquisition, at least by the measurements we have so far been able to employ. This analysis is complicated by the fact that media reports might be most likely to pick up on international arms transfers. Nevertheless, as might be expected given the vagaries of warfare, it appears that ethnic groups most often pursue multiple approaches to obtaining weapons. In two conflicts—Bosnia-Herzegovina and Sri Lanka—groups acquired arms through indigenous production, domestic procurement, and importation. In fourteen cases, groups used two approaches to acquiring arms, most frequently through the combination of domestic sources and importation. In twenty-eight of the thirty-nine cases for which we could determine the arms source(s), ethnic groups received arms through importation. In nineteen cases, there was evidence suggesting domestic procurement, and in only seven instances was there evidence of indigenous production.

Table 2.5   Modes of Arms Acquisition by Ethnopolitical Groups

Evidence of Indigenous Production	Evidence of Domestic Procurement	Evidence of Importation
Bosnia-Herzegovina	Afghanistan	Afghanistan
India	Angola	Angola
Northern Ireland	Azerbaijan	Azerbaijan
Papua New Guinea	Bosnia-Herzegovina	Bosnia-Herzegovina
Philippines	Burma	Burma
Sri Lanka	Chechnya	Burundi
West Bank/Gaza	Indonesia (E. Timor)	Chechnya
	Indonesia (W. Irian)	Croatia
	Indonesia (N. Sumatra)	Djibouti
	Iraq	Ethiopia
	Kenya	Fiji
	Mali/Niger	Georgia (Abkhazia)
	Mexico	India
	Moldova	Iran
	Papua New Guinea	Iraq
	Peru	Kenya
	Somalia	Liberia
	South Africa	Mali/Niger
	Sri Lanka	Moldova
		Morocco
		Northern Ireland
		Philippines
		Rwanda
		Senegal
		Serbia (Kosovo)
		Somalia
		Sri Lanka
		Sudan

In the case of the Basque movement in Spain, for example, the rebel ETA organization had small arms, including rifles and explosives, but the media never identified the source of these arms. Most probably, they were domestically acquired. Domestic acquisition is likely to affect certain phases of warfare, but arms importation seems necessary for sustained struggle.

It might be further expected that ethhnopolitical groups in combat would import arms from multiple suppliers rather than a single source. Two reasons underlie this proposition. Groups can expect a higher probability of safe shipment over multiple purchases if they seek arms from more than one source. To paraphrase the maxim: do not put all your weapons on one ship. However, a second reason to pursue multiple import sources concerns availability. Different suppliers are likely to have different types of arms on offer at different times and terms. More than one country stocks Russian and American equipment, so that quantities and spare parts might be augmented through a supply network. Additionally, ethnic groups might realize cost savings by shopping around, raising the probability that they can afford weapons by seeking lower prices among competitive suppliers. However, for these savings to be realized, a group would require sufficient information on arms availability as well as the foreign connections to make the deal.

Although in many instances ethnic groups have turned to more than one foreign supplier, the hypothesis that this will generally be the case is not clearly supported by the available data (table 2.6). In thirteen of the twenty-eight cases where importation occurred, arms came from more than one supplier. This finding is muddled, however,

Table 2.6   External Suppliers for Ethnopolitical Groups in the 1990s

Location	Suppliers	Intermediate Locations
Afghanistan	Albania, Pakistan, Russia, Turkey, Uzbekistan	
Angola	Bulgaria, France, South Africa, Ukraine, United States, Zaire	Namibia, Zaire
Azerbaijan	Armenians, Russia	
Bosnia-Herzegovina	Serbia	
Burma	Cambodia, China, Thailand	
Burundi	Rwanda	
Chechnya	Russia, Turkey	Azerbaijan, Cyprus, Dagestan
Croatia	Serbia	
Djibouti	Ethiopia, Somalia	
Ethiopia	Sudan	
Fiji	Libya	Australia
Georgia (Abkhazia)	Russia	
India	Afghanistan, Pakistan, Thailand	Pakistan
Iran	Iraq	
Iraq	Iran	
Kenya	Uganda	
Liberia	Burkino Faso, Libya, Nigeria	Côte d'Ivoire
Mali/Niger	Libya	
Moldova	Russia	
Morocco	Algeria, Libya	
N. Ireland	Libya	Malta
Philippines	Pakistan	
Rwanda	Albania, Belgium, Bulgaria, China, Egypt, France, Romania, South Africa, Uganda, Zaire	India, Zaire
Senegal (Casamance region)	Mauritania	
Serbia (Kosovo)	Albania	
Somalia	Ethiopia, United States	
Sri Lanka	Bulgaria, Burma, Cyprus, Hong Kong, India, Lebanon, North Korea, Singapore, Thailand, Ukraine	
Sudan	Ethiopia, Uganda	

by lack of data on the amount of arms sent by each supplier; in cases of multiple supply, the overwhelming bulk of arms might have come from only *one* source.

Two conflicts tied for the most suppliers: Rwanda and Sri Lanka. In Rwanda both Hutus and Tutsis, whether controlling the government or not, have established a diverse supplier network. Likewise, in Sri Lanka, the Tamils have built an unprecedented supply network over the years (Bonner 1998a). UNITA in Angola followed in second place with six suppliers. Five suppliers supported the main factions in Afghanistan during the 1990s. In the other eight cases with multiple suppliers, ethnic groups appeared to rely on two or three sources. The fact that groups tend to use few main suppliers may mean that these are generally sufficient or that they are all that they can afford or rely on. In other words, constraints on group armament still appear to be significant.

In addition, when ethnic groups acquire arms from sources outside the state, the immediate sources are likely to be geographically close to the state. This means that while the weapons may have been manufactured or originated elsewhere, their accumulation and shipment for the war in question was from proximate locations. Three reasons suggest that proximity is a factor. Ethnic groups might extend or migrate across state boundaries, as with the Kurds living in Iraq, Iran, Syria, and Turkey, or Tuareg nomads living in areas encompassing Mali and Niger. Aid from one ethnic community or portion of a community to another seems more likely to take the form of arms when the ethnic community is contiguous or nearby, as across the Albanian border into Kosovo. This relates to the level of interest in affairs across the border as well as more general concerns about the cost and security of shipments. Even a major power like the United States generally shipped arms to regional fighters through nearby staging points, as in the CIA Angolan operation of the 1970s (see chapter 4). To intervene directly in a state undergoing conflict can risk identification, embarrassment, and charges of sovereignty violation for the supplying power.

As arms are sent from abroad, potentially involving black market or redirected transfers, costs as well as the possibility that they will be discovered, blocked, or confiscated rise with distance. Thus, notwithstanding occasional North American shipments to Ireland, ethnic communities living far away from an ethnic dispute tend to send financial aid rather than military goods themselves.

A final reason for the importance of geographic proximity in arms supply depends on the regional nature of hostilities, where, for example, one state seeks to undermine the other by arming the latter's ethnic minorities. In the extreme case, a state might arm a group in a neighboring state as a proxy in its own conflict with that state, such as Ethiopians arming Sudanese rebels (though Libya also appears to have attempted long-distance subversion through arms to Northern Ireland). This argument also raises the question of the original source of arms supplies, since the delivery path can be concealed and circuitous.

Changes in the nature of the arms trade since the Cold War ended can be introduced as a critique of the proximity hypothesis. After all, if anything, the Cold

War's end has reduced the importance of ideological or strategic motivations for sales and to some extent arms trade relationships based on bloc politics. Therefore, arms suppliers would be theoretically freer to sell to any actor they choose, regardless of region or political affiliation, particularly as the economic rationale for arms exports increases relative to political and strategic incentives. However, while this is most likely the case for states as arms importers, based on the empirical evidence it does not appear to be generally true of ethnic groups. Their resources and negotiation opportunities are more tenuous, which makes it more difficult for them to engage arms sellers reliably at a distance. Additionally, in many of these ethnic conflicts, the major arms supplier—particularly the United States—also seems to want to remain uninvolved in the fighting or to dampen it, and often sides with the government in the interest of "stability." Bosnia and Kosovo may be exceptions, but the overall situation seems far different than during the Cold War when Washington or Moscow would undertake massive weapons delivery by air and sea either clandestinely or openly to compete with each other. To conclude, the most likely immediate sources of imported arms for warring ethnic groups are nearby regional actors with arms to spare, perhaps accumulated as a result of Cold War politics, imported, or leftover from earlier conflicts or from a longer arms trail.

A corollary might suggest that when ethnic groups import arms, they tend to do so from immediate neighbors. An examination of the twenty-eight cases where importation occurred reveals that in the majority (fifteen) of cases, all the suppliers were contiguous with the location of the ethnic conflict. In seven additional cases, at least one of the suppliers was contiguous. Only in five cases were none of the suppliers next door (although in one of these conflicts, Moldova, the Slavic minority received arms from Russians stationed inside the country). Focusing on the *region* in which the conflict occurs also supports this hypothesis. In all but a few of the twenty-eight cases, all the suppliers were in the same region. Exceptions, usually involving ethnic kinship and major power or postcolonial intervention, include: arms sent from Albania and Turkey to Afghanistan; American, French, and Belgium arms to UNITA in Angola; West and East European states selling arms in Rwanda; American arms to Somalia; and the far-flung Sri Lankan networks mentioned above.

Despite the contiguity finding, when arms are acquired from abroad, we would expect shipments to ethnic fighters to have had at least one transshipment point. Although greater distance between the group and a potential supplier and added stops along the way raise the costs and risks of acquiring arms, the nature and frequent secrecy of importation suggests that arms are very likely to make several stops before reaching their final destination. Black market and private dealers especially, and occasionally even states, are likely to seek a covert roundabout route for shipments, forging manifests and destinations, changing vessels or carriers, and so on. This is evident in news reports that detail the port where weapons arrive, as well as their next destination, but not their origin. As a result, unlike state-to-state transfers that are most often direct, we hypothesize that transfers to ethnic groups generally would be indirect.[10]

In line with our findings about contiguity and proximity, however, when we test the hypothesis of multiple transshipment points with the available data, we find reason to doubt the transshipment hypothesis. Allowing for imprecise or incomplete reports, in only seven of the twenty-eight reported cases of arms imports was there media mention of transshipment. Of course, it is possible that media focus more on the existence of arms than on how the weapons get to the ethnic groups. In the 1970s, Namibia and Zaire provided stopping points for American and South African arms to Angola, while the Russians tended to ship directly, via air and sea, to the Angolan government.[11] In Chechnya, Turkish arms were shipped via Azerbaijan and Dagestan, while Russian arms were shipped via a brokerage in Cyprus. Alleged Libyan arms on their way to Fiji were discovered in Australia. Pakistan has been both a starting point and a midpoint for arms bound for Kashmir and India. The Côte d'Ivoire facilitated weapons supplies to Liberia, while Malta was a transfer point for Libyan arms bound for the IRA. Zaire and India in one instance were way stations for arms to Rwanda.

For the other ethnic conflicts where few "middlemen" were in evidence, further data refinements are necessary before definitive conclusions can be drawn. It could be that long and multipoint arms routes are more the exception than the rule, and that most arms for ethnic fighters originate nearby or next door.

States in Conflict

As with groups in conflict, states also encounter basic constraints in seeking to acquire weapons. The first of these is economic and essentially boils down to how much money can be spent on defense, and what portion of the defense budget finances arms acquisition. The other constraint occurs infrequently when a state becomes the subject of an arms embargo. In 1998, for example, due to fighting in Kosovo, the United Nations recommended an embargo on the area, including Albania. The goal was to keep Albanians from arming ethnic Albanians in Kosovo as well as to prevent Serbs from acquiring more arms. As noted earlier, though, such embargoes often leak. The embargo on the former Yugoslavia failed dramatically, while the one in Kosovo was hindered both by the lack of effective monitoring and enforcement along remote borders, and by the mixed motives of outside powers and their intelligence agencies (Crossette 1998).

Among the varied reasons why states arm and why they choose supplies and suppliers are considerations of politics, power, and prestige, as well as military advantage. Politics can involve forging links and ties to certain patron states, often arms suppliers, for purposes of influence or leverage. States also can be pressured to buy certain types of systems in relation to their perceived foreign threats and in conjunction with their alliance and bloc affiliations, as when Poland, Hungary, and the Czechs were Warsaw Pact members as compared to their prospects as NATO members after the dissolution of the Soviet Union.

Surprisingly, though, not much has been written on the subject of arms acquisitions by governments seeking to start or expand repression against their citizens or that find themselves on the defensive, facing an ethnopolitical rebellion. A state facing a rebellion has a menu of options that might or might not include further arms acquisitions; common sense suggests that the options boil down to some form of military, economic, or political response.

Based on this thinking, we might suggest a tentative first proposition that states are more likely to increase arms acquisitions when they are involved in ethnopolitical conflict than when they are not facing such disruption. However, we can as yet find little empirical evidence to support the hypothesis. Table 2.7 shows the dollar value of arms imports for fifteen sampled countries experiencing ethnopolitical warfare after 1970, using ACDA data. These countries were selected based on two additional criteria. First, we focused on countries where the conflicts began after 1967 and before 1992, because of limitations in the coverage of ACDA data, which begins in 1963 and ends in the mid-1990s. Second, common wisdom suggested that there would be little correlation between the outbreak of fighting in Spain or in Northern Ireland and the arms imports of major powers such as Spain and the United Kingdom. Thus, we selected relatively smaller countries, which were more regionally focused.

As the table indicates, the results are mixed. Several of the states did import considerably more after conflicts erupted, in particular, Angola, Indonesia, and Morocco. Bangladesh and the Philippines displayed modest increases, and the change in Sri Lanka was more than 150 percent.[12] In just under half of the cases, though, states imported less or the same amounts of arms after the fighting began.

Table 2.7   Change in Average Reported Government Arms Imports (in constant $U.S. million) Prior to and During Ethnic Conflict

Country	Prior to Conflict	Average Arms Imports	During Conflict	Average Arms Imports
Angola	1970–74	0	1975–79	702
Bangladesh	1977–81	49	1982–86	64
Chad	1985–89	75	1990–94	25
Ethiopia	1986–90	749	1991–95	16
Fiji	1982–86	0	1987–91	0
Indonesia (E. Timor)	1971–75	67	1976–80	335
Kenya	1986–90	93	1991–95	11
Liberia	1984–88	16	1989–93	3
Morocco	1970–74	25	1975–79	743
Papua New Guinea	1985–89	22	1990–94	16
Peru	1976–80	613	1981–85	357
Philippines	1967–71	64	1972–76	85
Senegal	1977–81	39	1982–86	6
Sri Lanka	1978–82	10	1983–87	26
Sudan	1978–82	196	1983–87	84

Source: Data from U.S. Arms Control and Disarmament Agency, *World Military Expenditures and Arms Transfers,* various years.

In some cases, as in Senegal in the 1970s, governments had gone on buying sprees before violence erupted, and the military seemed to have all the arms they needed.

This is not necessarily to suggest that leaders predict outbreaks of fighting and arm in anticipation; the patterns displayed here could be coincidental. It should be noted that some of these countries experienced *international* conflict, which probably had an impact on their decision as to the amount of arms to acquire. Fighting, such as that which occurred between Angola and Zaire in the second half of the 1970s, Bangladesh and India in the mid-1980s, Morocco and Algeria in 1979, might help to explain increases in arms acquisitions. However, it should be noted that some countries that saw fighting had diminished imports, such as Peru (which fought with Ecuador). Additionally, some countries with no external involvements, such as Sri Lanka, increased their imports; others, such as Papua New Guinea, decreased theirs. In any case, the data suggest that more nuanced government arms studies are required to make further progress on the question of whether states respond to violence by increasing arms.

Table 2.8 shows the number of suppliers that exported arms to states before and during the outbreak of ethnopolitical warfare, with the assumption that the num-

Table 2.8   Shares of Major Suppliers to Governments Experiencing Ethnopolitical Conflict, Prior to and During Conflict

Country (Outbreak)	Prior to Outbreak of Conflict			During Conflict		
	Number of Suppliers	Top Supplier (%)	Top 3 Suppliers (%)	Number of Suppliers	Top Supplier (%)	Top 3 Suppliers (%)
Angola (1976)	2	67 (Other)	100	5	94 (USSR)	98
Bangladesh (1982)	5	67 (China)	96	7	76 (China)	92
Chad (1990)	3	68 (U.S.)	100	n/a	n/a	n/a
Ethiopia (1991)	5	60 (USSR)	91	n/a	n/a	n/a
Fiji (1987)	n/a	n/a	n/a	2	75 (France)	100
Indonesia/E. Timor (1976)	2	56 (U.S.)	100	6	46 (France)	90
Kenya (1991)	4	50 (France)	99	n/a	n/a	n/a
Liberia (1989)	1	100 (Other)	100	n/a	n/a	n/a
Morocco (1975)	4	81 (U.S.)	98	5	59 (France)	98
Papua New Guinea (1990)	2	60 (USSR)	100	n/a	n/a	n/a
Peru (1981)	8	37 (USSR)	71	7	30 (France)	72
Philippines (1972)	2	85 (U.S.)	100	6	78 (USA)	94
Senegal (1982)	2	84 (France)	100	2	94 (France)	100
Sri Lanka (1983)	2	63 (China)	100	5	37 (Other)	91
Sudan (1983)	5	48 (U.S.)	85	5	68 (Other)	97

Source: Brzoska and Ohlson (1987, Appendix 7) and SIPRI (1991).

ber would increase under the stress of active combat. For these fifteen exploratory cases, we cover the time period approximately five years before the conflict erupted, using SIPRI data on shares of major suppliers of major conventional weapons to Third World countries. The results are again mixed. In the cases of Angola, Bangladesh, Indonesia, Morocco, the Philippines, and Sri Lanka, states expanded their arms sources. These also tended to be states with the largest-scale internal struggles. However, particular circumstances varied in these states. While Angola expanded its array of suppliers, they accounted for only marginal sales; the USSR consistently supplied 94 percent of Angolan arms after the outbreak of fighting with UNITA. Indonesia largely switched from American to French arms, as did Morocco, which moved from four to five suppliers while converting to its French arms connection. This can possibly indicate a tendency to seek alternatives to Washington's sometime restrictions on arms shipments to conflict situations involving human rights concerns. The Philippines, in spite of some other relatively smaller purchases, continued to buy most of its arms from Washington (85 percent before the conflict compared with 78 percent during civil violence). Bangladesh, which expanded its list of suppliers, also relied more heavily on its primary source, China, which provided 67 percent of Bangladeshi arms prior to the conflict in the Chittagong Hill Tracts, and 76 percent afterward. Sri Lanka represents the best case of a country diversifying its arms import patterns.

Other states responded to ethnic violence in somewhat different ways. Senegal and Sudan both stayed with the same number of suppliers. The former increased its dependence on France, which supplied 94 percent of Senegalese arms after the fighting began. Peru slightly decreased its suppliers and also switched primary suppliers. Sudan, while keeping the same number of sources, also seemed to seek alternatives to dependence on the United States.

Ultimately, then, it appears as if states experiencing especially intense or widespread internal security problems or wishing to repress popular movements or segments of the population search among a larger group of suppliers for a *primary* arms source that will provide effective armament while imposing as few restrictions as possible. The mixed acquisition pattern also might result from the fact that many states acquire arms periodically, and thus when internal fighting does erupt, states already have existing stockpiles to rely on and existing deals for arms in the pipeline.

It is also possible that for some conflicts these data are a bit too coarse to reveal the importance of specific shipments of specific weapons. We know, for example, that there was a large arms shipment prior to the outbreak of the Rwandan conflict. Whether this equipment empowered the government toward its ethnic "cleansing" or even made a difference in its genocidal calculations is generally difficult to determine a priori. Certainly Boutwell and Klare argue that the common impression of Rwandan violence with machete hacking and clubbing is oversimplified:

> Before the killing began, the Hutu-dominated government had distributed automatic rifles and hand grenades to official militias and paramilitary gangs. It was this firepower that made the genocide possible. Militia members terrorized their victims with

guns and grenades as they rounded them up for systematic slaughter with machetes and knives. The murderous use of farm tools may have seemed a medieval aberration, but the weapons and paramilitary gangs that facilitated the genocide were all too modern. (Boutwell and Klare 2000, 48)

When faced with ethnopolitical conflict, states also are likely to respond with particular types of weapons based on the terrain and level of opposition. For example, when Turkey drove its forces into Iraq in the mid-1990s to attack Kurdish rebels who were making cross-border forays into Turkey, the Turks employed state-of-the-art military hardware, including American-made F-16 fighter aircraft (Washington sometimes formally objects to such cross-border uses by high-profile clients such as Israel). Likewise, the Sri Lankan government has resorted to aerial bombardment of Tamil Tiger bases. On the other hand, in some disputes, such as in the crowded West Bank administered by Israel, much of the weaponry used against the Palestinian uprising, at least before the renewed outbreak in late 2000, were small arms and antiriot gear. Governmental forces thus appear to deploy heavier equipment under four conditions: when the rebellious group is concentrated in one relatively isolated area, when the ethnic group is located or takes refuge inside another state, when there is little concern about collateral damage (in particular when domestic or international political costs from killing civilians is low), or when the ethnic group itself has only small arms.

CONCLUSION

Two practical findings emerge from our analysis of approximately fifty contemporary ethnopolitical conflicts. First, for most ethnopolitical groups, access to weapons is a challenging but not an insurmountable obstacle. As we have demonstrated, ethnic groups can acquire arms through a mix of strategies, including domestic procurement (especially in cases of state breakdown or in countries already awash in arms) and foreign import. Groups can turn to a large number of states and nonstate actors, often close by and willing to supply arms either on the open commercial market or on the black market. Finally, in a much smaller number of cases, ethnic groups can remanufacture what they need or supplement their arsenals by making homemade bombs, mortars, mines, modified launch platforms, and other small or mobile equipment.

States' arms acquisitions are also affected by conflict, particularly in larger-scale ethnic disputes. States tend to increase both the quantity of arms they acquire and the number of sources they tap for supplies under the stress of acute conflict. However, many also tend to rely on a primary arms source even under such circumstances.

All of these findings have practical and policy implications, which we will explore in chapter 6. The simple fact that people interested in studying arms and ethnopolitical conflict cannot readily peer into the fog of war to see relevant quantities, types, and sources of arms, and that intervenors find it difficult to patrol remote areas, suggests that conventional arms control is likely to be difficult. The different types of weapons used, as well as their varied sources, suggest that arms control and disarmament measures need to be complex to keep pace with the arms involved in ethnopolitical war.

Among this study's surprising findings so far are: (1) the evident predominance of groups' arms *imports* over domestic arms procurement, (2) the predominance of a few main arms suppliers for both groups and governments, (3) the tendency for government arms imports to be unaffected initially by the outbreak of fighting, and (4) the relative scarcity of confirmed transshipment of arms coming to ethnic fighting groups.

NOTES

1. The resolution creating the *Register* was adopted in 1991, and during 1992, procedures for operating it were identified and adopted. The first submissions of arms transfer information occurred during the spring of 1993 (Laurance 1995).

2. For good reviews of the history of the arms trade, see Harkavy (1979), Krause (1992), and Laurance (1992). Keller and Nolan (1997/1998) examine the question of whether the trade in major conventional weapons has changed since the end of the Cold War.

3. See Bonner (1998c), for example, on the case of Bulgarian arms sales after the Cold War.

4. As part of a moratorium on small arms in West Africa, largely springing from the Malian peace process in the mid-1990s, ACDA created such a list (Smaldone 1999).

5. We use the terms "small arms" and "light weapons" interchangeably in this volume.

6. Klare and Andersen (1996, 2) believe that about 15 percent of the arms trade consists of small arms. However, there is no way to know the percentage of an individual country's imports of small arms. Current estimates place the annual legal trade in small arms at between $7 billion and $10 billion, and the black market trade at $2 billion to $3 billion (Boutwell and Klare 2000).

7. Because the *Register* is relatively new compared with the other sources, scholars have not used it much in analyses of the causes and consequences of the arms trade. Instead, most scholars have focused on descriptive trends and the adequacy of UN reports. The concern for statistical analysis is that some sort of persistent systematic bias will result from gaps or disagreements in the data as in the United States-to-Finland example.

8. Early on, the Tibetans reportedly received arms and military equipment clandestinely from United States intelligence services, but evidently not in recent decades.

9. A second example involves Sarkis Soghanalian, a Lebanese citizen, who brokered arms on several occassions. Recently, he appears to have been part of a deal by which AK-47s from Jordan were to be sent to the Peruvian military. Some of these weapons turned up in the hands of the Colombian guerrillas FARC (Revolutionary Armed Forces of Colombia). Soghanalian claims to have been set up by Vladimiro Montesinos, then chief of Peru's intelligence service (Rempel and Rotella 2000).

10. Complicated routings both raise and lower shipment safety for the group. In the former sense, transshipment points hinder accurate tracking and obfuscate weapon origins and

descriptions. However, each transit point is also a possible locale for detection and confiscation. Moreover, arms might be siphoned off from the shipment at each stop, so that the final delivery is smaller than contracted. Secondhand arms are frequently passed on through wars in several states; quality control is certainly suspect.

11. Recently, it was alleged that Zambia was a transshipment point. The Zambians denied any role in arming UNITA (Keesing's 1999).

12. The Angola case is misleading since the preconflict period occurred prior to the state's independence. It is likely that arms imports did increase after the conflict broke out, but there were few arms imports prior to the conflict, so the change is not as large as seems here.

Chapter Three

Arms and the Onset
of Ethnic Conflict

After seven years of unheeded "early warning," the ethnic violence of Kosovo finally commenced on a major scale in the spring and summer of 1998. Disillusioned with the slow pace of political accommodation, an extremist nationalist group seeking to represent ethnic Albanians living in the Serbian province launched a violent rebellion against Serb authorities in the once autonomous region. In the process, moderate Kosovar-Albanian nationalists were displaced at least temporarily in the resort to arms. Serb police and military units responded with harsh and bloody crackdowns on suspected leaders, recruits, and their families. The entire process looked alarmingly familiar, as in the scenes of ethnic carnage witnessed in places such as Bosnia since the end of the Cold War. To many, the pattern of "ethnic cleansing" that resulted, as hundreds of thousands of refugees were uprooted from their homes, also brought back horrible memories of the period that preceded the holocaust and genocide in World War II, or in the case of Armenians in Turkey, early in the twentieth century.

One intriguing question is whether the Kosovo uprising was dependent on acquisitions and infusions of armament. There is a good deal of controversy about the extent and source of arms for the KLA, the fighting force that confronted the Serbs after 1997. Analysis of this question requires piecing together some sort of arms and war chronology, a task attempted later in this chapter. Nevertheless, this specific case raises a set of critical questions for analysts and policy makers alike: are arms infusions necessary or sufficient conditions for the triggering of ethnic or identity wars? Do significant arms buildups generally precede or follow the start of fighting or escalations in combat? If the pattern generally shows buildups preceding warfare, then arms acquisitions by governments or ethnic groups in the midst of rising tensions could be a valuable early warning indicator, giving outside parties time to step in before violence explodes.

Many scholars are interested in the preventative aspect of theories on the causes of ethnopolitical conflict. Van Evera (1994), for example, has suggested that the catalytic factors or preconditions leading from nationalism to war can be useful predictors to determine when nationalism will be dangerous. There has been increased interest in using changes in arms flows or accumulation as warnings of violence (Harff and Gurr 1998; Laurance 1999). In the 1990s, this has been the case for major conventional weapons, as suggested by the *UN Register of Conventional Arms,* which was designed to increase the transparency of arms flows, identify "destabilizing" and "excessive weapons" buildups. Husbands (1995, 131) suggests that "monitoring the flow of light arms to regions of tension can be a useful measure of incipient conflict." This is a very logical conclusion if in fact arms acquisitions do play a clear and discernible role in the onset of ethnopolitical conflict.

Beyond this rationale, examining the impact of arms on the onset of political violence is worthwhile for other reasons as well. It is important to know whether concepts such as arms balances, arms races, and deterrence used to explain or predict incidents of international conflict also apply in domestic war contexts, especially in light of the growing importance of internal disputes. If applicable, the insight gained from these concepts can help determine when ethnic conflict might or might not turn violent. For example, Spear (1996) has argued that ethnic conflicts can entail arms races between an identity group and a government. Posen (1993) has sought to apply the concept of "security dilemma" (the phenomenon whereby those who arm competitively for security end up feeling no more secure because their opponents also arm in return) to substate actors. These scholars are on the right track in that more can be done in searching for analogies between international and civil war, especially as regards the role of armament and arms acquisition.

As peace and conflict scholars are quick to point out, most armed political violence under way today occurs within states, and the majority of these disputes at least have an ethnopolitical component (see Wallensteen and Sollenberg 1997). Scholars note that many variables play a direct or indirect role in the occurrence of ethnic war and that research is at the beginning of a process of identifying and testing those factors. We believe that armament patterns, once more systematically considered, could play a significant role in understanding civil violence.

This chapter, then, is divided into four parts. In the next section, we discuss the concept of the initiation of ethnopolitical violence. Following that, we explore the antecedents ("causes" may be too strong a term) of such violence within two strands of research: the literature on rebellion and the literature on arms and warfare. In the third section, we hypothesize about the role of arms in affecting these outbreaks in cases of ethnic conflict. Finally, we turn to empirical analysis of data on these issues.

From a reading of the Kosovo example, particular arms acquisitions themselves are unlikely to be a necessary or sufficient catalyst for ethnic violence in general. However, accumulations of arms, and in some instances particularly empowering acquisitions, may make it easier and more tempting for ethnic groups with strong grievances to choose violent forms of political action. Moreover, such accumulations can create insecurity in relevant political actors, insecurity that might subsequently find expression in preemptive attacks or in state repression—although judging from the Kosovar example, it was the initial armed attacks themselves, rather than arms accumulations, that seemed to spark Serbs into especially repressive action.

THE ONSET OF ETHNIC VIOLENCE

Many countries are heterogeneous, consisting of multiple ethno-cultural and communal groups. Ethnic or identity groups are defined in terms of a shared history, language, or culture among other distinguishing characteristics. A subset of these groups might have politically defined economic or social grievances that represent a perceptual shortfall between what the group expects in the way of resources, protection, or treatment, and what it actually receives. When these grievances are expressed in political action, ethnopolitical conflict and possibly violence result. Such conflict, which can overlap with other forms of domestic strife, such as class, caste, or economic disputes, can take form between two or more ethnic groups or between groups and a government over "important political, social, cultural, or territorial issues" (Brown, 1993, 5).

However, despite appearances to the contrary, most of the ethnic groups worldwide are not at each other's throats most of the time (Fearon and Laitin 1996). Many cases of ethnic tension do not spill over into significant violence. The Quebec secession movement, for example, generally (at least since the 1970s) has been "fought" in the framework of electoral politics and referenda. Ethnic tensions thus can be played out within the arena of conventional politics, and depending on the nature of the regime, might involve a variety of tactics. In Western democracies, ethnic groups can, with sufficient resources, form interest groups to lobby for change, offer candidates for office, vote along ethnically distinct lines, air their grievances through the media, or stage legal demonstrations and bring lawsuits. Such groups also might choose more unconventional approaches, including violence. As we consider less democratic regimes, the conventional choices appear to shrink.

When ethnopolitical conflicts, often referred to as political "identity disputes," take on a violent nature, the violence can be similar to other forms of internal war, for example, war over economic or class issues (e.g., economic unrest in Albania in 1996, the Tupac Amaru rebellion in Peru, and the guerrilla movement in Colombia). In the dozens of identity disputes under way since 1990, violence, as measured in annual casualties, ranges from relatively low, as in the cases of Northern Ireland and Spain, to much higher in the more deadly conflicts in the Balkans, Rwanda, and Sudan. As noted in chapter 1, violent conflicts can involve one or a combination of three scenarios: rebellions undertaken by ethnopolitical groups against ruling governments, state repression by the government against a particular ethnic group, and interethnic fighting.

The onset of fighting can be thought of as a demarcation between two different behaviors. In the study of international violence occurring between two or more states, initiation separates "peace," however tenuous and strained, from war. However, this demarcation may or may not be clear in practice. It might not be clear when the first shots were fired or the first "border skirmishes" took place, and whether these are the appropriate demarcations for subsequent "wars." The concept of war implies rather sustained bilateral or multilateral combat. Once behavioral scientists defined international war as an armed conflict between two or more members of the international system (e.g., states) with at least 1,000 battle casualties, it became possible to identify and analyze the phenomenon at least somewhat more precisely. Moreover, most of the time states are at peace with one another, so that wars—relatively infrequent events when measured against possible dyadic relations—are that much more distinct (Small and Singer 1985). Likewise, military "interventions" undertaken by one state inside another's territory are a relatively discrete form of action, as for example, when the United States moved troops into Grenada and Lebanon during the Reagan administration. However, there may still be ambiguities concerning when intervention ceases, and in contexts when inaction might itself be a form of intervention (as when inaction by potential intervenors allows one faction inside a state to win power over another).

The beginning of internal identity wars also can be difficult to establish with precision. Indeed, initiation dates for international conflicts, such as the Gulf War, generally are more identifiable and readily accepted than the start dates of civil wars. Most people would accept the fact that hostilities between Iraq and Kuwait began on August 2, 1990, while hostilities between the coalition of UN-sanctioned forces and Iraq began with a massive air offensive on January 16, 1991. Unlike international conflict, however, in domestic situations, scholars, reporters, and officials often cannot agree on the *year* the fighting began, let alone the exact date. Contemporary hostilities in Sri Lanka between the government and the ethnic Tamil minority, for example, are variously thought to have begun in 1982, 1983, 1984, or 1985 (for 1982, see Regan 1996a, 1996b; for 1983, Brown 1996; for 1984, Sivard 1996; for 1985, Gurr and Harff 1994). Part of this confusion is that scholars have yet to come up with as clear a set of operational definitions for civil or identity conflicts as they have for international wars and military interventions.

Klare and Andersen (1996) note that the study of light weapons—arms most often used in ethnic conflicts—must be made in the context of what they term the "culture of violence" that is pervasive in such regions as Central and South America, or central and south Asia. In many countries, the use of guns and associated political violence are common phenomena. The idea that violence is so ordinary has prompted some scholars to adopt the 1,000 battle casualty figure to separate "conflict" from other politics within the state (see Licklider 1995; Wallensteen and Sollenberg 1997).

However, in line with others who focus on escalation of a dispute to violence (e.g., Carlson 1995; Dixon 1996; Sample 1997), we define the initiation of violence simply in terms of the onset of the first escalation to attributable acts of intrastate political violence. That escalation can vary from a short step to a massive leap. For example, in studying rebellion in the *Minorities at Risk* project, Gurr and Moore (1997) present a scale ranging from 0 to 7, where "0" represents no rebellion and violence increases thereafter. Subsequent escalation ranges from (1) sporadic terrorist acts, to (2) more organized and frequent terrorism, (3) local rebellion, (4) small-scale guerrilla activity, (5) participation by ethnic group in civil war, (6) large-scale guerrilla activity, and finally, (7) to protracted civil war.

Thus, ethnic conflicts sometimes break out at very low violence levels, as in the Kosovo case, or at much higher levels, as in Bosnia and Serbia. The entire range is worth study because significant disruption to local polities can result from even sporadic acts, and because we wish to determine the role of armament in the escalation of conflict to various levels of violence. Consider an ethnic group at time t that has some set of grievances against the state, but is not using violent means to express its dissatisfaction. At time t + 1, the group may continue to use nonviolent means, such as a strike or demonstration; it might shift to sporadic and limited terrorism by detonating a few bombs or attacking a few outposts or individuals; or it could leap to more substantial forms of rebellion. In this chapter, we are interested in the first violent move by an ethnopolitical group. As seen in the case studies below, for example, we would date the Kosovar rebellion in Yugoslavia as beginning in 1995, and escalating thereafter.

ARMS AND ONSET

What role do arms play in the onset of ethnopolitical violence? We can apply the basic concepts identified in chapter 1: opportunity and willingness, where opportunity is largely seen as a function of capabilities, and willingness involves intentions. In the recent literature on internal wars, it is apparent that arms are a factor in the opportunity for ethnic groups and governments to use violence as a form of political expression, and in their willingness to do so. Studies of civil war emphasize the importance of group identity and grievances. This literature focuses primarily on willingness to struggle and tends to treat arms as related most closely to opportunity for violent action.[1]

Ethnic or identity-based violence is the product of the interaction of states, their policies, and the responses of resident ethnic communities. One way to think about such violence is that it is the result of two choices by a group (or a specific subset of entrepreneurs within the group) to undertake a particular action. A group that is the subject of perceived discrimination or state repression first has to choose whether or not to mobilize in order to redress its grievances, that is, to organize more formally and obtain needed resources for action. Then it has to choose one of three responses: take no action and continue suffering, protest (either conventionally—through means such as voting—or unconventionally—through such methods as strikes or riots, and either peacefully or with some violence), or rebel (always violent, to varying degrees). Mobilization and action are separate but interdependent choices. If mobilization happens first, it is unlikely that an ethnic group will choose to continue to do nothing and bear the costs of their grievances. Mobilization tends to push groups toward protest or rebellion. Rebellion without prior mobilization and preparation, often in the form of armament, would be difficult though it might consist of spontaneous rioting.

In explaining the outbreak of ethnopolitical conflict, many scholars look at both the group and its environment. One component, stressing "exogenous" factors surrounding the group, argues that ethnic communities view certain aspects of social or political change as a threat to their identity/security and respond or mobilize to try to protect themselves. Included in this aspect, is the role of the government, whose responses can favor ethnically inclusive or exclusive policies. A second argument, centering on "endogenous" factors peculiar to the group itself, emphasizes the pursuit of group goals, material or political in nature, as a force shaping collective action, as well as the degree of cohesion of the group, and its capacity for action. This view also tends to highlight ethnic elites or entrepreneurs, who can mold group support to achieve a particular platform (Gurr 1993; Gurr and Harff 1994; Gurr 2000). Fundamentally, violent conflict is the product of community grievances and political mobilization.

Grievances and mobilization, and ultimately the nature of ethnic conflict are in turn affected by a myriad of factors. These have been the subjects of several scholarly typologies. Brown (1993 and 1996) and Van Evera (1994) focus on four clusters of factors favoring domestic political, including ethnic, violence: structural, political, socioeconomic, and cultural/perceptual. These factors create and shape grievances, elicit mobilization, and affect the degree and form of state repression. Among the structural factors contributing to ethnic violence are states' weaknesses, internal security dilemmas, and heterogeneity of ethnic groups within a single country. Relevant political factors include authoritarian, illegitimate or unrepresentative regimes, exclusionary ideologies, ambitious ethnic groups with conflicting goals, and aggravating elite politics (such as the passage of discriminatory legislation regarding such fundamentally sensitive matters as citizenship, property rights, education, employment, and language usage). Economic problems and economic discrimination are a third set of issues that can promote the outbreak of violence by highlighting intergroup differences and disparities. Cultural discrimination and an ethnic group's own myths about its proper place in a state can favor such violence as well. Other scholars have conceptually organized their work around the nature of the actors involved (the ethnic groups and the regime) and the sociopolitical environment (Gurr 1993; Gurr and Harff 1994; Gurr and Moore 1997; Kaufman 1996).

One environmental component relevant for our purposes is the notion of external support, which can include arms flows. According to Singh (1995, x), the "supply of small arms and training in their use is the most frequent assistance provided by external states and non-state actors" to disputants in internal conflicts. Sending arms is a ready and concrete act that signifies support without initially risking the donor's own personnel in a direct intervention. The literature on how arms affect ethnic conflict remains at only the most general level and centers mainly on support of rebellious ethnic groups. There is little consideration of how government arms acquisitions or deployment might influence group rebellion, or how one ethnic community's arms acquisitions might affect other groups' rebellious tendencies. This interactive dynamic has not been explored much in the civil conflict literature, but is a hallmark of the arms and international war literature.

Some ethnic conflicts are not so much disputes between ethnic communities as they are reactions to state repression or complicated state policies directed against minority communities. Gurr and Moore (1997) note that such repression is likely to be the result of several factors. One is the amount of real or anticipated ethnic rebellion. A second factor is the state's coercive capability, which might include, for practical purposes, the size of the military or internal security forces, training, and armament. A third element concerns past repression, which if successful, can lead to the institutionalization of repression within the state.

Still, the role of arms is considered at only a general level in such analyses, as a capability of the state for carrying out repressive policies. The interactive dynamic between government and group armament is missing. Would not government and the ethnic group fear each other's arms acquisitions? Moreover, if past rebellion is an antecedent of current repression, then more complex arms relationships might be involved, if only indirectly.

The literature on arms and war in general can offer some guidance in teasing out the nuances of the impact of arms on ethnic fighting in particular. Most scholars seem to believe that weapons acquisitions themselves do not directly lead to war. However, arms appear to be a contributing factor, an antecedent variable affecting the relationship between two states in ways conducive to war by, for example, creating insecurity through arms races. Arms acquisitions have been associated with increased conflict or bellicose behavior, while, occasionally, arms embargoes have been associated with declining violence (Kinsella 1994a, 1994b, 1995; Sanjian 1995, 1999; Sylvan 1976; Pearson, Baumann, and Bardos 1989). Stedman (1996) notes that the cutoff of military aid by the Soviets may have facilitated a political settlement in Nicaragua; a similar cutoff of U.S. aid supposedly helped push the Salvadoran government to make concessions in its long civil war.

Weapon supplies, however, also can lead to the increased propensity for hostility among actors in an arms race.[2] This is because they take arms as a sign not just of capabilities for harm, but of intentions to do harm as well (Baugh and Squires 1983). In a realist-conceived international system based on power balances, mutual threat, and self-help, what state could take the risk that a potential enemy was arming solely for defense?

The contrasting view is known as the *para bellum* hypothesis: if you want peace, prepare for war. This approach suggests that the outcome of arms buildups is likely to be peace through deterrence. At first glance, it would seem as if deterrence theory, derived from interstate relations, would be difficult to apply to interethnic or group–government relations. While a state might arm to provide security for internal groups, it seems unlikely that an ethnic group would acquire arms to deter a state. In a sense, though, an ethnic community that arms in a campaign for autonomy or secession might in the long run achieve a form of deterrence stability, although in the short run, deterrence might be likely to fail as the government tries to stifle the uprising. Just enough armament to convince authorities that the group can and will persist in rebellion, employing such means as "hit-and-run" tactics, can tip the scales in favor of serious negotiations in some circumstances. Of course, the state might also be provoked into ever harsher repression.

The ethnic conflict literature provides a detailed examination of the critical factors involved in rebellion and repression, but largely ignores the question of armament (external support) and arms balances or races. The role of arms in the "run-up" to identity wars is likely to be complex. Weapons acquisition is one aspect of the mobilization process, while resources are gathered for action. Acquisitions also are a means for ethnic groups to express grievances, and a reason or a means for states to respond, since the state's sovereign monopoly on political armament is threatened. Thus, arms acquisitions and supplies can be perceived as a beneficial resource to protect one's interests, but they also can lead to diminished security and increased threat perception. While an ethnic group might see arms as an opportunity to advance its interests, states see danger; while states see security in arms, ethnic groups might see increased repression directed against them. Specific minority groups might feel extremely vulnerable in the face of well-armed ethnic opponents and militia as well.

Nevertheless, since armament is seldom likely to be a sufficient condition for war, just because a country is awash in arms does not necessarily mean that ethnic violence is imminent, though it might certainly be a warning sign. As noted above, identity group grievances can be funneled through both conventional and unconventional politics. By making violent political acts more feasible and by possibly raising the tension and reaction levels, however, weapons acquisitions, either by identity groups or by the state, can contribute to the outbreak of civil unrest. Arms, thereby, are not likely to be a direct cause of violence, but through their effect on threat perception, might constitute an interactive variable or catalyst, combining with group grievances, governmental policy changes, and tactical decisions to produce violence.

As a first proposition, then, we suggest that major arms or great new access to weapons are not needed for violence to break out, nor does the mere presence of widespread armament in a conflict zone reliably predict violence. To evaluate this proposition, and to better understand the dynamics and variety of ways in which arms relate to ethnopolitical warfare, we survey four cases that illustrate each of the outcomes created by combining arms access (high or low) and the onset (or not) of ethnopolitical uprisings (see table 3.1).[3]

In the case of Sri Lanka, Tamils initially had access to light arms, and this facilitated the outbreak of the violence that began in 1983 and continued for more than seventeen years. This case, in which armament did seem to catalyze rebellion, can

Table 3.1   The Relationship between Arms and Outbreak

	Outbreak of Rebellion	*No Outbreak of Rebellion*
High Access to Arms	Tamils in Sri Lanka	Berbers in Algeria
Low Access to Arms	Palestinians in West	Magyar (Hungarians) in
	Bank/Gaza	Romania

be contrasted with the *Intifada*—or Palestinian uprising—in December 1987, which occurred at relatively limited levels of violence despite the general absence of manufactured weapons. In Algeria, on the other hand, weapons were available at least generally in the area, but the Berbers there, as a rule, chose not to pursue a violent course and over the years undertook protests and demonstrations to address their grievances. Finally, ethnic tensions concerning the position and power of the Hungarian minority in Romania have not yet produced a sustained violent outbreak; in part it appears due to the general absence of weapons.

CASE STUDIES

Tamils in Sri Lanka

The beginning of the most recent violent phase in an enduring dispute, rooted in the days of colonialism, dates to July 1983 (Tambiah 1986; Singer 1996). The conflict involved the two main ethno-linguistic groups on the island: Sinhalese and Tamils, of whom the latter were a minority at 18 percent of the population (11 percent Sri Lankan Tamils and 7 percent Indian Tamils). Additionally, these groups were distributed unequally across the country where the Sinhalese have enjoyed a strong majority, except in the north (Austin and Gupta 1988).

The conflict between the two (or three) identity groups stems from issues regarding political power (with underlying economic tensions) and ethnic identity. The Tamils have felt threatened on both fronts. The Sinhalese believe that they descended from Indo-Aryan tribes and that Buddha himself entrusted the Sinhala with the island (Spencer 1990, 20). The Tamils, on the other hand, practice Hinduism and claim they have lived on the island for more than 1,000 years as an autonomous group, especially in the Jaffna Peninsula. In the extreme sense, some Tamil legends hold that they were the original inhabitants and that the Sinhalese are only Tamils converted to Buddhism. During British colonial days, there were religious clashes between Buddhists and Hindus, but never at the level seen after 1983. The colonial administration created a structure that divided the population into ethnic, language, and religious factions and bred mutual resentment; in addition, large numbers of Tamils were moved to the island from mainland India. Tamils generally were given greater access to colonial administration and generally elevated over the Sinhalese majority.

The postindependence unitary parliamentary system, patterned after London's Whitehall, gradually evolved into ethnically based parties and coalitions, with the majority Sinahalese gaining ascendency. In 1956 a language act was passed, making Sinhala the official national language, effectively alienating the Tamils. Riots broke out when additional efforts were launched to make Buddhism the official state religion. Protests ensued again in 1961 when language diversity provisions of the Tamil Language Act of 1958 remained unfulfilled (O'Ballance 1989, 4–6), leading to arrests and crackdowns on Tamil organizations. As a result, Tamil independence groups, such as the Tamil United Liberation Front (TULF), developed in the 1970s. The LTTE, an extremist military wing, was created in 1976 to launch guerrilla-style attacks on government installations.

In addition to growing ethnic unrest, a class struggle emerged as a Marxist revolutionary group, the People's Liberation Front (JVP), reportedly used Chinese and North Korean arms and ammunition to launch armed attacks aimed at destabilizing the government in the countryside and even in Colombo. The North Korean Embassy in Colombo was identified as a supply depot, leading to the expulsion of the ambassador in 1971. The Colombo government, which finally succeeded in squelching the JVP, received considerable military aid from countries such as the United States, Britain, India, Pakistan, Yugoslavia, and the Soviet Union (e.g., six MIG-17s from Russia, six helicopters each from India and Britain, and two more from Pakistan, see O'Ballance 1989, 8–9).

With this as a stage-setting background, in July 1983, the LTTE ambushed and killed fifteen soldiers outside Jaffna using remote-controlled land mines stolen from army storage outside the city.[4] Although the government attempted to keep the incident quiet, the news quickly spread. Sinhalese, inflamed by reports and rumors about the ambush, rampaged through Colombo attacking Tamils and burning their houses and businesses. A Sinhalese mob broke into the Walikade prison and killed some fifty-two Tamil inmates with knives and clubs. According to O'Ballance (1989, 23–26), the July riots, with death tolls reportedly reaching 362 ("Death Toll in Ethnic Violence in Sri Lanka Revised to 362" 1983), were a watershed event that "divided the nation into two hostile camps, and pitched Sinhalese and Tamils irrevocably against each other" (for similar views, see Singh 1995).

Those events do not appear to have been highly premeditated; rather, they seemed to be part of a larger series of tit-for-tat attacks and counterattacks that had occurred during the summer (Tambiah 1986). Indeed, after August, things evidently quieted back down until early 1984 when a new Sri Lankan government began diplomatic overtures to Pakistan, China, and South Korea, thus alarming India. New Delhi up to that point had worked relatively cordially with the Sri Lankan authorities out of concern over the flow of refugees and tales of atrocities as Tamils spilled into the Indian state of Tamil Nadu. Colombo's ties to India's enemies, however, soon brought Indira Gandhi to aid the various Tamil liberation organizations, providing weapons and training in Madras, thus sending the Sri Lankan authorities a strong message.

At the outset, the Tamil Tigers were armed relatively lightly, with shotguns, rifles, automatic rifles, and submachine guns. Some of these weapons were taken from government soldiers, others were imported from southern India. Much of the early fighting in Sri Lanka, as a result, consisted of ambushes, political assassinations, and bombings (Claiborne 1983; Weaver 1983). Thus, available arms supplies can dictate the style and pacing of early ethnic violence.

The pattern developed further in 1984, as the LTTE reportedly picked up arms from the PLO as well as from India and other international market sources. Thus, the Tamils began to carry out insurgent attacks and kidnappings not only against the Sri Lankan government, but also against other Tamil factions, eventually weakening and eliminating these rivals. In this case, the type and level of available arms seemed to condition the type of violent strategies and tactics adopted by the insurgents. The rebellion began with rather light armament, locally available or derived from India and sufficient to forestall a quick government victory. Added arms sources, including foreign patronage, allowed the subsequent expansion of the military campaign and broadening of goals.

The *Intifada*

Despite the Tamil example, arms are not always necessary for the onset of violence. A motivated ethnopolitical group can turn to violence even when the opportunity to acquire arms is quite low, especially if there is a political incentive to do so. Such an example is the case of the Palestinian uprising in Israeli occupied territory that began in 1987. In this instance, arms were widely present in both Israel and the occupied territories on the West Bank and Gaza, but mainly in possession of Israeli authorities and occupiers (especially settlers).

The Palestinians had long had a wide range of grievances with the Israeli state, which came to include human rights issues such as press censorship, detentions, and travel restrictions; economic hardships, such as taxation and land and property confiscation/demolition; and political issues of rights and equity (see Pressberg, 1988; Siniora 1988). Alongside these grievances were increasing nationalism and frustration with the lack of progress achieved through PLO strategies. Both trends were fueled in part by changing demographics in the West Bank and the Gaza Strip. Specifically, a majority of Palestinians were under thirty years of age. On the one hand, they had access to education, but no concomitant rise in economic prospects and opportunities. This produced a growing realization that a better future was not forthcoming. Additionally, the younger Palestinians tended to be more radical and, with fewer conflicting business and social interests, more willing to undertake active struggle.

Fueled by the disillusionment generated by the Egyptian-Israeli Camp David Accords of 1978, Arab League states and the PLO allocated some $150 million annually for ten years to build an organizational infrastructure inside the territories. This involved increased trade union activities, as well as an upsurge in women's, students', and youth organizations (Shalev 1991, 14–42). Islamic groups, including the soon-to-be infamous HAMAS, ironically initially assisted by the Israelis as a foil against the better-armed PLO, began to campaign for a religious *jihad*. Thus, the uprising, while indigenous to the territories, could relate both to a viable organizational structure and an outside support network (that may have even assisted in eventual acquisition of some light arms).

Other external factors also may have contributed to the uprising. The most notable was perhaps the gradual and unexpected collapse of the Soviet Union and cessation of the superpower rivalry from the late 1980s. By this time, the two superpowers had begun encouraging a series of regional conflict settlements, ranging from Angola to Afghanistan. The *Intifada* might have been designed partly to catch their interest and bring added pressure on Israel. Also, Palestinians felt that Arab League attention had begun to wander, especially at the league meetings in Amman in November 1988, toward the Iran-Iraq and Gulf area.

On December 9, 1987, tensions came to a head. A traffic accident involving an Israeli truck killed four Palestinians in the Gaza Strip, leading to immediate protests that spread to the West Bank. The uprising, termed *Intifada,* or "shaking off" in Arabic, was indeed defined by the lack of Palestinian arms inside the "territories." In its first year, the uprising was called "the war of the stones," and was carried out by large groups of Palestinian men, women, and children. The participants deliberately used no "arms" in order to establish a sharp contrast to the armed Israeli authorities (Mishal and Aharoni 1994, 1). The use of stones, slingshots, petrol bombs (technically a form of armament), and leaflets was meant to grab attention in Israel and throughout the world. While clearly the *Intifada* involved forms of violence and primitive arms, it was described by Fatah Central Committee member Abu Iyad (1990) as "an unarmed Palestinian revolt against loss of Palestinian rights and lands."

As a result, the Israeli response appeared brutal. A number of Palestinians were killed in the clashes. An article appearing in the *Economist* one year after the outbreak of the fighting summed up the situation:

> Although it has been a ghastly year for both sides, the 1–1/2m Palestinians of the occupied territories have suffered more. Well over 300 have been killed and thousands more injured; ordinary life has collapsed under the weight of strikes and curfews. The Israelis, in contrast, have got off fairly lightly. Army reservists have had to do long spells of riot patrol in the territories but the duty is miserable, seldom dangerous. In a year of disturbances only eight Israelis—two soldiers and six civilians—have been killed. (Year of Living Dangerously 1988, 50)

In addition to Palestinians killed by Israelis, and vice versa, Palestinians also killed each other in a struggle against collaboration with the Israelis. By 1992, it was estimated that Israelis had killed 900 Palestinians, while Palestinians had killed 450 of their fellow countrymen (Deadlier Intifadah 1992, 43).

Within a year of the uprising, its character began to change. In place of large groups of rock-throwing youths blocking streets, the disturbances were increasingly carried out by a smaller "hard-core" group of Palestinians, who had, aside from rocks, taken to using knives (attacks on Israeli settlers by young unorganized knife-wielding individuals killed fifty-two between 1985 and 1987) and firebombs. Freed, writing in February 1988, noted that an ambush of an Israeli security patrol in the Gaza Strip marked both the changed nature of the conflict as well as its escalation. The attackers used explosives and automatic weapons, "the first reported use of firearms by Palestinians against any Israeli—military, security or civilian—since the uprising began" (Freed 1988, 1; see also Salpeter 1988, 6–7; From Dream to Nightmare 1991). This tactical shift, which ultimately resulted in at least 39 incidents involving hand grenades, 127 bombings, and 102 attacks involving knives and hatchets (Shalev 1991, 70–76), was largely attributed to tougher Israeli countermeasures.

What were the consequences of the *Intifada*? For the Palestinians, the first year marked major political gains. In particular, during the Palestine National Council meeting at Algiers, November 12–15, 1988, Yasir Arafat, spurred to action, announced intentions for an independent Palestinian state. Perhaps more important during 1988, "Palestinians, buoyed by a new-found sense of community, talk of asserting economic independence and replacing violence with massive civil disobedience. In Arab villages and Palestinian refugee camps, self-appointed grassroots committees to administer community life have sprung up for the first time" (Montalbano 1988). Essentially, the uprising, at least in its first few months, was seen to enhance Palestinian morale and sympathy for the cause more than any other action undertaken since Israel's independence in 1948. However, the gains and euphoria seemed to fade as the *Intifada* matured.

As the Palestinian fortunes initially improved, those of the Israelis declined. Analysts began to draw the analogy of Israel, historically cast as David, now playing Goliath's brutal role. Certainly, Israel's prestige dropped in the eyes of the international community. The *Intifada* also caused an economic drain as money was shifted to domestic security concerns. It deeply affected Israeli domestic politics and military strategies in an army never before confronted with massive civil unrest. The use of supposedly "nonlethal" but highly disabling rubber bullets, for example, was to become standard fare.

This episode demonstrates that ethnopolitical groups can rebel even in situations where arms are not readily accessible to them or when the group does not, at least initially, seek to use those arms it can obtain. Palestinians inside the territories chose a form of civil disobedience during the outbreak and early stages of the uprising. In the early stages, which did not appear highly coordinated but nevertheless reflected a degree of planning, and which essentially expressed pent-up rage, the participants picked up whatever was at hand—rocks. Demonstrators were apparently conscious of how far they could (relatively) safely push the Israelis, and tried as the uprising evolved to reach that edge but not go past it.

The Berbers in Algeria

Just as the onset of ethnopolitical violence can occur regardless of the presence of large amounts of weapons, the presence of weapons need not always produce the onset of violence. Such is the case with the Berbers in Algeria. The Berbers are thought to be the original inhabitants of North Africa.[5] Arab settlement, beginning in the seventh century, challenged the Berbers' way of life. Berber areas became concentrated in regions that were hardest to reach, including the mountains of Kabylia and Aurès. The Berbers have sought to resist the Arabs, Turks, and French, who attempted to impose rule on them. Today, Berbers make up around 30 percent of Algeria's population. Partly as a result of a long history of resistance and population density, the Berbers have a strong identity.

Berbers are predominantly distinguished by linguistic and cultural differences. These differences became the rallying point for Berber identity after Algeria became a state in 1962. While the government sought to Arabize the country, the Berbers sought to maintain their unique heritage. They were challenged on two fronts.

The National Liberation Front (FLN), the dominant political party, has been able to keep the Berbers at bay, limiting their ability to participate in official policy making and in conventional politics. The Islamic Salvation Front (FIS), among other Islamic parties, became the second threat. During elections in December 1991, the FIS showed surprisingly strong returns. The army intervened and a civil war erupted in 1992 between the government and the FIS (represented through its military wing, the Islamic Salvation Army (AIS), which has killed up to 80,000 Algerians (Peace of a Kind 1999). Added to this mix is the Armed Islamic Group (GIA), which seems to have emerged in 1993, and has been linked to killings and massacres. While fighting the government, the FIS represents a worse alternative for the Berbers, in particular through its calls for mandatory Arabic in education and government.

The civil war that broke out in 1992 between the FIS and the government had its roots in political, economic, and sociocultural crises (Pierre and Quandt 1996; Stone 1997). After independence, the Algerian leaders feared that a multiparty state might weaken the country, so a one-party system, led by the FLN was created. In the 1980s, Islamic groups began to challenge the government as being out of touch, corrupt, and insufficiently devout. Ironically, the government's liberalizing response opened the door to the creation of the FIS, the elections in 1991, and the subsequent civil war. The cohesiveness of the Islamic groups was aided by a sense of countering the Berber minority and the remnants of French colonialism, as well as a heightened awareness of the latent power of Islam demonstrated in the 1979 revolution in Iran (Quandt 1998). In addition to the challenge in the political realm, the nation saw social and economic problems, such as substantial unemployment, economic barriers to advancement, and a more noticeable gap between rich and poor.

On July 5, 1998, Algeria enacted an Arabization law, which had been in the works since 1991. The law stated that Arabic would be the only language in official documents and at official meetings. Cinema and television would also be broadcast (or dubbed) in Arabic (*Africa Research Bulletin* 1998, 13184). At the same time, a famous Berber singer, Lounes Matoub was killed in June 1998, infuriating the Berbers.

Arms appear to have been available to the Berbers among the many weapons entering the country. Islamic groups had developed complex import networks, and one source was Europe. The Islamic Salvation Front (FIS) was buying small arms (mainly Czech-made) in Switzerland, which were shipped to Algeria through Austria, Germany, Switzerland, France, and Spain (Czech Weapons for Islamic Extremists in Algeria 1996). Further evidence for this arms route was demonstrated in two trials that took place in Europe. In 1997, four Algerians were convicted in Germany of smuggling weapons to radical Algerian Islamic groups in 1999; a similar trial was under way in France (German Court Convicts Four Algerian Smugglers 1997; Islamic Militants Face Up to Eight Years in Jail 1999). A second pipeline to the Islamic groups might have come from Osama bin Laden, the Saudi millionaire who has been linked to terrorism and the Afghan weapons network (Algeria Accuses bin Laden of Financing Islamic Terrorists 1998). The Polisario in Morocco was also believed to be selling light arms to the FIS (Polisario Reportedly Selling Arms to Algerian FIS 1997). While the Berbers did not have the same access that the Islamic groups had, it seems that they would have had some access to arms if they had been willing to play sides against each other. Homemade bombs could have been produced and arms could have been acquired domestically through theft, if weapons were not acquired through negotiation or importation.

The Berber response, however, remained mostly confined to the realm of conventional and peaceful politics. First, they formed political parties in an effort to compete in the political arena. These included the Socialist Forces Front (FFS) and the Rally for Culture and Democracy (RCD), as well as a cultural organization, the Berber Cultural Movement (MCB). Second, they engaged in protest action.[6] In 1998, however, some of the Berbers took up armed struggle. As a result of continued violence against them and these catalytic events in 1998, the Armed Berber Movement (MAB) formed, pledging to "avenge the death of the singer and kill those who apply the Arabisation law" (*Africa Research Bulletin* 1998, 13184). It should be noted that this is not the only instance of violent acts. In 1976, a group of Berbers bombed the headquarters of a FLN newspaper. Violent unrest occurred in 1980 in protest of government efforts to restrict Berber media and education. Thirty deaths were reported (Stone 1997). However, for the most part, the Berber response has been peaceful.

In January 2000, the AIS dissolved (80 Per Cent of Islamic Fighters Lay Down Arms 2000). An amnesty program was enacted and the GIA was still active in 2000. Whatever the outcome of the battle between the FLN and the Islamic movement, the Berbers will continue to face challenges to their culture and language.

In spite of the presence of weapons and eight years of civil war and the growing culture of violence that accompanies it, the mainstream Berber organizations have reacted in a remarkably peaceful manner most of the time.

Hungarians in Romania

Magyars or Hungarians make up about 10 percent of the population in Romania. Communal tensions are long standing, dating to World War I. In 1918, the Transylvania area, previously controlled under the defeated Austro-Hungarian empire, was given over to Romania and formalized in the 1920 Treaty of Trianon. Hungary, then under a fascist regime, took back the area at the beginning of World War II. After the war, it was again awarded to Romania. During the postwar years the two governments have been at times suspicious of each other's motives, a feeling carrying over to the majority and minority populations in each country.

During the 1970s and 1980s, Romanian leader Nicolai Ceaucescu took particularly harsh measures against the Hungarians, including resettling Romanians in Transylvania, bulldozing Hungarian villages, closing Hungarian-language schools, and removing Hungarians from administrative positions (Vachudova 1996). With Ceaucescu's violent downfall and the revolution of the 1990s, Romanian politics were heavily infused with nationalism and Hungarians were again perceived as a threat.

In March 1990, violence broke out between the two groups. The violence was short lived and confined to Tirgu Mures, a city in Transylvania. Three died and scores were wounded. Light weapons and implements including axes, scythes, and clubs were featured in the fighting, which was finally broken up by the military (Blood in the Square 1990, 23).[7] Overall, the violence was quite limited, in spite of the fact that as the 1990s continued, Hungarian expectations of better treatment after Ceaucescu foundered in mutual misunderstanding or distrust.

Events in 1994 illustrate many of the problems between ethnic Hungarians and the majority Romanians. In 1992, Gheorghe Funar, a Romanian ultranationalist, had become mayor of Cluj, the Transylvanian capital (Barber 1994). One rallying issue developed over an archeological dig around a statue of King Matthias, a medieval Hungarian leader in Cluj. Hungarians seemed to think the Romanians would take the opportunity to remove the statue. A second example concerns a law passed in late 1994, which prevented citizens from flying foreign flags or singing foreign anthems—a policy seemingly aimed at the Hungarians (Marsh 1994). Finally, during the mid-1990s, as Hungary and Romania negotiated a peace treaty—at least in part to improve their chances of joining NATO and the European Union, the Hungarians began to push the Romanians to grant autonomy to ethnic Hungarians in Romania. This move infuriated Romanian leaders, confirming their fears that Hungarians were out to cause trouble.

The Hungarian response, however, generally has not been to turn to arms, in spite of their grievances. Soon after the Romanian revolution of 1989, the Hungarian Democratic Federation of Romania (HDFR) was formed. Hungarian efforts went into supporting this party, which allowed them to apply more conventional politics and to have wider ranges of choice in pursuing their political goals. However, the problems continued to worsen, as increasing nationalism pushed the Romanians to squash as much of Hungarian ethnicity as they could, while the Hungarians increasingly called for autonomy. Romania's interests in joining the Western community of international organizations and its beliefs about how it should act to do so tended, however, to dampen any motives for outright mass violence. Romania's inability to gain admission to Western organizations might cause the government to remove the gloves in this struggle at some future point however. While the government is obviously armed, Hungarians' arms access reportedly has remained low, so that rebellion is at least not favored and would be difficult to carry out unless foreign arms were injected.

Considering all four cases, then, we see that in Sri Lanka and Algeria, arms access was reasonably high at the outset of hostilities, but with varying results in the face of significant interethnic grievances. Regional political developments also affected the outcomes in both cases. Likewise, where group arms access was low, violence, albeit on a relatively limited scale, did occur in Israeli-occupied territory, but not in Romania where again there were exogenous regional pressures tempering the outcome. All of this suggests, not too surprisingly, that arms are only one factor in determining whether violence will break out. There is a second finding of this analysis, although not apparent from the four cases. It is very difficult to find cases for the combination of high arms access and little or no violence. The Miskito Indians in Honduras and the Copts in Egypt are two other possible cases. More often it seems that ethnic groups with strong grievances are hard put to ignore the temptation of a ready supply of weapons.

BROADER ANALYSIS

A further proposition relating arms and the escalation of ethnic tension to rebellion is found in groups' ability to take advantage of arms to defend ethnic identity, redress perceived grievances, or attempt to advance other goals (Ganguly and Taras 1998). Gurr and Harff propose that the greater the external support—including weaponry—available to groups, the greater the "chances groups will use violent means to challenge authorities"(1994, 85). The point here is one of both possibility and probability. We believe that the greater access to arms an ethnic group has, the greater the chances it will employ them.

Although the Sri Lankan case supports this proposition, to show that as arms access increases, the probability and level of violence increases, we need to examine a wider array of cases. We turn to the *Minorities at Risk* data set as a starting point. The focus of these data is a list of more than 200 ethnopolitical groups in countries around the world. Some of these groups turned to rebellion as a means of redressing grievances; others chose nonviolent approaches or did nothing. The first step in our analysis was to collect a sample of cases of ethnopolitical groups that rebelled and those that did not.

We began by removing two types of cases from the data set. First, we removed ethnopolitical groups from Western democracies, Japan, Australia, and New Zealand. In so-called First World countries, the full range of arms access and of rebellion is seldom represented in the same country. Rather, we focus our attention on countries in the former Soviet bloc (the new states of the former Soviet Union and Eastern Europe) and countries in the global south. Second, we focus on ethnopolitical groups that either rebelled in the 1990s or never rebelled. Therefore, to facilitate analysis of arms access, we drop cases of ethnopolitical groups that rebelled during the period from 1945 to 1989; the more recent the conflict, the more likely there is information regarding arms in the conflict. The result of these two steps was to reduce the original list of ethnopolitical groups to 133 cases.

Of the 133 cases, we recorded twenty-six instances of ethnopolitical groups in rebellion in the 1990s, and 107 cases where no group rebellion was undertaken at any time. Approximately 20 percent of the groups mounted rebellions. Of the 133, we randomly selected thirty cases during the 1990s for further examination. It is our expectation that in cases of rebellion, arms would generally be widely available (high access) prior to the conflict's initiation. Moreover, in cases of no rebellion, the group should have had low prior access to arms. We can illustrate our expected outcome and identify the thirty cases in table 3.2. As the table shows, in our sample we have six cases of rebellion, and twenty-four cases of no sustained rebellion, a similar ratio to the population of the data set.

The next step is to determine whether arms access was high or low in these various cases. We did this by studying the geographical context in which the conflict took place to determine whether the conditions were conducive to such access or if access was reported. This means (1) whether or not there was "state breakdown," that is, the dissolution of existing governmental structures that would erode the sovereign control of arms arsenals by central authorities in the area; or (2) whether there was direct evidence or reports of arms possession by disputing groups. We consulted *Keesing's Record of World Events* and major newspapers indexed in *Lexis-Nexis* from 1990 onward for each case in the sample. Of course, if there were no reported violence, the press might be unlikely to cover, and therefore might overlook, arms shipments to particular ethnic groups. This is a potential flaw in the methodology, but at the moment it is the only practical method to survey arms flows in a group of cases. We include the narratives in *Keesings* to supplement press reports. The results are displayed in table 3.3.

As expected, in most cases of conspicuous rebellion and violence, there had been high arms access among ethnic group(s) in the sample. Only in the 1991 Avars conflict in Georgia and the Gagauz and Moldavian nationalists in 1990 was there no apparent ready arms access. The violence confronting the Avars, a population of roughly 4,000, evidently consisted of attacks by militant Georgian

Table 3.2   Expected Relationship between Arms Access and Initiation of Rebellion by Ethnopolitical Groups

	Rebellion	*No Rebellion*
Arms access high	Gagauz (Moldova), Serbs (Bosnia), Serbs (Croatia), Ingush (Russia), Croats (Bosnia), Avars (Russia)	
Arms access low		Tatars (Russia), Indians (Malasia), Ogani (Nigeria), Mossi-Dagomba (Ghana), Yoruba (Nigeria), Russians (Kyrgyzstan), Indigenous Peoples (Honduras), Blacks (Peru), Ngbandi (Zaire), Indigenous Peoples (Argentina), Copts (Egypt), Lozi (Zambia), Tuvinians (Russia), Bemebe (Zambia), Russians (Uzbekistan), Roma (Macedonia), Hungarians (Yugoslavia), Russians (Latvia), Blacks (Venezuela), Karachay (Russia), Slovaks (Czech Republic), Ahmadis (Pakistan), Pushtuns (Afghanistan), Bamileke (Cameroon)

nationalists, backed by the local Georgian authorities (therefore with access to arms), attempting to force the Avars to move to neighboring Dagestan. The nationalists blocked food shipments to Avar villages, set homes afire, and beat up Avar peasants. Georgia finally agreed to bear part of the cost of Avar resettlement in Dagestan, which opened the possibility of further conflicts in that economically and socially stressed state. The highly outnumbered Avars themselves appeared to stick to peaceful tactics (Leontyeva 1991).

In the Gagauz/Moldovan case, it is possible that Russian or Eastern European arms supplies seeped into the populace and preceded the uprisings, which nevertheless remained at a relatively low level of violence. The press narratives seemed to stress the use of makeshift weapons:

Moldovian nationalists attacked border posts in the southern republic today, threatening to kill border guards and their families if Soviet security forces do not withdraw, Tass reported. The more than 3,000 militants also set a fence on fire and threw stones before being persuaded to leave the checkpoints on the Romanian border. . . . It was the first report of violence in Moldavia since members of the Gaguaz [sic]

Table 3.3   Observed Relationship between Arms Access and Initiation of Rebellion by Ethnopolitical Group

	Rebellion	No Rebellion
Arms access high	Serbs (Bosnia), Serbs (Croatia) Ingush (Russia), Croats (Bosnia)	
Arms access low	Avars (Russia), Gagauz (Moldova) Ogani (Nigeria),[a] Yoruba (Nigeria),[b] Hungarians (Yugoslavia)	Tatars (Russia), Indians (Malasia), Mossi-Dagomba (Ghana), Russians (Kyrgyzstan), Indigenous Peoples (Honduras), Blacks (Peru), Ngbandi (Zaire), Indigenous Peoples (Argentina), Copts (Egypt), Lozi (Zambia), Tuvinians (Russia), Bemebe (Zambia), Russians (Uzbekistan), Roma (Macedonia), Russians (Latvia), Blacks (Venezuela), Karachay (Russia), Slovaks (Czech Republic), Ahmadis (Pakistan), Pushtuns (Afghanistan), Bamileke (Cameroon)

[a]Violence flared up in 1996 after the hanging of the political activist/playwright Ken Saro-Wiwa and eight other Ogoni nationalists by the government of President Sani Abacha (*Los Angeles Times,* November 12, 1995).

[b]The Yorubas, who had sided with the Hausa during the 1967 Biafran war, clashed with the Hausa-Fulani in 1998 after the death of the chief of the Yoruba, Mashood Abiola, in July 1998 (*[London] Guardian,* July 9, 1998; *New York Times,* July 19, 1998, sec.1, p. 3). Also, as recently as November 1999, the violence between the Yourba and Hausa-Fulani left 100 people dead (*New York Times,* November 29, 1999, p.5).

minority launched a drive to secede from the republic earlier this month, and underscored the conflicts that have mushroomed since President Mikhail Gorbachev loosened the Kremlin's grip on ethnic groups. . . . "The militants pelted the Stoyanovka checkpoint with stones and then set the fence around it on fire," Tass said. . . . Moldavian leaders flew to the scene and persuaded the militants to give up the two checkpoints they were blocking. . . . The Gagauz claimed control over part of the republic earlier this month and on Sunday planned elections for an autonomous government. But ethnic Moldavians opposed the move, and the elections were called off. Tensions had been reported yesterday to be easing, as talks between the opposing sides were under way. (Moldovan Militants 1990)

Thus, despite a few exceptions, it appears that some degree of arms access would be a prerequisite for significantly violent rebellion.

While Moldavia and the Avars cases illustrated the circumstances of low-level violence without much weaponry, the Ingush case was a good illustration of the way arms available in a large conflict zone have an impact upon the initiation of rebellion. In 1992 violence flared between Ingushis and Ossetians in the former Soviet republic of North Ossetia, a territory with a long history of conflict and resentment inflamed by Stalinist forced-resettlement policies during World War II. When the Chechen Republic declared its independence and initiated warfare against Russia in 1991, "the status of the Ingush people, to put it mildly, became uncertain," with the group divided among newly split republics of Chechnya and Ingushetia, as well as North Ossetia (Stalinist Repressions Trigger Ossetian-Ingushi Conflict 1992). Among the 100,000 or so Ingushi, thousands lived in North Ossetia where, in 1991, they demanded control over the historically significant Prigorodny District. Fighting broke out between Ingushi and Ossetians in the district in late October 1992. Russian interior troops and paratroopers rushed to the area to keep order and particularly to neutralize Ingushi "armed formations." Continuing skirmishes were reported with the use of firearms and artillery. Ingush units had begun the fighting against local police, taking hostages and seizing further arms and ammunition from Russian Interior Ministry installations (Stalinist Repressions Trigger Ossetian-Ingushi Conflict 1992; Russian Forces Fighting Alongside Ossetian Volunteers 1992). As the Russian-backed Ossetians initiated a counteroffensive of reportedly "ethnic cleansing" proportions, they claimed that the Turks and other Islamic countries were arming the Muslim Ingushi. The Russians may have been particularly sensitive to disorder in North Ossetia because nuclear weapons were reportedly stored there (Ethnic Purification Taking Place in North Ossetia: Official 1992). Thus, arms were clearly available to both sides as this dispute got under way, with the Russians upping the ante by arming the Ossetian counteroffensives.

In the twenty-four sampled cases where sustained violence was not conspicuous, though there may have been sporadic incidents, as reported in the notes to table 3.3, arms access by the aggrieved group was judged uniformly low. This result does not, however, mean that arms were entirely absent from the scene in these conflicts. For example, in the case of Russia's Tatarstan in 1991, the more than six million Muslim Tatars desired to form an independent state, but the Russians reacted strongly to the prospect of being unable to project power east of the Urals to reach the rich resources of Siberia. As with the Avars in Georgia, armed Russian vigilante groups reportedly sprang up "spontaneously" to repress the Tatars, without the overt support of the Russian army, KGB, or Interior Ministry (Beecher 1991). Thus, unarmed or lightly armed ethnic groups in tense situations can become the victims of state-backed counterethnic groups, militia, and vigilantes. In Nigeria, Yoruba and Hausa merchants and militant youths vying for control of major Nigerian food markets clashed in November 1999 using guns and machetes. Hostilities and fears intensified as Nigeria reverted to democracy after military rule ended amid a sagging economy and widespread poverty. The election of President Olusegun Obasanjo, a southern Yoruba, worried northern Hausa and Fulani clansmen (Hundreds Flee Ethnic Battles That Killed Dozens in Nigeria 1999), previously dominant groups with traditional ties to the military that certainly could have given them access to armament.

Table 3.4   Arms Imports and Subsequent Rebellion in 133 Countries

	Did the country experience a rebellion?	
Arms Acquired	Yes	No
Yes	6	1
No	19	107

A second test on these 133 cases was then conducted. We associated cases of ethnic rebellion from 1991 to 1998 with external support for ethnic groups (specifically the provision of military equipment) from 1990 to 1998. We expected to find that importation of military equipment would precede cases of rebellion, but that there would be no such arms acquisitions in cases where rebellion did not occur. Table 3.4 presents the results of this test.

In six cases, the expectation was fulfilled. The Mayans in Mexico, Serbs, Croats and Muslims in Bosnia, and Abkhazians and Ossetians in Georgia all received arms prior to the outbreak of fighting. Arms to the Pashtuns in Afghanistan did not spark a rebellion by this group, although there was fighting going on in Afghanistan at this time. For most of the cases (107), where there was no rebellion, there were no reported arms being imported. However, in nineteen cases, there was an uprising without prior arms importation.[8] As we noted in chapter 2, there are three ways to acquire arms and it is possible that in some of these cases, arms were acquired domestically or produced indigenously. From this table, it does seem that if ethnic groups mobilize and arm, they are likely to rebel, that without arms imports, rebellion is unlikely but far from impossible.

Thus, while arms access is probably not a sufficient condition for violence, and while there are isolated examples of rebellion without new armament and violence with light armament falling short of full-scale rebellion, arms access still comes close to being a necessary condition for ethnic violence. If one group lacks arms, there is no guarantee that the other side in the dispute will not obtain them anyway because of opportunity, fear, or insecurity. Governments increasingly appear to contribute to this possibility by selectively arming one side or another.

If this is so, then accurate tracking and agreed transparency (voluntary reporting) of arms flows prior to violence in ethically tense areas could provide an important component of early warning. Even a consistent account of state breakdown in the control of weapons arsenals or the regional spread of weapons could provide such warning in time for third parties and international organizations to attempt diplomatic remedies.

CONCLUSION

The role of arms in sparking ethnopolitical rebellions is somewhat more complex than might appear at first glance. As hypothesized, rebelling ethnic groups generally have prior access to significant arms supplies, though not always from outside sources. Ethnic groups that do not rebel generally are not well armed. Nevertheless, groups such as the Palestinians, Gagauz, Zapatistas, and Yoruba have resorted to violent tactics on at least a small scale without much initial armament, when they felt that such a step was in their political and social interest, sometimes as a plea to the outside world.

Because arms accumulation by ethnic groups or in conflict zones seems a relatively good predictor of impending violence, steps for future policy and research should focus on gathering information about what arms ethnopolitical groups and militia have or are likely to be in a position to obtain. Secondly, efforts to measure ethnically relevant (i.e., internal security) government arms and government arms transfers (e.g., to ethnic militia) also are urgently needed. In addition, a test of the impact of arms on state repression needs to be devised, which will require a better measure of repression than is available at the moment.

This discussion has been confined mainly to the initiation of uprisings. In the next chapter, we turn to arms effects on escalation and de-escalation of violence once under way. We have already seen here that arms have a way of seeping into a fight once begun, and that increasing arms levels appear to take civil violence to new levels as well, thus enabling the combatants to modify or raise their tactics and revert to more shows of force. It will be important to determine whether that is a common phenomenon, and what the consequences are for the parties and populations involved.

NOTES

1. Studies of international war tend to focus on arms possession, trade, and races in relation to conflict, but a review of their main findings also might yield insight into the impact of arms on the onset of intrastate fighting. Much of this research focuses on the question of state security. Arms are either seen as deterring violence or fostering the security dilemma, wherein the search for security through armament itself can promote insecurity.

2. Although this proposition has not been rigorously tested, some scholars believe that arms races can occur in ethnic conflicts as well as international ones. Such arms races would presumably be largely qualitative in nature (Klare 1999; Posen 1993; Spear 1996).

3. It is unlikely that there would be situations where there is no access to arms. Even in countries where guns are subject to extensive controls, a few guns could fall into the hands of ethnopolitical actors. This is important because a few weapons might be all that are needed to start a rebellion, which was the case in Liberia (Boutwell and Klare, 2000).

4. According to O'Ballance (1989,12) there were a number of Tamil resistance groups— at one point over forty, but of these, five were "durable, active and effective." They were the Tamil Eelam Liberation Organization (TELO), the Eelam Revolutionary Organization of Students (EROS), the LTTE, the People's Liberation Organization of Tamil Eelam (PLOTE), and the Eelam People's Revolutionary Liberation Front (EPRLF). The Tamil United Liberation Front (TULF) was an active group, but not in the same sense, as it did not have a military wing.

5. This discussion of the Berbers comes from the *Minorities at Risk* Web page and the assessment prepared by Jonathan Fox and Victor Assal, updated in June 1999.

6. For example, the assessment of the Berbers on the *Minorities at Risk* Web site lists several peaceful protests, including those on January 25, 1990; May 31, 1990; April 20, 1993; and January 12, 1995. Berbers also engaged in various strikes and boycotts during the 1990s.

7. According to Woodward, eight persons were killed and 300 were injured over a period of three days. It is suggested that the Romanians were acting on directions from local officials (Woodward 1998).

8. The cases are: Other indigenous people in Mexico and Venezuela, Blacks in Columbia, Greeks in Albania, Avars in Russia, Russians in Lithuania and Georgia, Malinka in Guinea, Ewe in Togo, Westerners in Cameroon, Ijaw in Nigeria, Hutu and Tutsi in the Democratic Republic of Congo, Amhara in Ethiopia, Zulus in South Africa, Shiites in Bahrain, Uzbeks in Tajikistan, Muslims in India, and Fijians in Fiji.

Chapter Four

Arms and the Progression of Ethnic Conflict

Analyses of the conflict in Sri Lanka involving the government, ethnic Tamils, and ethnic Sinhalese present a picture of a "spiral of violence that has not stopped" since anti-Tamil riots in July 1983 (Isaac 1996, 179). After seventeen years of fighting, more than 62,000 people have died (Jayamaha 2000). Efforts to resolve the conflict have failed so far and the fighting has generally worsened over time. At critical junctures, as for example in 1987 when Indian interventionary forces arrived in Sri Lanka, and in 1990 when those forces left, the conflict has tended to escalate. Peace talks initiated by President Chandrika Kumaratunga, elected in 1994 on a peace platform, broke down, which in turn prompted a major military campaign in 1995, and perhaps indirectly, an assassination attempt by the Tamils on the president in 1999. On May 4, 2000, the Sri Lankan government introduced emergency measures "as it faced possibly its greatest crisis in the 17-year war against Tamil separatists" (Sri Lanka Introduces Crisis Measures 2000, 22). In June, the conflict appeared "to be reaching a critical and decisive juncture" (Smith, 2000) and every succeeding crisis in this war is described as the most serious to date.

One of the factors that may have contributed to the escalation of this and similar disputes is the acquisition by both sides of armaments, providing fuel to continue the fight. Both the government and the Tamils—particularly the LTTE—have had access to and have obtained a variety of weapons throughout the years. The impact of arms acquisitions *during* warfare is an important consideration, but one that has taken a back seat academically to the study of the initiation or termination of violence.[1] Yet much of the damage occurs in the midst of conflict. Identifying factors that make violent encounters endure and worsen, or that shorten and ameliorate them is, therefore, vital. If arms are one such factor, either selective arms shipments or steps toward practical arms control and reduction could help end or at least mitigate ethnopolitical violence. For those studying the dauntingly persistent or recurrent civil ethnic violence in places like Sri Lanka, understanding the pattern of violence, and by implication rearmament, during warfare might offer keys to success-ful intervention and eventual conflict management. The purpose of this chapter is to assess the role of mid-war arms acquisitions in escalation and de-escalation pat-terns, and in the severity and duration of ethnopolitical fighting.

We proceed with an underlying expectation: the relationship between arms and escalation is not automatic. As with the initiation of wars in the last chapter, we do not expect arms by themselves to be either necessary or sufficient to spark esca-lation. Escalation might occur without new prior arms infusions, while fighting can also be *followed* by increased arms flow, to replenish spent equipment. Like-wise, efforts to remove arms from ongoing conflict or prevent future imports, for example via arms embargoes, do not always produce de-escalations.

Because of the prolonged nature of conflicts as in Sri Lanka, it is also useful to speculate about the effects of ongoing warfare and logistical considerations on the pattern of arms acquisition. In other words, does the course of violence itself or the geopolitical landscape dictate the types of arms in demand and the timing and source of acquisitions? If so, then we have a predictive indicator relevant to policy planning for those interested in dampening warfare or stemming the flow of fuel to battle. For example, it has been argued that in the context of Philippine rebellions, ranging from the leftist "Huqs" of the 1950s and 1960s to the Islamic *Moro* rebel-lion of the 1990s, the rebels put a premium on acquiring easily replenished arms and ammunition. In other words, it is of little use to acquire exotic arms, such as Israeli Uzi machine guns, if resupply routes are uncertain. It is much wiser to acquire local arms directly from the enemy, that is, to pick them up on the battle-field, steal them from storage sites, or buy them from corrupt government officials, soldiers, or military bases (such as those of the United States) (Nemenzo 2000).

Before we examine whether these various expectations are met and determine more about the circumstances under which we would relate arms levels to escala-tion/de-escalation, we first identify four ways of conceptualizing the "middle" of conflicts: by way of duration, intensity, escalation/de-escalation, and volatility.

POST-ONSET CONFLICT CHARACTERISTICS

Once ethnopolitical warfare is under way, the conflict can undergo a series of changes reflecting ebbs and flows in the fighting. One such change involves scope. Scope entails the location or geographic spread of the violence and the number of parties involved. A second type of change concerns the degree of international-ization of the conflict, which involves the entrance or exit of outside actors into the conflict. Both scope and internationalization have implications for the extent and type of armament needed to continue fighting. However, available data sources generally fail to provide consistent coverage of the location and partici-pants of ongoing conflicts. Therefore, we focus on five other pertinent indicators of changing levels of fighting: severity, duration, intensity, escalation and de-escalation, and volatility.

One of the most frequently reported statistics concerning conflict refers to severity of fighting, or the number of civilian or military casualties. Severity is an absolute, though not always readily estimated measure. It is often expressed in terms of the number of deaths from the onset of the war up to a certain end point — either the termination point or a recent point in time. Annual yearbooks offer casualty statistics, which generally cover a period from the war's outbreak to a year or two prior to publication and are updated in each succeeding volume (see Sivard 1996). Severity, however, is a simple measure, which does not take into account the length of the fighting or size of the populations involved. Deaths of 5,000 in a war lasting a year have very different implications as to severity than the same number of casualties spread over a ten- or twenty-year period in an ongoing struggle such as that of the Basques in Spain. Because the measure of severity tells us little about a conflict's dynamic, we prefer more sophisticated and revealing ways to peer into conflict dynamics and effects.

A second relevant characteristic of internal wars is duration. Duration, the length of the violent period from onset to termination, is frequently measured in months or years. Many scholars believe that arms acquisitions produce not only more severe wars, but also longer ones. This is the idea of armaments as "fuel" for the violence. For many policy makers the primary goal of disarmament efforts is to bring a conflict to a conclusion faster and prevent recurrence by reducing the fuel.

The combination of severity and duration leads to a third characteristic, namely conflict intensity. Casualties are divided by an appropriate time period, usually years or months, to obtain an average estimate of casualties per unit of time in order to facilitate the comparison of multiple conflicts. (Casualty figures could also be divided by the population figures for the groups in conflict to provide a comparative estimate of impact intensity.) Intensity is a more useful statistic than its two components alone, since it raises important questions about why some conflicts are more damaging than others. Rwandan killing in the 1990s, which was about as long in duration as the first Chechen war from 1994–96, produced about twenty-five times more casualties. This was in spite of the fact that for the most part heavy weapons were not used in Rwanda, but were readily employed in Chechnya. Intensity might tell us that a conflict saw harsher more vengeful and personal violence — more killing in a shorter time span, or that it entailed slogging it out in heavy fighting over many years.

Escalation, a fourth conflict dynamic, refers to changes in the level of violence.[2] Such changes might be "routine," as in the cycle of fight and wait during dry and rainy seasons in many tropical countries, or, as indicated below, they may involve calculated and strategic decisions, some of which also entail a form of deterrence against new offensives. Zartman defines escalation as "a significant change in the nature of the conflict in the direction of increased violence as distinct from a gradual intensification of conflict with no definable change in its nature" (Zartman

1995a, 19). We define escalation and de-escalation in terms of the intensity of fighting, where intensity is the severity over time.

Manifestations of de-escalation include a contraction of the scope of the fighting, a lessening of the intensity of the conflict, the declaration of a cease-fire by some or all of the parties, or the initiation of negotiations among the disputants. Of course, sometimes these efforts are designed mainly to give breathing space — time for regrouping or rearmament — so that one or both parties can reescalate the violence.

A still more dynamic measure to identify how many were killed at varying times during the war could add even more to our understanding of the nature of ethnopolitical conflicts once under way. Thus, a final dynamic characteristic concerns conflict volatility. Some conflicts tend toward relatively stable levels of violence — high, moderate, or low — over long periods of time. Other conflicts see steadily mounting or escalating violence, while still others swing back and forth between escalation and de-escalation. Arms acquisitions could play a role in determining such swings and how frequently the conflict moves between violent outbursts and lulls in the fighting. Conflicts with many ups and downs are considered "volatile."

WHY CONFLICTS EVOLVE AS THEY DO

In explaining why disputes evolve, we employ two basic assumptions. First, each actor — whether government or ethnopolitical group or groups — makes multiple choices throughout the contest in an effort to steer toward a more desired resolution, or as argued about some recent African and Central Asian conflicts, to keep the fight going in order to benefit from control of key resources in the country, such as diamonds in Sierra Leone and Angola or oil in former Soviet republics of Central Asia (Multiplicity and Complementarity in Conflict Resolution 2001). As Gurr (1998, 24) notes, in "the final analysis, whether or not ethnorebellions begin, rise, or fall depends on decisions taken by governments, ethnopolitical leaders, and external actors." Each actor tries to intensify or dampen the fighting, or continue it at the present level in order to approach certain goals or needs. The degree of change also can vary. Actors' ability to exercise these options depends in part on available resources such as armament and related equipment.

Second, the outcome of actors' choices depends on interactions once the fighting is under way. In a bilateral dispute, such as that in Moldova in 1991, six outcomes are possible at a given time, ranging from both sides doing nothing, to both seeking to escalate or de-escalate, or to one or the other escalating or de-escalating.[3] As we have posited elsewhere in the book, an actor's decision to adopt one of these options at a given time is a function of both willingness and opportunity. Willingness is the actor's desire to take a particular action; opportunity is the actor's ability or occasion to do so. Four combinations are supported: actors can be willing and able, neither willing nor able, or one but not the other. We examine each component in turn, beginning with willingness.

One motivation for conflict expansion is to negotiate from a stronger position. This motivation realizes the act of escalation as one of several tactics within a larger tacit bargaining process. By taking control of more territory, a group or governmental authorities try to improve bargaining position. Capturing territory, to continue with this example, can improve that position in two ways. First, it reinforces the threat that the party will capture even more ground in the future, thus pushing the other side to yield then rather than face a worse position down the road. Second, it allows the party to offer a concession relatively painlessly—the territory is captured so that it might later be given up. Of course, the danger here is that escalation forces the other side to respond similarly, or that somehow the negotiations are aborted so that the land is not soon returned (as in the Israel-Palestine dispute).

A second reason for expansion is to achieve outright victory, that is, to win or to force full concessions from the other side. A government might make a final push against an opposition group, seeking to kill, capture, displace or otherwise disable a sufficient number effectively to finish the ethnopolitical group as a unified or viable force. Israel's strategy in invading Lebanon in 1982 reputedly entailed such hopes in breaking Palestinian resistance once and for all. An aberration of such a strategy, seen elsewhere, is the harrowing tactic of "ethnic cleansing" to remove whole populations from a region and establish "new facts" about territorial control.

A third reason might be preemption. One side or the other expands the conflict in the belief that the other side is about to do the same. The advantage of going first is the ability to dictate the terms of the fighting or the peace talks. Finally, escalation might occur as a disputant seeks to demonstrate strength. An ethnopolitical group might seek increased status or greater media attention through escalation, particularly in raising awareness and support in the outside world.[4]

De-escalation also occurs for a variety of reasons, not all of which are by choice or preference. For example, a government or an ethnic group might conclude that it could face a worse situation in the future and decide to talk now. Conflicts might also de-escalate as disputants tire of fighting or run out of personnel or supplies. Environmental changes, such as economic upturns or downturns or natural disasters, also can affect the combatants' perceived prospects and willingness to continue fighting. Burma appears to illustrate several such factors: over decades of sporadic fighting, many of the antigovernment ethnic groups quit because of ultimate exhaustion or more alluring economic incentives. This caused a reinforcing pattern favoring the government: as each group opted out, the government increased its strength against those remaining, making them more likely to see an end or lull to the fighting as more attractive or palatable. Overall, escalation and de-escalation, in terms of willingness, reflect actors' varying goals and underlying interests, as well as the costs of either achieving them or not doing so through violence.

Opportunity, as just noted, also plays a role in the course of fighting. In addition to advantages or disadvantages posed by the overall conflict environment, opportunity can be thought of more specifically in terms of resources available to the actors. Capability is largely seen in terms of personnel and equipment. Thus, arms might enter into the actors' calculus, combining with factors of willingness or motivation in deciding on new offensives or revised tactics (as from guerrilla war to standard combat). Arms themselves give actors the requisite opportunity to take or persist in military action, and relative armament levels also can be a psychological factor influencing the cost-benefit calculations outlined above.

Duration, intensity, and volatility then, all result from these strategic choices. As opportunity changes, for example, actors are likely to flip between choices over time, thus creating more volatility. Where opportunity and willingness are both high for the actors, the conflict is likely to last longer and more likely to be severe in nature.

THE IMPACT OF CHANGES IN AVAILABLE ARMAMENT

In ethnopolitical disputes, both governments and ethnic groups generally possess a variety of options to obtain substantial amounts of arms (Goldring 1997; ICRC 1999; Karp 1993; Wood and Peleman 1999). However, in prior chapters we have seen that the level and types of weaponry possessed by the sides can vary, and are often characterized by a prevalence of small arms (Sislin et al. 1998). Governments rely heavily on imports for their armament needs and some also produce weapons in indigenous arms industries; however, most developing countries are unable to produce a broad range of weapons. Domestic procurement is a viable method for mobilized ethnic groups, where the group obtains weapons through raids on police or military installations or as a result of battlefield capture or illicit local purchases. Many groups also are able to import weapons from states, sympathetic kin or nearby supporters, and private foreign dealers. Presumably, if sources of outside arms are made available prior to the start of hostilities, the suppliers' stake in the recipient group's success increases during the war. Since they do not want to see their initial investment in the cause fail, suppliers might be more likely to follow up, despite Philippine skepticism noted earlier, as the fight goes on.

All of these methods of acquiring arms were employed in the case of Sri Lanka, illustrating patterns seen in whole or in part in many local wars. The government imported arms in large quantities from a variety of states, including the United Kingdom, China, and Israel. O'Ballance notes that the Tamil rebels also were quite resourceful. "Most trained guerrillas were armed with miscellaneous weaponry, either stolen in raids on armouries or stores, seized in attacks on security forces personnel, obtained by bribery or from the Black Market; a few, however, had been obtained from the PLO, India, or international arms market sources" (O'Ballance 1989, 39). The LTTE bought arms from dealers in Hong Kong and Lebanon, from corrupt military officers in Thailand and Burma, and from states eager to export for cash, such as Ukraine and Bulgaria (Bonner 1998a). O'Ballance also describes the "Munitions Factory," established by the Tamil Tigers in 1986, which was capable of producing mortars, grenades and land mines, and of repairing small arms. Few ethnic groups in other states have had such a well-developed supply system; most often groups are limited to portable light infantry arms as well as various means of sabotage.

At the most general level, a two-dimensional matrix (see tables 4.1a, 4.1b, 4.1c, and 4.2a, 4.2b, 4.2c) captures the intersection of changes in levels of armaments and changes in the nature of the conflict. The first dimension measures relative increases or decreases in arms size and supply either flowing into or out of the conflict zone. (At this point, we do not specify a time period, except to note that the changes in arms precede the change in combat or violence.) The second dimension measures changes in the fighting, specifically duration and intensity as forms of escalation/de-escalation. Such matrices suggest a series of basic expectations concerning the impact of changes in arms on changes in the nature of the conflict.

Arms and Duration

The essential assumption about arms and duration is that increases in armament provide greater opportunity for actors already willing to fight, and that changes in arms to one actor alter the willingness of the other actor. As we saw in chapter 3, prior to the explosion of available small arms in Albania in 1997, even the most radical elements in Kosovo had little opportunity to vent their frustrations through violent means. Guns allow for more violent forms of politics and for carrying out struggles longer. As a first proposition, then, we suggest that increased arms are more likely to lead to longer wars; decreased arms are more likely to lead to shorter wars. This pattern occurs because as arms continue flowing into conflicts, fighting can continue unabated. In addition, as arms flow to one side, this is likely to increase the other side's arms search and its willingness to continue fighting, a form of internal arms racing seen in Sri Lanka.[5]

Enlightening variants on the arms-duration relationship are seen in the cases of the IRA in Northern Ireland or the ETA in the Basque region of Spain. The former group has had access to large accumulated arms caches, sometimes reportedly stored across the border in the Irish Republic. The IRA's arsenal included forty rocket-propelled grenade launchers, 650 AK-47 rifles, hundreds of handguns, more than two tons of explosives, tons of ammunition, grenades, and more than one surface-to-air missile (Stohl 2000). Yet it has been noted that the full range of available weapons was not generally put to use in Ulster. Both Catholic and Protestant paramilitary groups have preferred headline-grabbing bombings and vengeance ambush attacks on collaborators and enemies in contrast to pitched battles.[6] The Basque separatists apparently possess fewer resources than the IRA, but like their Irish counterparts tend to employ what are commonly labeled "terrorist" tactics. Thus, despite the varied armament levels, both struggles have been waged with relatively similar tactics and have continued for decades (though with the Basque campaigns, more sporadically). Additionally, particular arms shipments to the British or Spanish governments do not seem especially associated with the pattern of violence, since both countries have NATO and international responsibilities and large arms stockpiles.

Thus, as noted earlier, arms acquisitions by themselves are neither necessary nor sufficient for the escalation or de-escalation of fighting. In the cases just mentioned, sheer willingness is often sufficient to continue the war, and tactics are determined by political needs and circumstances. Nevertheless, we posit that arms inflows from abroad raise the *probability* that wars will be longer and more intense by increasing the recipients' sense of long-term opportunity. There are likely to be exceptions and cases that do not fit this pattern. Again, analysis will be useful to highlight the general role of arms, along with the accompanying salience of other factors.

Finally, in cases where arms are pulled out of the conflict, either through attrition or sanctions, conflicts should tend to be shorter. We would expect to see more calls for negotiations or cease-fires in these cases, though the willingness to negotiate might precede the arms decline and allow for it to take place. It should be noted, as a mitigating factor, however, that since most governments have significant amounts of arms, and since many fighting groups gain armament domestically and not simply from abroad, arms embargoes by foreign powers might not have a decisive immediate effect on internal wars. Spare parts and fuel shortages could squeeze some developing states and groups, however. A government's access to high technology and intelligence on opponents' strength and location, as in satellite data transmitted by foreign allies (such as NATO for Britain and Spain), becomes increasingly important as combat intensity creeps upward or rebellion persists.

We argue as well that the greater the number of external arms suppliers, the longer the war. The logic here is similar to our first proposition, whereby arms provide opportunity. The more suppliers, the more their long-term commitment to continue backing their client; the combatant thus feels secure that resupply will be forthcoming. As a result, wars are likely to persist as peace talks are deferred.

A related proposition is that supplies of heavy weapons are more likely to lead to longer wars than are light weapons. In a sense, the use of heavy armament is a manifestation of the sum of several factors, which together suggest a greater commitment to violence. The use of heavy weapons necessitates the involvement of more personnel, more extensive training, and greater logistical and transport capabilities. It would also be likely to involve heavy "collateral damage" to civilians and property, instilling more grievances and presumably ongoing revenge motives. Finally, the political and social conditions allowing for the use of heavy weapons, such as strongly ingrained nationalism, might themselves also make the conflict more intractable.

To reiterate, we expect that all of the following conditions will favor longer domestic wars:

- Increased quantity of available arms
- Increased number of suppliers
- Deployment of heavy weapons

The next step in examining our expectations about the role of arms is to measure variables such as duration and severity and relate them to conditions of escalation and de-escalation.[7]

Preliminary analysis can be conducted on arms and duration. We start with our list of forty-nine conflicts, drawn originally from Gurr and Harff (1994) and modified by Sislin et al. (1998). The duration of many conflicts is, of course, still being established. For our preliminary test, we draw on data from Brown (1996), Gurr and Harff (1994), and Sivard (1996) to identify duration, and since there is disagreement, we dichotomize the duration variable into short (less than ten years) and long (equal to or greater than ten years) categories. Tables 4.1a and 4.1b illustrate the association between arms type and duration, and between arms sources (group importation or not) and duration. Table 4.1c examines the affect of government arms acquisitions (high or low) on the duration of conflict.

As shown, the relationship between type of weapons and duration appears to be the reverse of what we proposed in our third proposition: heavy weapons are somewhat more associated with shorter conflicts, and light weapons with longer wars.[8] Perhaps the disputants, the international community, or regional powers see heavy weapons as a danger signal indicating severe instability and unacceptable attrition rates. More pressure to end fighting sooner could result. The use of heavy arms also could lead to faster attrition and ultimate exhaustion of the combatants as well. However, since many of these cases have yet to end, this finding should be taken with

Table 4.1a   The Impact of Group Arms Type on the Duration of Ethnopolitical Conflict

	Duration	
Group Arms Type	*Short (<10 years)*	*Long (≥10 years)*
Heavy Weapons	Abkhazia, Afghanistan, Bosnia, Chechnya, Croatia, Iraq, Moldova	Angola, Azerbaijan, Burundi, Morocco
Light Weapons	Cambodia, Djibouti, Ethiopia, Ghana, Indonesia (N. Sumatra), Kenya, Liberia, Mali/Niger, Mexico, Papua New Guinea, Rwanda, Serbia (Kosovo), S. Africa	Bangladesh, Burma, India, Indonesia (E. Timor and W. Irian), N. Ireland, Peru, Philippines, Senegal, Somalia, Spain, Sri Lanka, Sudan, Turkey, W. Bank/Gaza

caution. Nevertheless, general availability of light armament, as compared to heavy, might allow a more sustained struggle at lower comparative costs, at least for the combatants.

Arms importation by groups (table 4.1b) is even less clearly related to duration. Imported arms supplies seem to produce both short and long conflicts, while many conflicts running on what arms are at hand (as in Spain) have run on for decades.

One of the more suggestive findings here is the evident relationship between average annual government arms imports and duration of violence (table 4.1c), even allowing for vagaries of arms import reports.[9] The bulk of the warring coun-

Table 4.1b   The Impact of Group Arms Source on the Duration of Ethnopolitical Conflict

Group Arms Source	Duration	
	Short (<10 years)	Long (≥10 years)
Importation	Abkhazia, Bosnia, Chechnya, Croatia, Djibouti, Ethiopia, Iraq, Kenya, Liberia, Mali/Niger, Mexico, Moldova, Rwanda, Serbia (Kosovo)	Angola, Azerbaijan, Burma, Burundi, India, Iran, Morocco, N. Ireland, Philippines, Senegal, Somalia, Sri Lanka, Sudan, Turkey
No Importation	Afghanistan, Cambodia, Indonesia (N. Sumatra), Papua New Guinea, S. Africa	Bangladesh, Indonesia (E. Timor and W. Irian), Peru, Spain, W. Bank/Gaza

Table 4.1c   The Impact of Government Arms Imports on the Duration of Ethnopolitical Conflict

Government Acquisitions	Duration	
	Short (<10 years)	Long (≥10 years)
High (≥ $50 million annual average)	Abkhazia	Angola, Bangladesh, Burma, China, India, Indonesia[a], Iran, Morocco, Nigeria, N. Ireland, Peru, Philippines, Spain, Sudan, Turkey, W. Bank/Gaza
Low (< $50 million annual average)	Afghanistan, Bosnia, Cambodia, Croatia, Djibouti, Ethiopia, Iraq, Kenya, Liberia, Mali/Niger, Moldova, Papua New Guinea, Rwanda, Serbia (Kosovo), S. Africa	Azerbaijan, Bhutan, Burundi, Guatemala, Senegal, Somalia, Sri Lanka, Uganda

Source: Duration information drawn from Brown (1996), Gurr and Harff (1994), and Sivard (1996). Group arms data drawn from Sislin et al. (1998) using mainly open-source newspaper and journal accounts. ACDA data are used for government arms, averaging government acquisitions over the period of the middle of the conflict in question. Some countries in our sample had missing data on one or more variables and are excluded from these tests.
[a]Indonesia is treated as a single case for analysis of government arms in relation to ethnic fighting.

tries with large average imports had long internal wars while the majority of the low-import states had short ones. It was quite possible, however, to have long wars with relatively low imports, but heavy imports with a short war appear to be very rare indeed. This could mean that long wars themselves suck in more outside arms through attrition, so that the arms are not causing the increased duration per se; thus it would be rare that new arms are needed for short wars. But arms in government hands also might give the wherewithal to pursue the military option longer in ethnic disputes without the perceived necessity for negotiated settlement. More study of this question is clearly merited.

Arms and Intensity

Next, we turn to arms and the intensity of ethnopolitical violence, recalling that intensity reflects damage per unit of time. The association between arms and severity is often considered obvious, and thus, often only implicitly stated: more arms or more sophisticated arms lead to greater killing. Beyond this, however, we suggest two other basic propositions: (1) supplies of heavy weapons (tanks, planes, artillery, etc.) are more likely to lead to intense fighting than are light weapons, and (2) the greater the number of arms suppliers, the more intense the ethnopolitical violence.

Intensity is measured as casualties divided by time, in this case in annual terms.[10] Preliminary analysis was conducted on intensity, with the same caveats as for duration. Tables 4.2a and 4.2b draw on casualty figures from Gurr and Harff (1994) and Brown (1996) for estimates over time. Again, given the preliminary nature of the analysis, we dichotomized intensity as less-intense conflicts, where average annual casualties were less than 1,000, and more-intense conflicts with greater than 1,000 average casualties.

As table 4.2a shows, heavy weapons do seem somewhat related to more-intense conflicts, although we see that Rwanda is certainly not alone among ethnic disputes generating heavy casualties with relatively light arms. Indeed, roughly half of the lightly armed conflicts also produced heavy casualties. There definitely seems to be some relationship between group importation and intensity of fighting; groups supplied by external actors are more often involved in intense struggles than those without foreign supply (table 4.2b). Here, external supply seems to fuel the fire and to sustain groups in their struggles. On the other hand, there seems little relationship between government arms importation levels and intensity of fighting. This might be due partly to the varied reasons that governments import arms, and also to the possibility that governments do not always employ large percentages of their arsenals in cases of civil violence. Hence, governmental arms might be a confidence boost in reserve, allowing authorities to prosecute longer wars, but not necessarily leading to frequent offensives. Clearly, a number of well-armed governments do engage in some very bloody civil violence, but in our sample, even more states with low import totals engage in high levels of violence.

Table 4.2a   The Impact of Group Arms Type on the Intensity of Ethnopolitical Conflict

	Intensity	
Group Arms Type	Less (≤1,000 annual deaths)	More (>1,000 annual deaths)
Heavy Weapons	Abkhazia, Morocco	Afghanistan, Angola, Azerbaijan, Bosnia, Burundi, Chechnya, Croatia, Iraq, Moldova
Light Weapons	Indonesia (W. Irian), Kenya, Mali/Niger, N. Ireland, Papua New Guinea, Sengal, Serbia, S. Africa, Spain, W. Bank/Gaza	Bangladesh, Burma, India, Indonesia (E. Timor and N. Sumatra), Liberia, Peru, Philippines, Rwanda, Somalia, Sri Lanka, Sudan, Turkey

Table 4.2b   The Impact of Group Arms Source on the Intensity of Ethnopolitical Conflict

Group Arms Source	Intensity	
	Less (≤1,000 annual deaths)	More (>1,000 annual deaths)
Importation	Iran, Kenya, Mali/Niger, Morocco, N. Ireland, Sengal, Serbia	Afghanistan, Angola, Azerbaijan, Bosnia, Burma, Burundi, Chechnya, Croatia, India, Iraq, Liberia, Moldova, Philippines, Rwanda, Somalia, Sri Lanka, Sudan
No Reported Importation	Indonesia (W. Papua), Papua New Guinea, S. Africa, Spain, W. Bank/Gaza	Bangladesh, Indonesia (E. Timor and N. Sumatra), Peru

Table 4.2c   The Impact of Government Arms Imports on the Intensity of Ethnopolitical Conflict

Government Acquisitions	Intensity	
	Less (≤1,000 annual deaths)	More (>1,000 annual deaths)
High (≥ $50 million annual average)	Iran, Morocco, Nigeria, N. Ireland, Spain, W. Bank/Gaza	Afghanistan, Angola, Bangladesh, Burma, China, India, Indonesia, Peru, Philippines, Sudan, Turkey
Low (>$50 million annual average)	Abkhazia, Cambodia, Kenya, Mali/Niger, Papua New Guinea, Senegal, Serbia (Kosovo),[a] S. Africa	Azerbaijan, Bosnia, Burundi, Chad, Croatia, Guatemala, Iraq, Liberia, Moldova, Rwanda, Somalia, Sri Lanka, Uganda

Source: Intensity information drawn from Brown (1996) and Gurr and Harff (1994). Arms data drawn from Sislin et al. (1998) and from ACDA, various years.
[a]The Kosovo conflict blew up into high-intensity violence after this data analysis was completed in 1998.

Arms and Escalation

As noted at the outset, duration and intensity are fairly static measures. With more refined data, we will be able to examine changes in the nature of the fighting more definitively. We expect a basic association between changes in arms and escalatory/de-escalatory periods: increased arms supplies leading to escalatory periods, decreased supplies to de-escalatory periods. The interesting challenge is to create a more sophisticated measure of escalation and de-escalation to see if that association holds.

Several measures are possible. One approach is to use the sum of scaled conflictive or cooperative events between the disputants (perhaps using event data such as Conflict and Peace Data Bank [COPDAB] domestic scales) over a particular time period (e.g., months).[11] A second measure could involve identifying expansions or contractions in the geographic space of the fighting.[12] Additionally, one might look at changes in the number of internal or external participants. Internal changes might involve the emergence of new, mobilized ethnic groups or splinter groups or increased participation in fighting through recruitment or the use of mercenaries. In Sri Lanka, the government instituted efforts to greatly expand the number of people serving in the police and security forces (O'Ballance 1989). Participation can also involve external actors. Fighting in Nagorno-Karabakh, Azerbaijan, between the Armenian population and the Azerbaijani government quickly brought Armenia into the conflict in support of Armenians living in Azerbaijan (Human Rights Watch 1994b). Russia was drawn in as a broker. In Sri Lanka, the main external player was India. Third-party involvement tends to raise the stakes and importance of the conflict and might exacerbate as well as relieve conditions and tensions.

We suggest a new measure built from monthly casualty figures reflecting the effects of increased or decreased fighting. We do this in full recognition of the potential shortcomings of casualty data because we seek a variable that changes often; outside interventions, for example, are relatively infrequent. Additionally, geographic scope and costs of war are difficult to measure. Finally, event data are lacking on a variety of ethnic conflicts over time.

We next examine four cases to see the relationship between arms and our measure of escalation. The cases were selected to illustrate key factors that can characterize the arms-violence nexus. Among these are varying length of struggle and need for resupply, degree of outside military or political intervention by third parties, degree of state breakdown and arms availability in the immediate environment, level and type of ethnic repression, type of insurrection and its reliance on political versus military means. The casualty trend lines for our cases are presented in figures 4.1 to 4.4.[13]

The fighting in Angola (fig. 4.1) had many periods of ups and downs between 1975 and 1998. Indeed, the violence persisted through the end of the decade, with UNITA forces using illegal diamond trade to finance weapon purchases to maintain the fight (Crosette 1999). Major escalations and immediate de-escalations were very frequent, with the largest in mid-1975, early 1977, the first quarter of 1978, late 1983, mid-1984 and mid-1985, late 1987 and 1989, and from late 1992 to the early months of 1993. The mid-1980s were the period of most sustained violence, although not always at ultrahigh levels.

Figure 4.1   Monthly Casualty Figures for the Angolan Conflict

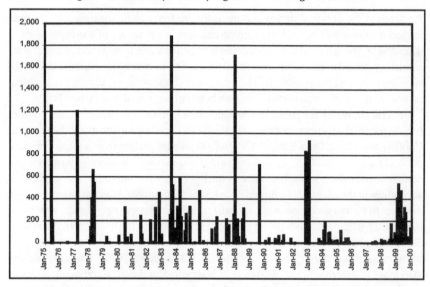

Despite low level hit-and-run attacks, Kosovo (fig. 4.2) did not become a fighting war until March 1998, with a two-month escalation, followed by de-escalation. The next combat episode was in the first three months of 1999, followed by a major spike in the spring and early summer. Obviously NATO's air bombardment figured prominently in this escalation and de-escalation of the fighting.

Figure 4.2   Monthly Casualty Figures for the Kosovo Conflict

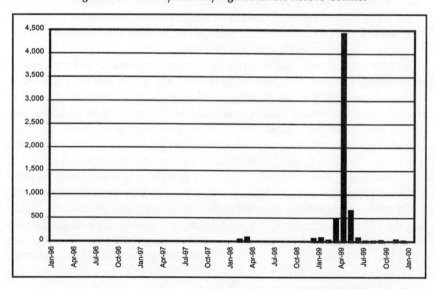

The Chiapas conflict (fig. 4.3) began with escalation in January 1994 and continued sporadically through the decade. We measured the conflict through December 1999. The initial escalation was followed immediately by an initial de-escalation in February and, for the most part, the conflict remained nonviolent until escalation in December 1997 between paramilitary forces and civilians, followed by de-escalation in January 1998. It is important to point out that the 1997 massacre was not the result of EZLN violence, but rather a response to the grievances of the indigenous people in the area and the greater prominence of their demands as a result of EZLN's efforts. Minor violence was reported in June 1998, while 1999 was relatively quiet, though the EZLN staged a referendum on human rights.

Figure 4.3   Monthly Casualty Figures for the Chiapas, Mexico Conflict

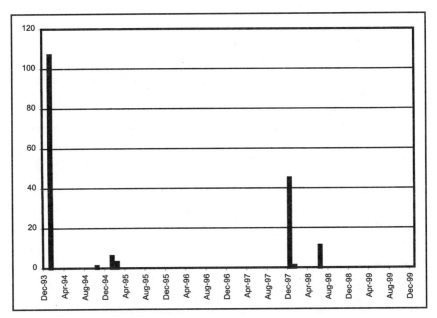

In the Moldovan case (fig. 4.4), the conflict "began" in December 1991 and concluded in August 1992, making it the shortest conflict we examined. There was one dramatic escalation in June 1992, followed by de-escalation in July. Violence had been evident between March and May of that year, but not at levels experienced over the summer.

Figure 4.4   Monthly Casualty Figures for the Moldovan Conflict

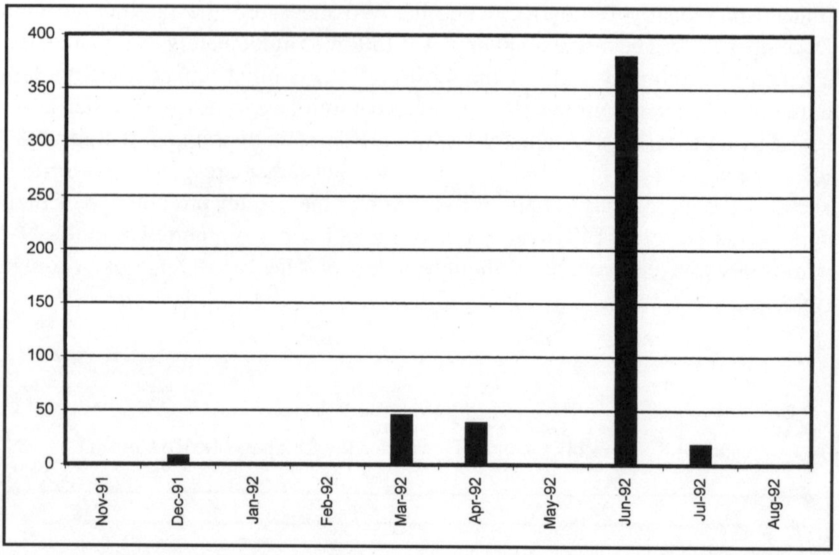

Aside from the ability to better trace escalatory and de-escalatory periods, the measure illustrated here also takes into account unique aspects of the intensity of different disputes. As the figures illustrate, escalation of one conflict can be of a very different order of magnitude and frequency than in another conflict. The Chiapas case is measured in tens of lives lost (according to Western news reports), the Moldovan case in terms of hundreds, and Angola in thousands. Angola was by far the most *volatile* case, with high frequency and fluctuation of fighting initiations and suspensions. The other cases were characterized by longer periods of relative inaction and political dispute. We now examine in more detail the role of arms in changing the pace of fighting in the various cases, allowing for the more extensive written histories available for some than for others.

Case Studies

Moldova

Moldova was created out of the politics at the outset of World War II. From the Molotov-Ribbentrop Pact of 1939, Stalin was able to take over land to the west and Moldova became one of fifteen republics of the Soviet Union in 1940. Stalin pushed Russians into Moldova, among other republics, as part of a plan to dilute the indigenous population and secure the region for Moscow. Once the Soviet Union broke apart and Moldova became an independent state, the ethnic Slavs certainly had to worry about their fate as a minority in the new state.[14]

The Moldovan conflict involved efforts by the Slavic minority, who made up the majority in the Trans-Dniester region, to secede from Moldova, whose ethnic majority was largely Romanian. The conflict became violent in December 1991, with a clash between police and the separatists. As Figure 4.4 shows, there was a major escalation in June 1992, followed immediately by de-escalation in July. The escalation appears to have resulted from several factors. First, it was only in mid-May that heavy weapons, tanks, and armored personnel carriers, were introduced in the fighting (Burke 1992). Prior to this, the separatists used light arms, some of which were taken from, or with the acquiescence of, the former Soviet 14th Army stationed in Moldova and sympathetic to the Slavic minority. For example, on two occasions in March ethnic militia members broke into military facilities and made off with small arms, "70 automatic rifles, about 2,000 rounds of ammunition and various hand weapons" (Dobbs 1992, 16) in the first instance, and "automatic rifles, ammunition, hand grenades, pistols and rocket-propelled grenades" in the second (21 Slain in Fierce Moldovan Clashes 1992, 12).

In addition, just prior to the escalation in late June, Romania had begun to supply the Moldovan government with arms. The Romanians shipped about forty armored vehicles, as well as AK-47 rifles, pistols, rocket-propelled grenades, and ammunition (Russian Army Admits Fighting in Moldova Civil War; Romania Says It Has Assisted the Ex-Republic 1992). These weapons raise an interesting question. They do not seem sufficient to have turned the tide for the Moldovans, but Romania's outside involvement might have seemed particularly threatening to the Russians. Thus, the course of violence is also affected by third countries' reactions to each other's arming of hostile sides in an ethnic war, a sort of proxy arms race.

A third change had to do with the Russian 14th Army, which more or less had stayed out of the conflict up to this point, with the important exception of leaking weaponry to the separatists. In June, as the Russians would later admit, soldiers began to take active part in the fighting, dramatically increasing the number of personnel and thus casualties involved (Shapiro 1992). Finally, the battle of Bendery, at which the bulk of these casualties occurred, represented something of a tactical change; prior to this, in April for example, the clashes were hit-and-run, and led to relatively few casualties. The fight for this town changed the nature of the conflict to more urban warfare, amid more dense populations.

It seems that in this case heavy weaponry and external suppliers did spur the overall escalation of the fighting. This escalation made it appear as if the conflict was about to spin totally out of control. Ironically though, the fear of more escalation might have contributed to the immediate de-escalation in July. A series of negotiations and cease-fires took place and the violence wound down quickly. In this way, heavy weapons and arms importation seemed to contribute to shortening the fight, which might otherwise have dragged on at much lower levels for months. This might be one explanation for our puzzling earlier finding that heavier armed disputes were not necessarily long lasting.

Chiapas

The rebellion initiated by the EZLN in Chiapas began on January 1, 1994 (perhaps the best-dated onset of an ethnopolitical conflict)—the evident catalyst being the launching of the North American Free Trade Association (NAFTA). The EZLN intended to champion the rights and welfare of the indigenous peoples of the Chiapas region of Mexico and to strike a blow at the apparent threat of "global capaitalism." News sources indicate that the EZLN were poorly armed, using only basic light weapons (e.g., pistols, rifles) and in some cases toy guns (Physicians for Human Rights 1994; *Keesing's Record of World Events* 1994, 39809). According to an EZLN communiqué, however, the EZLN's "arms and equipment were gradually gathered and readied during the 10 years during which our forces were secretly training" (Russell 1995, 133). The communiqué went on to assert that during the opening days of the conflict, the EZLN captured 207 weapons, ammunition, and dynamite.

After the initial hostilities in January, which saw somewhere between 107 (official figures) to something less than 400 killed, the conflict de-escalated. The next major escalation occurred in December 1997 when right-wing paramilitaries, suspected of being in league with the Mexican government, massacred forty-five civilians. This was followed by another immediate de-escalation. Up to the end of 1998, these were the only evident, substantial changes in the violence. According to Klare and Andersen (1996), the EZLN obtained arms by buying weapons from gun stores in the United States and smuggling them back to Mexico, buying arms on the black market in El Salvador and Nicaragua, or buying arms from the Mexican police or military. Russell (1995) concurs with this, and it appears that these weapons were acquired prior to January 1994, but this is not entirely clear from news reports.

The EZLN did not employ heavy weapons, a fact that seems to support the above hypothesis about degree of escalation. However, the EZLN did have a few sources of arms and it is not clear, by looking at arms alone, why there were not more escalations. The escalation in 1997 especially needs more study; a third-party group, possibly paramilitary or militia armed by the government, carried it out. In this way, arms supplies might indeed be salient in a conflict where they did not appear to play a prominent role.

This case demonstrates the interaction of opportunity and willingness: neither side—the EZLN or the Mexican government—apparently wanted to greatly escalate the violence. Peace talks began quickly and, although mostly nonproductive, if anything they became the focus of the dispute. In a sense, after an initial attention-getting uprising, the conflict was fought at the bargaining table, although villagers continued to feel imperiled by roving military forces.

Kosovo

Preparations for the conflict in the Kosovo region of Serbia centers on two important historical events. The earliest origins of the conflict date to 1389, when Serbs,

Ottoman Turks, and Albanians fought. The Serbs lost to the Ottomans, and Albanians began to settle in the area. Many Serbs explain that this placed Kosovo as close to their hearts as a territorial issue as Jerusalem is to the Jews and Arabs. The Ottoman Empire controlled the area until the early twentieth century, when fighting during the Balkan Wars led to the creation of the independent state of Albania, and also to greater Serbian regional influence. Beginning in World War I, the tide shifted toward the Serbs, who at times repressed the Albanians and attempted to move more Serbs into the area. In World War II, the process was reversed, with thousands of Albanians brought in by the invading Germans to displace the Slavic Serbs, a fact still remembered vividly in Serbia.

During the Communist era, beginning in 1945, Marshal Josip Broz Tito, struggling to keep the six Yugoslav republics unified, attempted to suppress ethnicity and create a sense of Yugoslavian socialist and national identity. Although Kosovo was given special treatment as an autonomous Yugoslav province, in practice the Albanians had little power, and at times the Serbs employed state terrorism and repression to attack Albanians living there.

Beginning in the 1980s, with worsening economic conditions, ethnic tensions flared anew, taking the form of rioting, protests, and demonstrations by the Kosovo Albanians. At the end of the decade, Slobodan Milosevic (head of the Serbian Communist party) seized upon the fears and grievances of the Serbian minority in Kosovo and, campaigning nationwide, used Serbian nationalism and control over the province as a rallying cry. Kosovo's special autonomy status was revoked. Subsequently, Serbs responded forcefully to the systematic breakup of Yugoslavia and supported the ruthless Bosnian Serb campaign to gain as much territory at the expense of Muslims and Croats as possible. It was this political change and President Milosevic's rise to the Yugoslav presidency using Serbian nationalism as a rallying point that provided the conditions for the worsening conflict between Kosovar Albanians and Serbs.[15]

During the 1990s, the Kosovar Albanians preferred greater political autonomy. They tried to obtain this goal by setting up a parallel state structure, including political institutions, linkage mechanisms (e.g., political parties), and policies.

The Albanians have responded not by taking up arms but by patiently constructing a parallel society and an alternative state structure. The Democratic League of Kosovo (LDK), led by President Ibrahim Rugova, rejected violence and public protests in order to avoid Bosnian-type massacres. The Kosovars built one of the Balkans' most impressive civic societies, with an alternative educational system, welfare service, youth organizations, and even a spectrum of political parties. (Bugajski 1997)

The environment and constraints on opportunity may have in part dictated Rugova's strategy. It would have been very difficult for the Kosovars to mount an effective campaign of violence. During the 1990s, they had no significant weapons, nor access to them. In any case, the Serb response continued to be one of repression, a response that began to have serious consequences.

For several reasons Kosovar preferences began to shift, and as we will see, so did their method for redressing perceived grievances. First, Albanian youth, who made up most of the Kosovar population, became increasingly radicalized because of the growing repression; they perceived themselves suffering significant, relative economic deprivation. Moreover, more moderate Albanians were under mounting pressure to show some results from their efforts to increase autonomy. Finally, there was a growing perception that the international community was not going to help. In such a situation, the views of the more radical elements tend to become more persuasive (Bugajski 1997).

The failure of the Dayton Peace Accords on Bosnia to treat the simmering Kosovo ethnic conflict in November 1995 appeared to lead younger Kosovars to consider the alternative of violence. Meanwhile, efforts to contain ethnic unrest through such means as negotiations and local councils continued in the province, but economic pressure grew with the collapsing Albanian economy next door, the international embargo on Yugoslavia, a Greek-imposed blockade of nearby Macedonia, and harsh International Monetary Fund (IMF) reform requirements. This led to an evident rise both in unemployment and the open and illicit regional trade of arms for goods such as oil and drugs, which could be resold on the European market (Chossudovsky 1999). These trends ultimately improved the chances for the Kosovo Liberation Army (KLA) to recruit discontented young fighters. As one author put it, "Thrown out of their jobs by the Serbian authorities and tired of waiting for [the moderate Kosovar leader] Mr. Rugova to deliver his promises of statehood and for the international community to get involved, a new generation of Albanians sees violence as the only way of gaining attention for their cause" (Dinmore 1997). However, with few members and few weapons, the KLA could as yet take little action.

The KLA had appeared in the newly emerging state of Macedonia in 1992 but had remained a relatively minute and isolated force.[16] In 1995, however, despite its still-small size and resources, the KLA carried out its first isolated attacks on Serb police forces in Kosovo, following with a series of public acts of sabotage (bombings) against police stations and officers in June 1996. Thus, Serb authorities came to identify the group as a "terrorist organization," a frequently used label in armed internal ethnic uprisings (seen in Spain, Turkey, Northern Ireland, Israel, etc.). Confining itself to ambushes of police patrols and attacks on Albanians "collaborating" with Serb authorities, the KLA refrained from major confrontations with Serb armed forces. This changed, however, in 1997 and 1998 as a series of events in nearby Albania and changing Serb strategies combined to spur the emergence/escalation of a larger-scale rebellion.

The regime of President Sali Berisha, who ruled Albania following the overthrow of Communism until his ouster in 1997, was notoriously corrupt and involved in a series of pyramid and Ponzi schemes. However, despite possible designs on a "greater Albania" to include parts of Macedonia and Kosovo, Berisha seems to have shipped few arms to the distrusted KLA (Berisha may have considered them agents provocateurs for Serb leader Milosevic). "It was the mass revolutionary uprising against Berisha in 1997 which freed up to a million guns from Albania's armouries and allowed the cash-starved KLA to get its hands on a lot of cheap weapons." Indeed, the KLA evidently had ties to the Albanian Socialist Party, which then came to power (Karadjis 1999).[17]

In the spring of 1997, as significant weapon supplies began to flow across the border, the KLA stepped up its attacks; the Serbs responded with greater repression. The conflict had begun to spin out of control.[18] Arms ended up facilitating the escalation of violence as the KLA shifted to a more sustained military campaign, "Emboldened by a massive infusion of arms from neighboring Albania, KLA guerrillas had stepped up their hit-and-run attacks on Serbian police stations and ambushes of military convoys" (Jensen 1998). The arms infusion consisted primarily of light weapons, including rocket-propelled grenades and the ubiquitous Kalashnikov assault rifle; the KLA also was seeking to acquire antiaircraft and antitank weapons. Although the United Nations enacted an arms embargo on Yugoslavia on March 31, 1977, arms smuggling continued, allowing the KLA to undertake larger and more frequent operations, though still producing relatively minute casualties.

Aside from the Albanian pipeline, arms also were reportedly purchased from within Serbia and Montenegro; as in many wars, rebels obtained weapons directly from the enemy or from enemy territory (Landay 1998). In May, news reports claimed that the KLA was also obtaining guns from pro-Iranian mujahedin groups (Buchan 1998). Evidently emboldened by these resources, the KLA's position came to focus on secession rather than a return to the political autonomy Kosovo enjoyed prior to 1989. As a result of the arms and the subsequent rise of the KLA, the moderate view was pushed aside.

KLA arsenals, originally stocked with old rifles acquired mainly inside Serbia or through the mountains from Albania, expanded still further. Assault rifles, Ambrust and Soviet-model RPG shoulder-fired antitank rocket launchers, mortars, recoilless rifles, and antiaircraft machine guns were now acquired. Thus, a mix of World War II vintage equipment and modern, often Chinese and Singapore produced, light arms, ammunition, and telecommunication gear was achieved (Smucker 1998).

Flush with arms, the rebels were able to further escalate the fighting in the spring of 1998 with the launching of bolder attacks and defense of villages. In response to heavy Serb police attacks on villages in the KLA-stronghold Drenica region, and in conjunction with the change of government in Albania, the rebels made a major power play for national independence. The Serbs responded militarily and large-scale fighting ensued with some 200 dying and 300,000 displaced before the first cease-fire in October 1998. Despite international inspection by the OSCE, violence mounted again sharply in January 1999, involving government "ethnic cleansing" strategies, leading to the abortive Paris peace talks in March and subsequent NATO bombardment and intervention (Kosovo Liberation Army (KLA), Intelligence Resource Program, Federation of American Scientists 1999).

Arms infusions thus also produced important strategic shifts among the Serbs, leading to tragic local and international ramifications. Aroused by KLA activity, in 1998 Serbia sought to crush the rebellion by any and all means. Shifting the fight from police forces, Serbia deployed more troops and heavy weapons including aircraft and tanks. Initial KLA successes may have been paradoxically harmful in the long run, since the organization was hard pressed to dig in and defend the region against Serb counterattacks. In addition, during the summer of 1998, the Yugoslav border was mined, successfully diminishing arms smuggling into the region (another paradox in light of the global campaign then under way to ban land mine use and trade) (Brown 1998).

In action-reaction sequence, the Serb countermeasures led to unexpected or unintended escalation and outside intervention. As Ambassador William Walker, U.S. representative to the Kosovo Verification Mission of the OSCE, put it,

> When the KLA was still weak, there was an overreaction by the Serbian government that went way beyond what you do to quiet the opposition. In fact, it did just the opposite. It led a lot of young people to what I would consider the mistaken belief that you take up guns and you go after your enemy in an equally vicious way. (Smucker 1998)

Thus, the KLA's ranks rose from about 500 members in early 1998 to a peak of 30,000 to 40,000 before being crushed—though not eliminated—by Serb forces before and during the NATO spring bombardment and occupation of 1999. Many KLA members reportedly were professionally trained former Yugoslav army veterans or former police or state security officers. About 1,000 foreign mercenaries from Albania, Saudi Arabia, Yemen, Afghanistan, Bosnia, and Croatia also swelled KLA ranks (Smucker 1998).[19]

In funding their foreign arms acquisitions, especially from sources in Albania, the KLA reportedly used connections with drug and criminal syndicates that sprouted in Albania and elsewhere in the Balkans during the war-torn and economically chaotic 1990s. Claims of a three-way drug-oil-arms connection involving Turkey, Albania, Serbia, Italy, and other neighboring states do not clearly show that the KLA, as opposed to other groups and other ethnic Albanians, dominated the trade. Such a network, however, would fit patterns of other lightly armed or poorer ethnic fighters seeking resources for arms acquisitions as well as the facility to "launder" or conceal such transactions (patterns seen in Ireland, Spain, Turkey, Burma, Lebanon, Africa, and elsewhere). It appears that the KLA was implicated in the misuse of Swiss bank accounts and gained funds from a 3 percent "Homeland Calling" tax on the incomes of many Kosovars working in Europe.[20]

In sum, the Kosovar Albanian armed revolt stemmed from growing ethnic insecurity and frustration coming to a boil between 1995 and 1997. Requisite levels of arms and bomb-making materials were procured gradually by the KLA both domestically (carried from former Yugoslav forces) and from neighboring Albania during those years, allowing the rebellion to start at low levels. The stakes were raised in a flood of Albanian arms and in Serb counterattacks in Kosovo, first by police and then by military units in a harsh crackdown when KLA resistance grew. KLA arsenals then expanded to include more modern light equipment from varied sources. A regular arms supply network was established, reminiscent of that seen in Sri Lanka, as the war escalated and as a new regime in Albania took a greater interest in the cause. The coincidence of mounting insecurity, frustration with outside powers, nearby state breakdown (Albania, Yugoslavia), a thriving regional arms-drugs-oil traffic, plentiful former Soviet bloc arms availability, growing world sympathy for the Kosovars, and rudimentary fund-raising all led the way to sustained combat in Kosovo.

Basically, it appears that arms acquisition followed initial political mobilization in this case, and that just enough arms were procured in the interim to allow fighting to break out at very low levels (hit-and-run bombings, raids, and sabotage). Further arms acquisitions set the stage for bolder attacks, and still more arms arrived as combat generated sympathies and the need for better equipment. Support networks developed in the latter stage among funding and arms sources, ultimately including intelligence agencies, especially as the KLA attained a place at the negotiating table. Ironically though, in the bargain for NATO intervention, KLA *disarmament* was one of the major demands (more about that in later chapters).

Arms both provided opportunity and affected parties' willingness to escalate in Kosovo. A complex "tit-for-tat" strategy developed between an ever more repressive government and the nationalist Kosovars, who were able to arm sufficiently to provoke but not defeat the authorities, and sufficiently also to bring on international sympathy. The KLA was already willing to use violence, but prior to the Albanian economic fiasco did not have the means to do so on a broad scale. For better or worse, therefore, armament was a key factor in allowing the KLA to emerge politically. The ensuing struggle hardened their goals for independence. The Serb-dominated Yugoslav government, already with a significant arsenal, was pushed into action and made more willing to pursue an increasingly violent course, despite growing international opposition. KLA armed action created insecurity among the Serbs who responded by stepping up state repression, thereby increasing Kosovar insecurity. This was the classic armed "security dilemma."

Angola

Arms supplied by interested third parties also largely paced the escalation/de-escalation patterns of the Angolan civil war, especially during its first decisive phase in the late 1970s. After that, stockpiled arms, and weapons purchased through illicit commodity (diamond, oil) trade, reportedly allowed at least one of the rebel factions, UNITA, to continue the fight sporadically up through the 1990s. We will concentrate our attention here on the earlier period, which has been especially thoroughly reviewed by Stockwell (1978), a centrally placed former American intelligence agent.

Modern ideologies, political aspirations and military organizations were attached to the various contending Angolan social forces in the aftermath of Portuguese colonial withdrawal, with divisions roughly along ethnotribal lines. Portuguese colonial rulers, intent on "dividing and conquering," had pitted Ovimbundu, Mbundu, and Bakongo peoples against each other throughout the first half of the twentieth century.

The postcolonial contest between armed Angolan factions was kicked off well in advance of Angola's independence from Portugal on November 11, 1975, with Chinese and American arms shipments to Holden Roberto's FNLA in 1973, a group with roots in the Kongo tribe (Stockwell 1978, 112). Moscow for its part supplied the Mbundu-based MPLA through the early 1970s, ceasing in 1973 but resuming on a limited scale in 1974. Not to be outdone in the context of opposing the Soviets and MPLA, the CIA continued to fund FNLA and also flirted with Jonas Sivimbi's UNITA, whose origins were among the Ovimbundu. This in turn led the USSR to escalate arms supplies, with more significant shipments and the dispatch of Soviet and Cuban advisors beginning in March 1975. Thus, Angola is a case with very heavy foreign arms investment.

Backed by both Washington and Zaire's President Mobutu Sese Seko, the FNLA set off major warfare in February 1975 by launching an offensive from Zairian sanctuaries against the MPLA in Luanda and the north. This controverted the Alvor Agreement of January 1975, which had set free elections for October among the three factions, just prior to Portugal's scheduled departure. In the face of early FNLA advances, the Soviets seized the occasion to undertake a massive arms airlift. AN-12 and AN-22 cargo planes ferried equipment into neighboring Brazzaville, capital of the Republic of the Congo, with subsequent air drops and boat deliveries to MPLA units defending Luanda.

> The fighting in Luanda intensified in July. With about equal force of arms, the MPLA had the significant advantage of defending the Mbundu homelands. It prevailed and evicted the FNLA and UNITA from Luanda. (Stockwell 1978, 68)

Inevitably, this level of commitment would catch Washington's eye. Because of its official opposition to arming the Angolan combatants, the Ford administration entrusted the CIA with a covert warfare operation. Secretary of State Henry Kissinger would perhaps have preferred a major undertaking capable of defeating the Soviets, but post-Vietnam congressional opposition necessitated a smaller-scale secret mission designed merely to harass and raise the costs for the Soviets and their African and Cuban allies. A CIA Angolan Task Force was created to oversee a program called "IAFEATURE," involving the infusion both of more sophisticated weapons and U.S. military advisors into the country. In fact, the National Security Council in Washington created rationales expecting that a judicious supply of weapons would prevent a "quick and cheap" MPLA victory and by establishing a military balance, "discourage further resort to arms in Angola" (Stockwell 1978, 20, 21, 46, and 54). This is tempting logic for an intervening major power, but proved entirely inaccurate in this case as in others.[21]

The hasty and makeshift nature of the IAFEATURE arrangements meant something of a mismatch between arms and their recipients. Some 622 "crew-served mortars, rockets and machine guns," 4210 antitank rockets, 20,986 outdated semi-automatic rifles (in addition to several thousand Chinese, South African, and Zairian rifles), along with 12 armored personnel carriers, 50 surface-to-air anti-aircraft missiles, 14 recoilless rifles, 180 rocket launchers, 64 heavy machine guns, 25 rocket grenade launchers, several thousand sub-machine guns and 9mm pistols, 96,000 hand grenades, 60 trucks, 20 trailers, 27 motorized swift and rubber boats, 1000 or so radios, field gear, vehicle parts, millions of rounds of ammunition, demolition materials, and combat rations were ferried via Zaire to a total of something under 10,000 combined FNLA and UNITA forces" (Stockwell 1978, 78 and appendix 5).

The state of warfare in the north was sporadic at the point of initial IAFEATURE supplies. The MPLA appeared to be poorly armed and led, and vulnerable to a knockout if sophisticated U.S. systems, such as Vietnam-era "Puff the Magic Dragon" flying C-47 combat aircraft, could be employed to clear whole areas through intense gunfire (Stockwell 1978, 79 and 134–35). However, the FNLA also proved to be ineffective, and the potential cost of escalating weapons technology too far was judged as unacceptable, precluding C-47s and deep overt American commitments in the wake of Vietnam. The Americans began to see Savimbi's UNITA as more reliable and better organized, if poorly armed with older weapons from various original sources. Savimbi was quoted as requesting,

> Big mortars, and bazookas with a lot of ammunition. Weapons that will shoot far and make the enemy run away. My men are not afraid to fight close, but when they do I can lose too many soldiers. I cannot afford to lose them. (Stockwell 1978, 141)

The effect of armament on the course of war is unusually well documented in this case.

> During September and October, the CIA, with remarkable support from diverse U.S. government and military offices around the world, mounted the controversial, economy-size war with single-minded ruthlessness. The lumbering USAF C-141 jet transports continued to lift twenty-five-ton loads of obsolete U.S. or untraceable foreign weapons from Charleston, South Carolina, to Kinshasa, where smaller planes took them into Angola. The USN *American Champion* sailed from Charleston on August 30 with a cargo of arms and equipment. . . . The deadline was November 11, 1975, when the Portuguese would relinquish proprietorship of the colony to whichever movement controlled the capital at that time.
>
> The war saw a seesaw of escalation. Momentum moved from side to side, as the United States and Soviet Union delivered obsolete weapons, then foreign troops, and eventually sophisticated systems such as wire-guided rockets and late-model jet fighter bombers.
>
> In early September the MPLA committed a devastating, ageless weapon, the Russian 122mm rocket, and set the FNLA troops running. . . . Supplied by the Soviet Union, the 122mm rocket, as much as any one thing, eventually decided the outcome of the civil war in Angola. (Stockwell 1978, 162)

Although the *katusha* rocket, using truck-mounted launchers called "Stalin's organs," had been around since before World War II, it packed a particular wallop in Third World fighting, as demonstrated in both Vietnam and the Middle East. Generally inaccurate and similar in caliber to mortars, it nevertheless struck terror into enemy towns and troop concentrations.

> The 122 had a simple advantage over the weapons we had given the FNLA—namely, range. It would fire twelve kilometers; our mortars no more than eight. From a safe distance the MPLA could lob 122 mm. rockets onto FNLA troops who were unable to return fire.
>
> Well-organized troops could endure such shelling indefinitely, by digging in or by aggressive patroling [sic] and maneuvering. The 122 could also be neutralized by coordinated artillery fire, tactical aircraft, or electronically guided rocketry, but these were not available to the FNLA.
>
> The United States had no simple weapon comparable to the 122 to give the FNLA. Our weaponry jumped from the less effective mortars to heavy artillery and modern rockets. These, and tactical aircraft, could have neutralized the 122, but they were prohibitively expensive and required highly trained crews to operate them. They would also have been conspicuously American and the [National Security Council] 40 Committee refused to authorize their use—until December, when it was too late. (Stockwell 1978, 163)

In the ensuing months, UNITA and FNLA tried to rally through direct South African and Zairian military intervention, with additional arms infusions coming from or through those countries.[22] Initially, South African-armored columns— armored cars and artillery—raced through MPLA lines on behalf of UNITA. A Zairian-FNLA column, supported by long guns manned by South Africans and Zairians (who obtained two malfunctioning 130mm guns from North Korea), advanced on Luanda. However, these forces merely further discredited the war effort and were ultimately defeated in battles against Cuban forces and MPLA elements, with the 122mm rockets playing a key role in scattering the FNLA and Zairians.

South African weapons and forces came up against the Cuban-MPLA firepower and organization, which finally turned the tide on the outskirts of Luanda and to the south. In addition to the dramatic effects of the *katusha* rockets, the MPLA-Cuban side employed missile-firing helicopters, T-34 tanks, and 122mm long-range (26km) cannon. Decision makers in the United States discussed responding with further sophisticated equipment (antiaircraft and antitank missiles, heavy artillery, tactical air support, C-47 gun ships) and even direct intervention, but the National Security Council refused to up the ante because of lack of funds and prospects of congressional disapproval. Even the addition of a few French missile-firing helicopters was meaningless in the absence of trained crews (mercenaries were constantly being sought) to fly them (Stockwell 1978, 216–18).

Because of Angola's geographic location, oil and mineral resources, and cold war significance, the warring factions drew an unusual array of patrons. The

United States, China, Romania, North Korea, France, Israel, West Germany, Senegal, Uganda, Zaire, Zambia, Tanzania, and South Africa at one time or another supported the FNLA and UNITA. The USSR, Cuba, East Germany, Algeria, Guinea, and other East European states backed the MPLA. Some of these collaborated (e.g., France, the United States, and Zaire) in arms deliveries. Gradually, more states shifted support to the MPLA side, and in October of 1975, China left the war effort (Stockwell 1978, 191–92).

> In the final and decisive phase of the war [in the 1970s], between December 1975 and April 1976, the MPLA with its socialist allies went on the offensive. The South African advance was halted 150 miles south of Luanda. The SADF [South African Defence Force] suffered serious casualties and several soldiers were taken prisoner before retreating to sanctuary in Namibia. The FNLA, after its encounter with Soviet-supplied "Stalin Organs" at the "Battle of Death road," was completely demoralized and ceased to be a factor in the civil war. Jonas Savimbi's UNITA rebels fought well against the joint MPLA/Cuban force in the south but were ultimately outgunned and outnumbered and fled to camps in Ovamboland.
>
> Thus, with the military equipment and advisers provided by the Soviet Union and soldiers sent by Cuba, the MPLA was able to cling to power. (Campbell 1988, 95)

Indeed, this was an era in which Secretary of State Kissinger, referring to a different dispute—the 1973 Arab-Israeli war—had vowed not to allow "Soviet arms" to defeat "American arms" in Third World struggles. It was the Soviets though who invested most heavily in the Angolan struggle, ultimately committing more than $400 million in assistance ($225 million by late November 1976), with a 7 to 1 advantage in shiploads and a 100 to 9 advantage in planeloads of arms delivered (by CIA estimates, Stockwell 1978, 180 and 216). Ironically, much of the Soviet and Cuban assistance through the years of fighting was paid for with Angolan oil revenues from U.S. companies, whose operations were protected by Cuban forces (O'Neill and Munslow 1995, 189).

Thus, arms themselves had come to symbolize the political stakes involved in such episodes. When MiGs were reported present, inaccurately as it turned out, in Brazzaville and Angola in 1975, U.S. decision makers discussed responding with the dispatch of portable "Redeye" antiaircraft missiles. But this weapon was highly classified and until that time had been released only to close clients such as the Israelis, and it clearly would have blown the cover of secrecy in America's war involvement (Stockwell 1978, 181–82).

In subsequent years the Angolan fighting would flare anew, in pitched cross-border battles with South African and UNITA pitted against Cuban and MPLA forces in the late 1980s. Approximately $2 billion to $3 billion in Soviet military resupplies to the MPLA, including additional sophisticated MiG-23 fighter jets, offset major South African arms expenditures in 1985–86, and immediately preceded the decisive battles of August 1987 through early 1988. This also led to at least $15 million of additional covert U.S. supplies, keeping UNITA somewhat

viable to forestall what was seen as a complete Soviet victory and to pressure
MPLA to negotiate. Reputedly, the U.S. aid package included shoulder-mounted
Stinger antiaircraft missiles, so effective in Afghanistan, though their employment
by UNITA could not be confirmed. South Africa's loss of air superiority meant
heightened death rates and thus growing distaste for and withdrawal from the war,
if not the beginning of the end for the apartheid regime itself (O'Neill and
Munslow 1995, 183–97).

In the 1990s, arms again demonstrated their importance to the course of conflict. A concerted effort of peace talks, furthered by the end of Cold War animosi-
ties between the United States and the Soviet Union, occurred during 1990 and
1991. The result was the Bicesse Accords in 1991, which led to general elections
in 1992 (Rothchild and Hartzell 1995). Savimbi of UNITA refused to accept the
outcome of these elections, and fighting renewed. However, during 1992–94,
UNITA's military prowess declined; while the army's strength increased. In 1993,
UNITA controlled much of the Angolan countryside, and by 1994, the army had
retaken substantial territory.[23] They were aided by $3.5 billion in arms and ammu-
nition acquired from abroad (Rothchild 1997). The United Nations instituted an
arms embargo against UNITA in 1993, but both sides were able to increase arms
acquisitions throughout the 1990s. As a result of the army's battlefield successes,
Savimbi became more interested in pursuing peace. This led to the Lusaka Protocol in 1994 (see *Africa Research Bulletin* 1994a, 11668, for the main points of the
Lusaka peace agreement).

The United Nations sent in a peacekeeping mission in 1995–96, the United
Nations Angola Verification Mission (UNAVEM III), and during these years there
was sporadic fighting. In part the government was trying to grab whatever gains
possible to cement their strong position against UNITA. In 1997 it appeared the
conflict had ended; demobilization of UNITA members was occurring, as well as
efforts to return refugees to Angola. On April 11, 1997, the new Government of
National Unity and Reconciliation (GURN), which included members of UNITA,
was sworn in.

However, the lull during 1994–96 seems to have been basically an occasion for
UNITA to resupply. As early as spring 1995, commentators were suggesting that
rearmament rather than peace building seemed to be the order of the day (*Africa
Research Bulletin* 1995, 11789–90). In addition, cease-fire violations occurred
throughout this period. Much of UNITA's efforts concentrated on maintaining
control over diamond-producing areas to finance arms buying. By 1997, the peace
process was viewed in serious jeopardy (*Africa Research Bulletin* 1997) as both
sides were openly rearming. The government was receiving supplies from Eastern
European sources, and UNITA was resupplying from sources in South Africa and
the Congo. By summer 1998, Angola was again poised on the brink of war, and
by the end of the year, it had gone over the edge (Human Rights Watch 1999).

Perhaps more starkly than in any of our other cases, escalating arms levels either
preceded or accompanied nearly all the military escalations of the Angolan wars.

In few cases has a single weapon (122mm rockets) played as integral a role in turning around the momentum and accounting for the initial basic outcome of the fighting. In the subsequent phase of internationalized warfare between the South Africans and Cubans, loss of South African air superiority, and a shift in the local power balance with overextended supply lines also worked to create a decisive turnaround, leading to South Africa's retreat from the war. UNITA itself has been sustained since then by weapons availability and resourceful trading.

Arms and Volatility

Having reviewed escalatory patterns, we offer the following propositions on the volatility of conflict. Volatility considers the overall pattern and frequency of escalations and de-escalations in the fighting. We suggest that certain types of weapons and certain methods of arms supply have an impact on overall volatility. First, heavy weapons are more likely than light weapons to lead to volatile conflicts, with more escalation and de-escalation. The basic reasoning here is that heavy weapons tend to produce major casualties, as seen in the last Angolan battles of the 1980s. Such weapons also are likely to be used episodically in many ethnopolitical conflicts, as forces regroup and resupply.

Second, in conflicts with one or a few arms suppliers, volatility is likely to be greater than in conflicts with no arms importation or importation from multiple suppliers. The idea here is that in conflict with little or no importation, the armament level is likely to be light and fighting drawn out over time. A conflict with many foreign suppliers, such as Angola, will tend to show more sustained periods of fighting and at a generally higher level of intensity. If heavy arms predominate, such fighting may tend to be of relatively shorter duration as we discovered earlier. In conflicts with a few suppliers, however, supply is more uncertain and there may be lags in resupply, resulting in more volatility as parties escalate and then fall back waiting for equipment to mount new offensives.

To test these suppositions, volatility can be measured from the escalation and de-escalation data presented above. Judging by figures 4.1 to 4.4, the most volatile of our conflicts were Angola and Moldova. In this sense, there were relatively large and/or frequent escalations and de-escalations given the conflicts' duration. Kosovo and Chiapas, on the other hand, seemed relatively more static, despite some escalatory spikes, with long periods of inaction. The frequency of escalations also was lower in these latter two cases.

Angola was the dispute in our small sample with the most outside arms suppliers and the biggest use of heavy weapons. We expected heavy weapons to be associated with volatility; we did not expect several suppliers to be so associated, however. Yet despite the various arms sources evident in Angola, the war mainly boiled down to American versus Soviet weapons funneled into the war zone through third parties, and particularly through Zaire, Brazzaville in the Congo, and South Africa (with South Africa having more autonomous control of the type and pace of armament than Zaire). Moscow and Washington had established such stakes in the fighting through the 1970s and 1980s that this became another of the major power Cold War proxy struggles.

The Moldovan case also saw arms from mainly only two sources: Russia and Romania. The introduction of heavy weapons characterized the escalatory period. On the other hand, arms levels appeared much lighter in Chiapas, and with little evident importation to the Zapatista side. As for Kosovo, the third most volatile dispute, the influx of arms from neighboring Albania characterized a telescoping of fighting toward the end of the period (figure 4.2). Volatility increased with the introduction of these heavier arms. Thus, the hypotheses appear to be supported by the limited evidence amassed so far if one counts Angola as a mainly dual-supplier war. With only four cases, however, it would behoove researchers to look more closely at the effects of multiple suppliers versus few suppliers in escalating civil wars.

CONCLUSION

The ongoing pattern of conflicts is a fruitful area of inquiry for conflict scholars. Obviously, conflicts vary in terms of duration, severity, escalation/de-escalation, and volatility, and these differences can be explained as the product of the combatants' choices. Those choices, in turn, are influenced by the parties' willingness to take the violence in different directions, and their ability to do so. Changes in arms type and availability are factors in determining those choices and capabilities.

The limited analysis conducted here supports the plausibility of several of the theoretical hypotheses about escalation and de-escalation. There does seem to be a relatively consistent relationship between arms flows and changes in the nature of ethnopolitical violence. Heavy arms appear to lead to shorter wars, greater intensity of fighting, and volatility in escalatory/de-escalatory patterns. External arms supply to groups in conflict also affect the fighting, leading to greater intensity, while more suppliers also appear to decrease volatility. Arms supplies to governments appear to equip forces for longer wars. Such preliminary conclusions suggest that future analysis and policies need to focus on the size and sources of weapons and their impact on government and ethnic communities' opportunity and willingness to manipulate violence to try to achieve their goals.

NOTES

1. It is also the case that much more analysis is focused on the initiation and termination of international conflicts. See, for example, Brzoska and Pearson (1994). For studies of the initiation of ethnic conflict, see, for example, Gurr (1993 and 2000b), Lake and Rothchild (1996), and Van Evera (1994). For studies on the termination of ethnic conflict, see Zartman (1995b) and Licklider (1995).

2. Escalation and de-escalation concern changes in casualties and intensity, and can be treated dynamically, however, they are far vaguer concepts than might be assumed. They can refer either to the outbreak and ultimate end of fighting, or to the patterns of increased or decreased fighting during the war. For example, some scholars are as much interested in how nonviolent disputes escalate to violence as they are in how wars become more or less violent during their course (Carlson 1995; Dixon 1996). Thus, the concept "deterrence" can focus both on preventing the escalation to violence in the first place, or on preventing the expansion of fighting once under way.

3. The Moldovan conflict basically was between the non-Slavic ethno-linguistic majority and the Slavic or Russian minority. Sometimes such majorities or minorities are themselves somewhat diverse, so that "two-sided" can be an oversimplification of conflict dynamics. During the Soviet period, the Soviet 14th Army was stationed in Moldova. After Moldova became independent in 1991, the army remained and sided with the Russians, providing an important source of armament during the short-lived violence.

4. This last motivation has important implications, since it is possible that one "good escalation" might attract sufficient media and public attention to validate the group's status as a "player." Further escalations might thereby become unnecessary, or might become necessary again to revalidate that status across long time periods, especially as the public and media become desensitized to the struggle over time.

5. In the case of international conflict, it might be suggested that as weapons technology improves over the centuries, wars would tend to get shorter. However, civil conflicts are fundamentally different from interstate wars. In the former, the traditional well-defined battlefield generally is not present. Rather, we often witness unconventional combat involving bombings, assassinations, and small-scale fighting and raids, with an occasional resort to pitched battles.

6. Such battles would likely have involved full-scale combat with British forces, something that neither of the disputing ethnopolitical groups would want; furthermore, the Unionist forces were probably not as well armed as their IRA counterparts.

7. Duration is fairly straightforward to define operationally as the total number of months of the conflict. Three complexities are noteworthy. First, as noted in chapter 3, scholars present different dates for the onset of fighting, which makes it difficult to assess overall duration. Despite such disagreements, however, focusing on casualties at the monthly level can help determine a more commonly accepted onset date, since months are more precise than years as a temporal demarcation. Second, many conflicts have not ended, so we do not know their ultimate duration. Finally, some conflicts have multiple combatants, not all of whom participate through the entire duration.

8. Of course, the decision to use ten years as the demarcation of "long" or "short" is subject to debate, since any war that goes on for ten years can be considered persistent to say the least. Some clear point was needed, however, for initial study.

9. Some country designations need explanation. Iraq obviously was a well-armed country in its 1990s battles with Kurdish and Shia minorities, but a UN arms embargo drastically reduced its actual arms imports, so it is classified here as "low." Similarly, while the country remained well armed, South African weapon imports were somewhat restricted during its long apartheid struggle. Sri Lankan government imports expanded greatly in the later years of its civil war, but the average was at lower levels during the middle years.

10. However, measuring changes in the intensity/severity presents several challenges. Existing data offer estimates of total casualties for the conflicts (e.g., Brown 1996; Gurr and

Harff 1994; Sivard 1996), but these data are problematic for at least two reasons. First, different scholars offer different casualty estimates. This could be due to a variety of reasons, such as different sources, counting rules (e.g., counting soldiers versus all battle-related casualties), or duration figures. Second, periodic updates create competing sets of casualty figures. For example, the *New York Times* reported on March 20, 1993, about ten years into the war, that the Sri Lankan conflict had produced 20,000 dead (Gargan 1993); on September 5, 1994, a report indicated 30,000 dead (Burns 1994); and on April 16, 1995, the number was raised to 34,000 (Burns 1995). Assuming the conflict began in 1983, this implies an average annual severity of approximately 2,000, 2,500, or 2,615 depending on the figure used. It also appears that the conflict was markedly worsening in the mid-1990s, but this would not be evident by looking only at average data. Therefore, average casualty data should be used in conjunction with the other measures to produce a fully accurate picture of violence intensity.

11. A concern in measuring escalation, particularly with event data, is the problem of the independence of events. Ethnic conflicts are complicated and can involve multiple actors on both sides. Escalations and de-escalations (e.g., offensives or unilateral cease-fires) can occur separately from one another, and conceivably even simultaneously. Governments might offer a carrot and a stick: an amnesty and a stepped-up military campaign to make the amnesty look more attractive. The point is that an adequate measure must be able to account for both processes. For example, killing is often an escalation of a conflict; not killing is not necessarily a de-escalation.

12. Other measures could include changes in the intensity with which issues are held by the disputants, possibly measured by examining grievances expressed in sources such as Gurr's *Minorities at Risk* data. One could also examine changing tangible costs of a conflict, aside from casualties, such as loss to economic productivity or environmental damage. For example, Grobar and Gnanaselvam (1993) sought to determine the opportunity costs facing the Sri Lankan government as a result of its focus on military expenditure—guns—rather than on investment for economic growth—butter—since 1983. Finally, another way of viewing escalation is to focus on changes in tactics. In Moldova, during the 1992 conflict, casualties were relatively low, until the fighting switched to an urban center and hit-and-run attacks were exchanged for sustained fighting.

13. We use Keesing's *Record of World Events, Facts on File*, and major newspapers (surveyed through *Lexis/Nexis*) to compile estimates of monthly casualties (including all reported fatalities of government soldiers and police, members of ethnopolitical groups, and civilians) from the beginning of each conflict through 1999 or the conflict's end, whichever occurred first. While casualty estimates are always problematic and subject to political bias, the figures at least are indicative of the pace of fighting. Claimed casualties tend to rise when combat levels increase. Note that the first time period we examine is the month prior to the onset of fighting. This means that each conflict begins with an initial escalation from non-violence to violence. We feel that this is consistent with commonly accepted notions of the concept of escalation.

14. For an alternative view that the Moldovan conflict was not ethnic in nature, but rather a fight between the old Soviet Union and the forces of change, see Evangelista (1996).

15. For a good review of the history of Kosovo, see the narrative on the Kosovo Albanians on the *Minorities at Risk* home page <http://www.bsos.umd.edu/cidcm/mar>.

16. Apparently, the KLA had its origins in the Popular Movement for Kosovo (LPK) party, established in 1982.

17. In spring 1997, approximately one in five Albanians lost most or all of their life savings when phony investments suddenly collapsed. Violence flared, and ordinary citizens, fearing for their safety, undertook raids on police stations and army depots. Hundreds of thousands of small arms were looted. Guns spread everywhere throughout Albania. This immediately raised the possibility that some of those weapons would find their way to Albanian minorities in nearby countries, including Kosovo (Neuffer 1997). Smuggling between Albania and the Kosovo province was already occurring for other goods, and it seemed inevitable that some of that smuggling would involve guns.

18. It is interesting to wonder if the international community could have done anything at this time to stop the crisis. The major players, including the United States, the United Nations, and the Serbs (who initially called the KLA terrorists), and the international community applied similar language to the Serbs' responses. However, as the Serb response became larger and out of proportion to the KLA provocation, and given perhaps a greater hostility to the Serbs, the international community became less objective and began to side with the Kosovo Albanians more and more.

19. Despite accusations that the United States (through CIA machinations with a so-called Government of Kosovo based in Geneva, and the use of drug cartels), Germany (through its security service), and other Western powers conspired to equip and unleash the KLA on Yugoslavia, there is scant evidence of much direct support, at least until the NATO-Yugoslav struggle of 1999. The KLA was on Germany's list of banned terrorist organizations, and, in contrast to its consent in Bosnia, Washington reportedly was lukewarm to Islamic arms going to Kosovo for fear of spreading terrorism of the Osama bin Laden variety. NATO did, however, provide KLA forces with satellite phones "with which [to] . . . relay intelligence on Serbian positions in Kosovo" (Karadjis, 1999), and, reportedly, Western arms turned up with the KLA in 1999. In a controversial report by Chossudovsky (1999), the Serb government claimed that the KLA also received heavy weapons training (rocket-propelled grenades, medium-caliber cannon, tanks, command and control) at camps in Albania.

20. Claims about KLA criminal ties are most boldly pronounced by University of Ottawa economist Michel Chossudovsky (1999). Karadjis (1999), citing a split in the ideological left concerning the Kosovo tragedy, takes issue with many of Chossudovsky's conclusions, while allowing for the possible drug connections and regional international ties.

21. As a side note, the Angolan operation illustrates the way unofficial or covert arms have been procured for ongoing ethnopolitical wars, at least in the highly competitive context of the Cold War. Although the CIA at the time lacked an efficient staff to plan and execute arms shipments, it maintained, "prepackaged stocks of foreign weapons for instant shipment anywhere in the world. The transportation is normally provided by the U.S. Air Force, or by private charter if the American presence must be masked. Even tighter security can be obtained by contracting with international dealers who will purchase arms in Europe and subcontract independently to have them flown into the target area. Often, the CIA will deliver obsolete American weapons. . . . In the Angola program, we obtained such obsolete weapons from the National Guard and U.S. Army Reserve stores. Initially, U.S. Air Force C-130 transports picked up weapons from the CIA warehouse in San Antonio, Texas, and delivered them to Charleston, South Carolina. U.S. Air Force C-141 jet transports then hauled twenty-five-ton loads across the Atlantic to Kinshasa [Zaire]. Inevitably, the air force billed the CIA for the service. . . . Repeatedly during the program we would place a token amount of certain weapons, such as the M-72 light antitank rocket (LAWS)

or the M-79 granade-launcher [*sic*], on an overt military air charter flight in the name of the Defense Department for delivery to the Zairian army, to lay a paper trail which would explain to auditors and prying eyes the existence of these weapons in Zaire and Angola." (Stockwell 1978, 58–59, 76)

22. The CIA had found South Africa a tempting ally and proposed sending arms and fuel to Angolan clients through Pretoria in October 1975. However, other elements of Washington's "working group" vetoed the idea because of a legal arms embargo against the apartheid regime (Stockwell 1978, 188–89).

23. According to one report, UNITA controlled as much as 75 percent of Angolan territory in 1993. In 1994, the balance had begun to shift in the army's favor, and UNITA's control dropped to 50 percent by mid-1994. Equally important was the perception that the military had a good chance of routing UNITA in most of the country within six months (i.e., by the end of 1994) (*Africa Research Bulletin* 1994b, 11406).

Chaper Five

Arms and Efforts to Resolve Ethnic Conflict

> When the sovereign state fails to manage conflict effectively and governance breaks down, the responsibility for dealing with disputes may fall for a limited time on external agents. (Deng et al. 1996, 207)

Ethnopolitical conflicts, entailing questions of group identity or survival, perhaps more than other forms of civil disputes, tend to become intractable. Disputes, such as those in Burma, the Sudan, Northern Ireland, and Israel, have dragged on for decades and generations.[1] Even when peacemaking breakthroughs occur, violence can flare up, undermining months or years of negotiations. A terrorist or "counter-terrorist" bomb or an assassination can be sufficient to jar, if not derail peace processes. In the case of Angola, dissatisfaction over election results and UNITA's role in power sharing was sufficient to cause that faction to return to violence two years after what appeared to be significant progress by the United Nations to resolve the long-standing dispute.

The resilience, dangers, and opportunities of ethnopolitical conflict are not lost on neighboring states, major powers, or international organizations. Outside parties at times try to resolve such disputes and wars. Efforts, in the form of mediation, military or economic sanctions, or military intervention, have increased in recent years but have had mixed results (Darby and MacGinity 2000; Regan 1996a and 2000; Licklider 1995).

As intervention success is not guaranteed, neither is third-party involvement per se. Some conflicts, as for example in Tibet, have witnessed few outside peacemaking attempts. In other cases, such as Kosovo, East Timor, Rwanda, and Zaire/Democratic Republic of the Congo, the outside intervention came after years of ignored early warning, while in still others, such as Liberia, the violence was relatively unexpected, did not involve well-known ethnic groups, and drew only belated and sometimes incoherent response. Political and strategic debates over the decision to intervene in the ethnic politics of a state or region are among the most divisive and heated within governments and international organizations, as seen in the painful 1999 UN secretary-general's report on belated peacekeeping in Rwanda. They involve questions of sovereignty and national interest calculation (see Roth 1999). Washington's postmortem on Somalia and controversies over lifting the arms embargo on Bosnia, as well as discussion among various observers (e.g., the United States, NATO, OSCE, and the United Nations) over intervention in Bosnia, Kosovo, and Chechnya illustrate the uncertainty international actors face in deciding whether and how to act.[2]

Scholars have identified multiple factors associated with a third party's decision to involve itself in situations of domestic violence abroad, or with the success or failure of such efforts (see, e.g., Assefa 1987; Kleiboer 1994; Regan 1996a and 2000). These factors might include the perceived interests at stake—such as historical notoriety for peacemaking, the international humanitarian outcry, the apparent "ripeness" of the situation for settlement, and the threat of the conflict to spread. One salient, though previously overlooked factor in such decisions is the impact of armament levels. When dealing with situations of conflict intractability, arms flows would appear to affect the probabilities of violence spreading, of continued fighting and wanton destruction, or of choking off violence. Arms and resultant levels of resistance and entrenched fighting also can influence the outcome of intervention, peacekeeping, and mediation in ethnic disputes, endangering the peacekeeping troops and personnel.

This chapter offers a rigorous assessment of the impact of arms supplies on the "endgame" of conflict, that is, negotiations and third-party conflict resolution efforts. What is the effect of arms acquisition by ethnic groups or the governments opposing them on the likelihood of effective conflict resolution efforts by third parties? A study of the role of arms thus speaks to the conditions under which certain policy tools of statecraft are effective, both for states and international organizations.

The chapter proceeds in four parts. We begin by defining key terms and concepts in conflict settlement. These involve negotiations and the prospect for third-party involvement to promote peace. We identify factors associated with partial and full success, that is, the suspension or resolution of the conflict. We then hypothesize about arms acquisition impacts on those factors and thus on successful strategies and outcomes. The final section analyzes these propositions using available data.

THIRD-PARTY DISPUTE SETTLEMENT

While disputants eventually find their own way out of most conflicts, often there is little incentive—and indeed a perceived disincentive—in making concessions. Some disputes end in military victories, others in negotiated settlements, still others seem to fade away. Arms can affect these outcomes, as for example by changing the military balance among disputants. Arms can also affect the probability that third parties will step in to help solve or affect the outcome of a conflict. It is this question of external involvement that we examine in depth here. Theorists have assumed that stalemates and conflict "ripeness" for settlement provide the best prospects for serious negotiations. Arms balances supposedly might foster either a victory or perceived stalemates, that is, the conclusion that neither side stands to win and that both will pay exorbitantly for continued fighting. The notion of ripeness also relates to parties' readiness to undertake serious peace talks, often driven by exhaustion, "war weariness," or pessimism about the war's outcome. Again, arms prospects can affect these calculations.

Third parties, states or international organizations, frequently step in to facilitate settlements.[3] Conflict resolution per se is essentially similar to the idea of influence, of getting others to do what you want them to do, and raises similar questions about the role of the actor trying to alter another's behavior, often in quite intricate and ambitious ways. For example, President Bill Clinton devoted long and arduous hours at Camp David in 2000 trying to broker a final Israeli-Palestinian peace agreement, confronting both the confounding technicalities of apportioning a city like Jerusalem, as well as the political obstacles each party faced back home. This process failure was a rude awakening for U.S. diplomacy. Third parties, in general, must contend with multiple interests of the disputants—both their interests relative to each other and their relationship with salient political groups in their own countries. A concession at one level might not be palatable at the other, and the pace of concessions usually cannot be forced.

Third-party actions aimed at conflict management can take many forms, including diplomatic protests, fact-finding, mediation, economic sanctions, offered enducements, arms embargoes, military assistance, air bombardment, or introduction of troops (Donnelly 1995; McCoubrey and White 1995, 225–54; Regan 1996b). Two of these have received the most attention—mediation, which is essentially diplomatic, and the introduction of troops, that is, military intervention. Zartman and Touval (1992) define mediation as a form of facilitated negotiation, which favors none of the participants in the dispute. In practice, mediation can take a variety of forms and encompass a variety of actions (Bercovitch, Agnagnoson, and Wille 1991). The involvement of major powers such as the United States, for example, has at times been labeled "mediation" even when such intervenors tend to favor one side. Powerful mediators, or perhaps more accurately "brokers," might push their own solutions and agendas or offer financial and other inducement for agreement (as in Camp David talks between Egypt and Israel and the Palestinians and Israel).

The role of foreign troops also is undertaken under a variety of names, including military intervention and peacekeeping, and potentially peacemaking and peace building. The goals here are often initially to separate the combatants, and then perhaps establish, extend, and nourish institutions to address the issues of perceived insecurity and injustice that often drive ethnic violence. Hesitantly through the years, such troops have taken on added combat responsibilities for enforcing peace accords, as in UN attempts to seal the East Timor border with West Timor against raiding ethnic militia in 2000. Multilateral (e.g., the United Nations or NATO) and unilateral military intervention (e.g., Nigeria into nearby Liberia) have gained increased attention recently, partly due to changing views on state sovereignty and international human rights enforcement, especially in the aftermath of the Cold War and the Iraq Gulf War (Cooper and Berdal 1993, 182).

A third party's decision to intervene is founded on both willingness and opportunity, concepts we have raised in earlier chapters. Willingness, in this context, focuses on the intervenor's interests; without interests in the dispute or its implications, the actor, regardless of its capability, is unlikely to attempt conflict resolution. Opportunity raises the issue of context, ripeness, and capability (Most and Starr 1989). Since we assume that third parties considering intervention in an ethnopolitical dispute have the requisite capability, the critical elements are willingness and the assessment of the conflict's likely trajectory given the third party's possible actions. The first step, then, is to assess the benefits of action versus inaction.

Third-party interests are essentially threefold: humanitarian, defensive, and expansionistic (Cooper and Berdal 1993; Touval and Zartman 1985). The latter two can also be thought of as strategic concerns, involving the maintenance and extension of power and influence abroad. Ultimately, increasing one's own influence also is an example of an expansionistic goal. Expansionistic goals are found when policy makers find new opportunities in ethnic conflict to increase ties, create dependencies, modify territorial boundaries, or project power.

These interests, which are not mutually exclusive and which can be difficult to distinguish, comprise the basic benefits expected through successful conflict resolution. Humanitarian goals are defined as the promotion of core human needs and values, including physical security and well-being (to be truly evenhanded, of course, implies security and well-being of all sides).[4] Defensive goals are defined in the context of threat perception. The possibility that a rival might gain power through manipulation of the ongoing dispute is one reason for outside peacemaking initiatives. Other intervenor interests include preserving stability or regional security. Ethnic ties represent a final defensive goal (they could also involve expansion), where states with the same ethnic group feel pressure to act in support of their kin across the border. In terms of multilateral defensive concerns, international governmental organizations (IGOs), while not possessing national interests, do have their reputations as effective actors in world politics to consider.

Third parties considering involvement in ethnopolitical conflicts are likely to hold a mix of such motives. Touval and Zartman (1985, 8) paint third parties as being concerned about both humanitarian goals and "less generous motives inspired by self-interest." It may be argued that states, particularly major powers, are more focused on national interest, while IGOs, which admittedly are composed of states but also have ongoing secretariats, are more concerned about humanitarian values (Ganguly and Taras 1998).

The cost of action as compared with inaction enters strongly into intervention decisions. Any intervention effort has costs, irrespective of outcome. These are primarily resource costs, including financing an operation (which could push toward mediation as a lower-cost solution than military occupation), as well as such considerations as potential casualties. An additional cost for third parties is political in nature, that is, domestic or foreign opposition to the peacemaking stance, which could include counter-intervention by rivals.

In addition to calculating benefits and costs, the prospective intervenor will in some way estimate success probabilities. If an effort is likely to fail, then it may not be very wise to try it, though this can depend on the perceived merits of the case. Success here at least partly depends on a favorable environment, which can entail factors such as the overall stability of the region, the geographical proximity of major or regional powers, the parties' political readiness and incentives to settle, and military balances.

These three features—benefits derived from third-party interests, costs, and estimated success probability—combine to form an expected-utility calculation. Intervenor calculations will be influenced by the overall pattern of the conflict at a given point in time, and particularly the perceived momentum toward a one-sided victory, a stalemate, or productive negotiations. The intervenor calculates the likely outcome of taking no action, considering the rough probability the conflict will be solved without its involvement, as well as the benefits inherent in such a resolution. This is weighed against the expected probability that the conflict will not be resolved—which can mean continued fighting and bloodletting or prolonged stalemate (that might or might not be to the intervenor's interest). Calculations here depend on the costs and benefits of continued ethnopolitical violence and third-party inaction.

On the other hand, the third party also presumably calculates the likely value of its involvement in the dispute, weighing the probability that the conflict will be resolved through its efforts and the expected resultant benefit, against the probability that the attempted conflict resolution will fail or backfire with the expected costs of failure. When the expected utility of conflict resolution efforts is greater than the expected value of inaction—either because the benefits or success probabilities are higher, or the expected costs lower—the third party is expected to act.[5]

The Role of Arms and Third-Party Involvement

Arms are one factor in these calculations, tending to affect expectations across all three types of third-party interests. As seen in the previous chapter, arms accumulations often are associated with increased violence and will likely have played a distinct role in the conflict as it developed. Whether accurate or not, there is a perception that death, injury, and population displacement all increase following infusions of weapons, ammunition, and spare parts. Thus, as humanitarian concerns rise, pressure grows on third parties to do something about armament in order to prevent greater loss of life and social, political, and economic disruption.

Arms flows also can increase defensive and expansionistic motives. However, the stakes for third parties are not affected uniformly by such flows. The effect seems strongest closest to the fighting, where interests in cross-border ethnic relations and potential threats to borders or regional power balances are greatest. Fighting in Sri Lanka, for example, seemed highly salient to India. Of course, once a state such as India becomes involved or committed, its regional adversaries, in this case Pakistan, also become more interested in the crisis. In the face of expected or expanded violence, nearby regional actors might seek to prevent contagion or political instability, spread their influence, weaken or preempt their adversaries, prevent incoming flows of refugees, or protect ethnic allies. Regionally powerful states such as Nigeria and Syria (in Lebanon) also might seize the banner of an international governmental organization (e.g., the Organization of African Unity or the Arab League) to legitimate their regional police role. Major powers might seek to promote their influence or maintain leftover colonial influence (as with France in Africa). Of course, military assistance also can raise the donor's stakes in the outcome, and hence increase the probability of its direct involvement or intervention to vindicate its arms shipments (Pearson, Baumann, and Pickering 1994). All of this suggests the following proposition: *as arms accumulations increase in a dispute, humanistic, defensive, and expansionist motivations increase, making third-party involvement more likely to occur.*

Of course, arms are also seen to raise potential costs of intervention in the tasks of containing, disarming, or defeating well-armed and entrenched fighters or government forces. Increased armament tends to raise uncertainty about outcomes by empowering more diverse groups or extremists and by funneling arms into resale and redistribution networks so that they threaten regional stability and predictability for years to come.[6]

It is likely that as conventional arms diffuse throughout a conflict zone, the threats perceived by potential third parties rise, though more for military involvement than for mediation. The intervenor might be impelled to act to stave off the unforeseen consequences of regional arms races, or it could be discouraged from action by the chaos likely to be encountered or generated. These risks are, of course, weighed against competing interests in preventing cross-border conflict contagion, refugees, and so forth. In Bosnia, NATO was constantly concerned about the potential for the conflict to spread to regionally sensitive areas such as Macedonia if the Serbs were pushed too hard by outside intervenors. All of this suggests a second, competing proposition: *as arms availability increases, the costs and uncertainties of third-party involvement rise, making third-party military intervention efforts less likely to occur.*

Thus, it appears that arms buildups exert contradictory pressures on would-be peacemakers. Arms in the hands of disputants increase the humanitarian, and at times political, benefits of third-party involvement and thus make intervention more likely. At the same time, arms proliferation also raises the risks and costs of military involvement, making third parties without strong interests wary and less likely to get involved.

SUCCESSFUL OUTCOMES

As we have noted, third parties are unlikely to intervene unless they believe they have at least a reasonable chance of success. Once intervention has occurred, arms balances can make a critical difference in outcome. Successful conflict resolution need not correlate with successful outcomes from the intervenor's point of view. Success might be defined in minimalist terms, for example, as denying disputed territory to an opponent or unstable actor. Efforts by the United States through the CIA in Angola could be characterized in this way, and of course involved injecting more arms and delaying any peace talks until the favored side was stronger. Thus, certain intervenors focus mainly on their own interests and goals in the conflict, whether or not the outcome brings peace or even victory to the favored side. Thus, Touval and Zartman (1985, 14) write that while a successful mediation is the "conclusion of an agreement promising the reduction of conflict," that agreement "should be in accord with the mediator's interests." Nevertheless, since mediation is generally conceived of as neutral, major power efforts to pursue their own interests can complicate strategies to end a dispute.

Successful conflict resolution, at a minimum, implies an end to the violence; at maximum, it represents the end of tensions between ethnic groups or between a group and a government. Bercovitch, Anagnoson, and Wille (1991, 8) define a successful mediation as "either a ceasefire, a partial settlement or a full settlement." On the other hand, Regan (1996a, 340) more modestly defines a successful third-party intervention as one that brings "an end to the violence associated with the underlying dispute." Operationally, the end of violence might be permanent or only for a relatively brief period of time.

The distinction between the minimum and the maximum is relevant, since it produces the subsequent typology of successful and failed efforts. There are more cases of success the less ambitious the definition of conflict resolution, and vice-versa. As of 2000, the Northern Ireland peace accords had resulted in a relatively successful two-year cease-fire, hesitant implementation of the power-sharing accords between Nationalist and Unionist parties, and an arms inspection scheme to verify that IRA arms caches were not being used. However, the process still fell short of a full reconciliation of the mutually suspicious populations in the province and short of meaningful disarmament of either side. Similarly, five years into the Dayton Peace Accords, under UN peacekeeping occupation, Bosnian guns remained silent, but a joint governmental and military apparatus and the return of refugees to towns and villages remained elusive. Touval and Zartman (1985, 14) note: "If we took success to mean the final resolution of all conflict and the reconciliation of the parties, then there would be very few successful mediations." Scholars have tended to take the weak definition (ending the violence to some degree), rather than the strong (ending the underlying tensions), though ending the violence is the first step, and certainly a worthy goal.[7] Nevertheless, we will see that widespread availability or even political stockpiling of arms complicates the prospect for prolonging cease-fires.

Armed with these definitions of success, the question then becomes "How can a prolonged cease-fire be achieved?" For many scholars, the answer lies in altering the disputants' cost-benefit calculus, regardless of their visceral or emotional involvement.[8] Whether consciously and explicitly calculated or not, a group might assess force as the best method for winning concessions from a government or from other groups in a particular context (time and place), while governments may or may not prefer force to concession. Each prospective outcome, thus, has some utility. A series of factors produces variation in the utility and probability of different actions. Third parties then might seek to take advantage of and manipulate these factors in mutual bargaining to facilitate conflict resolution processes (Benjamin 1995).

Essentially, there are two relevant components to a model of successful conflict resolution either by negotiations or through third-party efforts. These are contextual elements and procedural factors.[9] Contextual elements are found in the environment of the conflict and the environment in which the third party must operate. The procedural category focuses on the nature of the conflict resolution strategies and efforts. In the contextual category, we first examine how the nature of the conflict affects efforts to resolve it. Second, we examine how characteristics of third parties affect resolution outcomes. Third, we examine characteristics of the disputants. In the procedural category, we examine third parties' conflict resolution strategies. Each of these four aspects encompasses several specific factors.

For many scholars, the linchpin determining mediation or intervention success is the nature of the conflict. Within this dimension, at least four factors are proposed as favoring settlement, including (1) the dispute's ripeness and the presence of a stalemate among the disputants, (2) the conflict's intensity, (3) third-party pressures, and (4) the stakes involved. The general idea, for example, that a conflict's duration can be associated with successful resolution strategies is not new (Assefa 1987; Kleiboer 1996). There is a supposed point of ripeness at which time settlement can be more easily reached. Several claims exist as to when and if this happens, and the overall concept remains vague. Some scholars argue that conflicts ripen over time; as duration increases, costs rise, and participants, reaching points of exhaustion, become more receptive to either mutual or third-party peace overtures. Conversely, others see the potential for ripeness early in disputes, before positions harden, grievances build, and alternatives to fighting seem increasingly untenable. It may be that both positions are partially correct. Mediations, for example, appear most efficacious after one year but before three years have elapsed. Perhaps, in a sense, conflicts must ripen but not be left to rot on the vine (see Bercovitch, Anagnoson, and Wille 1991).

We showed in chapter 4 that ethnopolitical conflicts are dynamic, and some scholars have argued that as conflicts evolve, "sunken costs"—that is, expended and irretrievable resources such as civilian and military casualties—rise, making it more difficult to stop the violence. Thus, longer conflicts are associated with a lower immediate probability of successful resolution. On the other hand, Zartman has argued that a conflict is ripe for settlement when a "hurting stalemate" occurs between the parties, presumably after long, costly, and indeterminate struggle. Stalemates generally take time to develop or become apparent, and therefore longer wars might be readier in general for settlement. Certainly a number of long-term international and civil conflicts lasted for the duration of the 1980s and then simultaneously moved toward settlement in 1989. Of course, the change in the international system affecting outside intervention (end of the Cold War) might have affected this transformation, for example in the Afghan civil war.

The idea of ripeness in conflict settlement, then, may be spurious in that underlying factors cause the stalemate leading to possibilities of conflict resolution. Ripeness as a concept is perhaps a substitute for multiple conditions of the dispute (Salla 1997). In this analysis, we will try to break apart the concept into its components—such as the presence of a hurting stalemate—and examine them in light of arms supplies.

The symmetry of pain in a conflict, which is related to a conflict's intensity, is a second important characteristic affecting termination. Scholars have pointed to the idea of a *mutually* hurting stalemate as a critical prerequisite to successful conflict resolution. A mutually painful stalemate means that neither side has the ability to win nor, however, is either likely to lose imminently, and both sides suffer increasingly unbearable costs in the process. When both sides recognize this situation exists and is likely to persist, conflict resolution efforts supposedly stand the best chance of succeeding (Assefa 1987).[10] Indeed, Zartman (1995c, 334) argues that stalemate is perceptual rather than strictly objective

> where both sides in a conflict perceived themselves to be in a stalemate that was painful to each of them and they saw a better alternative through negotiation (as in Sudan in 1972, Mozambique, South Africa, Colombia, and possibly Angola and Sri Lanka in the mid-1990s), they negotiated an agreement; and where the government (as in Spain, Sudan, and the Philippines) or the insurgency (as in Eritrea) felt it was winning, or where the pain of the stalemate was bearable or justified (as in Angola, Afghanistan, and Sri Lanka, and among the Colombian extremists), no settlement was negotiated.

Of course, the notion of "bearable and justified" can dissolve in tautology; if the violence persists, it must, by definition, be bearable.

In the case of mediation, as opposed to other forms of intervention, stalemate has particular implications for third parties. Pessimists argue that intervenors should wait for the ripe moment, while optimists look for ways to create that moment. In the latter view, "Paradoxically, this may mean temporarily reinforcing one side to keep it in the conflict, maintain the stalemate, and preserve the triangular relationship [between the mediator and the parties]" (Touval and Zartman, 1985, 11). This was certainly illustrated by the U.S. opinion that the best solution to the Bosnian crisis would be obtained by arming and assisting the Bosnian federation so that they would not be defeated by the other forces in the area.[11]

The difficulty for third parties in this context is that it is not clear when or how a stalemate is achieved. It is not clear how often all sides use the same definitions and criteria, including views of relative "power."[12] Thus, although mutually hurting stalemates are associated with improved chances for successful conflict resolution in theory, in practice they may be difficult to achieve and recognize, let alone measure precisely.

Intensity of fighting, a conflict characteristic that was considered in the last chapter, has been linked along with widening geographic scope or internationalization with both increased and reduced chances of successful conflict resolution (Kleiboer 1996). Regan (1996a) offers a persuasive argument that as intensity increases, successful resolution is less likely. Essentially, intense conflicts produce a combination of higher sunken costs, smaller perceived marginal costs in continuing the fighting, and a myopia among the disputants because of the greater bloodletting, all of which hinder negotiation prospects and third-party efforts. A state or international organization would have to bring greater and greater resources to bear to alter the disputants' perceptions. Yet it also might be assumed that intense fighting is likely to lead to quicker exhaustion, and hence greater readiness to seek relief through negotiation. The key would appear to be *mutual* pain.

The disputants' and outside parties' stakes in conflict represent a final success-determining conflict characteristic. The threats facing minority and identity groups as well as their goals will vary. Cultural assimilation or loss of status pose different threats than genocide, for example, although in given situations, the former might be taken as warnings of the latter. One key factor driving ethnic rebellion is systematic exclusion or repression by governmental authorities of sizable minority populations. As stakes rise, the room for negotiation, or the overlap between the disputants' positions, tends to decrease. As seen in the Palestinian-Israeli "final status" negotiations, this makes mediation much more difficult. However, the fact that these negotiations took place at all meant that the parties' positions also had unfrozen somewhat, probably because one side or both perceived possible concessions from the other in the interest of "getting on with it" toward a settlement that would allow other pursuits (such as economic ventures). This is an example of relative stalemate, at least in political terms, leading to a process of seeking new accommodations or solutions. Likewise, in the case of military or peacekeeping intervention, higher stakes will often be translated into fiercer resistance, making intervention less likely to succeed, but also will make the conflict more important to outsiders so that they are tempted to intervene nevertheless.

The second cluster of conditions favoring successful peacemaking concerns third-party characteristics and strategies. Several elements have been proposed here, including the third party's impartiality, its leverage, and legitimacy (Rudolph 1995; Stedman 1996, Ryan 1992). These factors, though, are often variations on a theme: the state *versus* the intergovernmental organization (IGO), and in some cases the NGO, as an effective actor in conflict resolution. IGOs and NGOs might possess a certain advantage in the legitimacy and perceived impartiality of their actions once they decide to move, while states possess advantages of decisiveness.[13] International organizations also are thought to be prone to try diplomatic techniques more thoroughly before attempting military action.

Again, though, success criteria vary and can influence the judgment about failed or successful strategies; one might ask "success for what?" UN machinery, employing major power intervention in Bosnia, finally achieved a modicum of peace through occupation and an enforced cease-fire. However, in addition to the failure to achieve all elements of the Dayton Accords, critics have noted that the human rights record has been spotty at best, with few arrests of accused war criminals. In 1999, an anguished UN Secretary-General Kofi Annon also reported on the abject failure of out-manned and out-gunned UN peacekeepers to protect ethnic minorities in Srebrenica and other supposed "safe havens" in 1995 (Crosette 1999). On the other hand, while U.S. and British warplanes have enforced "no-fly" zones over ten years to protect ethnic Kurds and Shiites both in northern and southern Iraq, they have not strongly objected to Turkish policies of chasing Kurdish militants into northern Iraq to destroy their base camps. Thus, one form of enforcement might promote human rights and another might diminish them in the interest of some notion of regional "stability" (not wanting to risk the stability of a key state such as Turkey).

The third contextual dimension concerns the nature of the disputants. One view argues that different types of internal conflicts have different probabilities of successful resolution. Scholars have argued that ethnopolitical conflicts are more *difficult* to solve than other forms of politically or economically motivated violence because of higher levels of intensity and commitment, and that ethnopolitical conflicts are *easier* to resolve because all participants desire increased security. Licklider (1995), however, finds no significant difference in the likelihood of termination of various types of internal conflict.[14]

The final cluster of determinants for conflict resolution success is procedural and involves third-party strategies and tactics. Across several studies it becomes clear that various tactics have different success rates depending, of course, on context. No type of conflict resolution effort always succeeds or always fails. In a rigorous study of varied intervention efforts, Regan (1996a) found that mixed strategies, consisting of a combination of military and economic intervention, are more likely to succeed than any single form of intervention. He also found (2000, 141) that intervening on the side of the government, especially militarily, boosts success chances as he defines them, with major powers having a 20 percent greater chance of success than lesser states.[15]

The Role of Arms in Successful Outcomes

The impact of armament on successful conflict resolution appears to be indirect, working through the contextual and procedural factors discussed above. Consider first the contextual factors. Arms are likely to have an impact on both stalemate and conflict intensity. Indeed, we saw in the last chapter that violent conflicts in which communal groups had access to imported arms were very likely to be highly intense, that is, to produce many deaths per unit of time. The presence of heavy armament likewise was associated with high intensity. Government arms imports were a less reliable predictor of high-intensity warfare. If what matters in hurting stalemates is the parties' relative strength, and if the parties perceive this strength in military terms, then by affecting relative military balances, arms acquisitions can play an important role in the creation or destruction of a hurting stalemate. When arms are acquired by the weaker side and thus allow it to continue fighting or raise the intensity of the fight—perhaps creating a stalemate—then the result theoretically should be more favorable for peace talks or third-party initiatives even though it is likely to be very unfavorable for those caught in the cross fire.

While arms can work as positive or negative influences on a stalemate, their impact on intensity is more likely unidirectional. Adding arms generally increases conflict intensity by increasing casualties per unit of time and allowing for the overall expansion of the fighting (Spear 1996). While improved or increased arms might allow quick decisive advantages that could turn the tide or shorten a war, as seen in some cases in chapter 4, thus reducing total casualties, most recent cases appear to show the opposite effect. In Afghanistan, Angola, Kashmir, Liberia, Rwanda, Sri Lanka, Sudan, and elsewhere, increased access to arms from a variety of sources appeared to contribute to the prolongation and intensification of fighting (Klare 1997).[16] Thus, irrespective of who receives arms, they are more likely to raise the violence than to decrease intensity in any meaningful way.

Regan (2000, 141) found that increased intensity makes it less likely that outside parties will risk intervention, but ironically, perhaps by generating hurting stalemates, raised intensity somewhat increases the chances that interventions will contain the violence. Increased violence makes it both more imperative and more taxing for any negotiations or third-party involvement to succeed. One must overcome the obstacles of sunken costs and vengeance motives entailed in bloody fighting over long periods. It would stand to reason that any military response to a more violent conflict is going to have to be larger, too. Mediators would have to work harder to reconcile differences; greater fighting is proof of greater stakes. This suggests our next proposition: *increased arms acquisitions increase the intensity of ethnopolitical violence, tending to scare off potential intervenors, though perhaps increasing the chances of intervention success.*

However, states in general would appear to have different chances of successful conflict resolution than international organizations, irrespective of the conflict resolution strategy. This is due to such factors as the actor's power base, cohesion, legitimacy, and interest in the dispute. By raising costs, increased armament challenges both states and IGOs as intervenors. However, IGOs appear at a greater disadvantage. In particular, increased conflict intensity and violence might undermine the cohesion and will of international organizations to intervene by raising different agendas and dissention among members. Nevertheless, when ethnic militia in East Timor attacked election monitors in 1999, it seemed to galvanize the United Nations Security Council in finally authorizing an Asian military intervention to stem the violence. As a general proposition, though, *states should fare better as intervenors than IGOs in highly armed conflicts.*

As arms levels escalate in a local war, military interventions particularly are likely to become more costly than other forms of involvement. Available arms can allow combatants to continue fighting rather than to give in to immediate negotiations by raising the hope of battlefield success and advantages in bargaining down the road. In Timor, it took considerable U.S. diplomatic and economic pressure on the shaky Indonesian government to clear the way for the entry of peacekeeping forces. Such a major power role would appear to be necessary to enable an international organization to be effective in a highly charged environment (see Regan 2000). Political efforts, such as mediation, also fall prey to arms' impact, but with fewer direct risks to the intervenor. *This suggests that the costs of third-party military intervention strategies will rise relatively more than the costs of nonmilitary strategies in highly armed conflicts.*

When the hypotheses are examined together, the contradictory impacts of arms accumulation are apparent. If obtained by ethnic minorities or weaker parties, arms might produce a hurting stalemate that in turn might favor successful conflict resolution. On the negative side, however, arms increase conflict intensity, which increases the parties' intransigence and the costs facing third-party peacemakers, particularly IGOs and military intervenors, thus necessitating more commitment by major powers.

ANALYSIS METHODS AND RESULTS

Given data concerns, the analysis here should be taken as a first look at the hypothesized relationships. Our approach is as follows: we seek to test the relationships between arms acquisition and determinants of third-party action on the one hand, and arms and the success of conflict resolution efforts on the other.

Partly this approach is motivated by the difficulties of operationalizing the two ultimate dependent variables: conflict resolution efforts and success. We cannot use a strict definition of success, that is, ending the dispute, since many conflicts recur. Even taking a more restricted definition, based on the notion of a cessation of hostilities over a specified period of time—as Regan (1996a) does—leaves problems. How many cease-fires have been broken in Northern Ireland and Bosnia? If they meet the duration requirement, it would be possible to have multiple "successes" and (certainly multiple failures) within one ongoing and continuously troublesome dispute at given levels of armament. It took five years of sporadic negotiations to achieve an agreement on a joint Somali government in 1997, and the ultimate success of that agreement remained suspect at least until efforts to form the government took hold in 2000. As previously noted, it is also sometimes difficult to gauge motives and determine whether intervenor efforts are aimed at conflict resolution or self-interest (or both).[17]

We chose again to focus on our sample of forty-nine cases (see appendix).[18] For this analysis, we focus on two measures of arms: the *type* of arms used and the actor's *access* to arms.[19] As before, the type of arms is generally divided into heavy and light weapons. Spear (1996) suggests that the introduction of heavy weapons has a distinctive impact on the course of fighting. In this chapter, we also try to gain a bit more refined measure of the degree of ethnopolitical group armament. Earlier we discussed the three channels by which groups acquire arms: domestic procurement (e.g., battlefield capture or raids on police or military facilities), indigenous production, or importation from friendly governments or groups abroad. Therefore, we created two measures of arms access by ethnic groups. The first identifies cases where groups imported arms (high) as opposed to cases where they did not (low). Seeking to go beyond just external arms shipments, we also constructed a measure combining all three sources, drawn from the data presented in chapters 2 and 4. We start with 0 for any conflicts where the ethnopolitical group(s) fighting did not appear to receive or amass weapons. We assign 1 point for evidence of domestic procurement or indigenous production by groups. We assign 1 point for importation from one or two sources, and 2 points for importation from more than two sources. This creates a scale from 0 to 3.[20]

For the forty-nine cases, we were able to identify the type of evident armament in forty-nine conflicts, and estimate the degree of group access to arms (three types of procurement) in forty-three cases. Heavy arms were used in eleven conflicts; light arms in thirty-eight. This finding is consistent with contemporary views that heavy weapons tend to be more an exception than a rule in ethnic fighting. Overall access to arms by communal groups in conflict, calculated on our 0 to 3 scale, showed five conflicts with level-3 group access, twelve with level 2, sixteen at level 1, and the rest either 0 or undetermined.

The first proposition focuses on the decision to intervene and suggests that arms buildups create situations of greater humanitarian need, which ultimately should foster a greater probability of intervention. We can measure the humanitarian costs of an ethnic conflict in two ways: casualties and refugees. We have already seen in chapter 4 the impact of heavier arms and group arms acquisitions in relation to conflict intensity. Information on the total number of refugees produced by a conflict is difficult to obtain; we rely on Gurr and Harff (1994) supplemented by Brown (1996), giving us data for only thirty of the forty-nine cases. We present this information as a dichotomous variable; high humanitarian need is defined as total refugees of at least 100,000 (which occurred in twenty-one cases), and low humanitarian need is defined as total refugees below 100,000 (nine cases). Tables 5.1a, 5.1b, and 5.1c illuminate the relationship between changes in government and group arms and humanitarian need.

Table 5.1a   The Impact of Government Arms Imports on Humanitarian Need

		Humanitarian Need	
		High	*Low*
Imports	High	8	3
	Low	12	4

N = 27; χ^2 = 0.015; p-value = 0.903

Table 5.1b   The Impact of Type of Arms Acquisition by Ethnopolitical Groups on Humanitarian Need

		Humanitarian Need	
		High	*Low*
Arms	Heavy	8	1
	Light	13	8

N = 30; χ^2 = 2.184; p-value = 0.139

Table 5.1c   The Impact of Arms Access by Ethnopolitical Groups on Humanitarian Need

		Humanitarian Need	
		High	*Low*
Access	High (2, 3)	11	1
	Low (0, 1)	9	6

N = 27; χ^2 = 3.481; p-value = 0.062

There appears to be no statistically significant relationship to humanitarian need when arms are measured either in terms of government acquisitions or when the arms are classified by type. Many of the cases where ethnic group arms access was high also coincided with high humanitarian need, but several cases of low access did as well. Thus, arms procurement does not necessarily generate increased refugee flows, though in many cases the fighting does produce disruption, panic, and flight. Presumably, when this happens, there is increased probability that outside parties will at least be called upon to take some action, even if belated and confined to diplomatic entreaties.

The second proposition suggests that arms imports or accumulations increase the costs of acting, so third parties are less likely to undertake conflict resolution attempts through interventions. Though we cannot measure the costs directly, we can examine efforts by all actors against changes in arms. Here we expect that as arms rise, third-party conflict resolution attempts (both military interventions, as well as nonmilitary efforts such as negotiations and economic sanctions) generally decline (see tables 5.2a, 5.2b, and 5.2c).[21]

As the tables indicate, and contrary to expectation, the impact of group armament in stimulating outside military and diplomatic interventions is evident, and

Table 5.2a   The Impact of Arms Imports by Governments on Conflict Resolution Attempts (CRA) of Third Parties

		CRA	
		Yes	No
Imports	High	9	10
	Low	20	5

N = 44; χ^2 = 5.116; p-value = 0.024 (Finding significant at the .05 probability level)

Table 5.2b   The Impact of Type of Arms Acquisition by Ethnopolitical Groups on Conflict Resolution Attempts (CRA)

		CRA	
		Yes	No
Arms	Heavy	11	0
	Light	20	18

N = 49; χ^2 = 8.236; p-value = 0.004 (Finding significant at the .01 probability level)

Table 5.2c   The Impact of Arms Access by Ethnopolitical Groups on Conflict Resolution Attempts (CRA)

		CRA	
		Yes	No
Access	High (2, 3)	15	1
	Low (0, 1)	15	12

N = 43; χ^2 = 6.949; p-value = 0.008 (Finding significant at the .01 probability level)

statistically significant in the case of group acquisition of heavy arms, and nearly as significant in the case of group access. When ethnic groups use heavy arms or when their access was high, third-party resolution efforts occurred in nearly all cases. Thus, despite our prior assumptions about the costs associated with heavily armed conflicts, evidently mediators and outside powers were readily drawn into such disputes. When group access was low or when light weapons were deployed, the rate of intervention was roughly fifty-fifty. *Low governmental* arms levels, however, appear to accompany either the perceived need for or occasion for interventions. It could be that well-armed governments tend to resist outside intervention or do not require it to reestablish order, thus dissuading potential intervenors most effectively.[22]

If costs were a great concern to third parties, we would expect to find that they would not get involved in ethnopolitical conflicts awash with arms. This does not seem to be the case except for arms on the government side. Evidently, the threat to regional stability or humanitarian concerns inherent in the use of heavy weapons or in rebel access to arms in civil violence may stimulate peacekeeping or self-interested intervention attempts. The results call for further analysis.

An additional set of assumptions concerned the generation of hurting stalemates, thought to be so crucial for conflict settlement. The concept "hurting stalemate" is quite difficult to operationalize, because it is a perception held by the disputants as well as by potential third parties. The best evidence for a hurting stalemate would thus likely be found in disputants' own statements; for ethnic groups particularly, this information is scarce.[23] At this stage of our analysis, we use a subjective measure of a hurting stalemate—scholarly interpretation of whether such a situation exists in a particular dispute.[24] We focus only on the existence or absence of a hurting stalemate at any time during the conflict and do not attempt to count them or identify their duration.

The hypothesis suggests that by redressing power balances, potent arms in the hands of ethnopolitical fighters should foster such stalemates. Tables 5.3a and 5.3b present the findings.

As the tables indicate, there is a quite statistically significant relationship between levels of arms and the presence of stalemate; the relation is present for measures of group arms acquisition, and significant for both arms type and access. As we move

Table 5.3a   The Impact of Type of Arms Acquisitions by Ethnopolitical Groups on the Presence of Hurting Stalemates

		Hurting Stalemate	
		Yes	*No*
Arms	Heavy	8	2
	Light	9	24

N = 43; χ^2 = 8.926; p-value = 0.003 (Finding significant at the .01 probability level)

Table 5.3b   The Impact of Arms Access by Ethnopolitical Groups on the Presence of Hurting Stalemates

		Hurting Stalemate	
		Yes	*No*
Access	High (2, 3)	11	4
	Low (0, 1)	5	17

N = 37; χ^2 = 9.306; p-value = 0.002 (Finding significant at the .01 probability level)

from disputants employing only light arms to conflicts with heavy or heavy and light arms, or as we move from conflicts with few arms sources to those with more, hurting stalemates are much more likely to occur. Conversely, most cases without stalemate also had only lightly armed groups or low group arms access.

This finding entails disquieting policy implications since peacemakers might be interested in the promotion of stalemates through the dispatch of arms; stalemates themselves seem to correspond with at least temporarily increased arms infusions. Note though that not all of these hurting stalemates identified in the appendix produced effective peace agreements, especially not in a reliably timely fashion. Furthermore, we are as yet unable to pinpoint the arrival or level of arms in the hands of fighters specifically enough to relate them to the *timing* of the stalemate.

Our fourth proposition links arms to the probability that a state will undertake or succeed in conflict resolution as compared with multilateral attempts through international organizations. Specifically, the rates for states and international organizations should decline as arms increase; however, the change for states should be relatively smaller than for international organizations. Thirty-one conflicts had third-party involvement. The results of our sample show that states played a peacemaking role in a total of twenty-five disputes, while intergovernmental organizations were somewhat less active, operating in twenty conflicts. Often, both types of third parties were active in the same conflict. Tables 5.4a, 5.4b, and 5.4c present the relationship between arms and third-party type.

Table 5.4a   The Impact of Government Arms Imports on the Involvement of Regional States and Major Powers versus International Organizations

		Conflict Resolution Attempt			
		Regional States/Major Powers		*International Organizations*	
		Yes	No	Yes	No
Imports	High	7	12	6	13
	Low	16	9	13	12

Table 5.4b   The Impact of Type of Ethnic Group Arms on the Involvement of Regional States and Major Powers versus International Organizations

		Conflict Resolution Attempt			
		Regional States/Major Powers		*International Organizations*	
		Yes	No	Yes	No
Arms	Heavy	10	1	9	2
	Light	15	23	11	27

Table 5.4c   The Impact of Ethnic Group Arms Access on the Involvement of Regional States and Major Powers versus International Organizations

		Conflict Resolution Attempt			
		Regional States/Major Powers		*International Organizations*	
		Yes	No	Yes	No
Access	High	9	4	8	5
	Low	15	13	12	16

There is some evidence (table 5.4a) that increased government arms access tends to retard interventions by both states and IGOs at roughly the same rate. States become more involved than IGOs at lower arms levels. However, heavier arms in the hands of groups and overall group access to arms (via trade, manufacture, or domestic procurement) appear (tables 5.4b and 5.4c) to spur outside intervention, particularly by states. IGOs are likely to become involved in heavily armed situations, but less so when group access to arms is high. Lower levels of group arms or access do not appear to attract as much intervenor interest.

Results therefore indicate that the hypothesis, emphasizing cost considerations, was too simple; government arms retard outsider efforts, but group arms appear to inspire such efforts. There appears to be little meaningful distinction between states and IGOs in these proclivities, except that IGOs themselves appear somewhat less likely than states to initiate action when group arms access is high.[25] Third-party cost calculations are probably not simply dependent on arms levels but relate to fears of instability and humanitarian pressures as well. A better operationalization of "cost" is required to refine the analysis, which will enable a clearer determination of how arms affect relative costs faced by different potential third parties.

The final hypothesis relates arms to the probability of success for different types of conflict resolution attempts (CRA). Conflict resolution attempts or efforts can be grouped into two major categories: military (including peacekeeping operations) and nonmilitary efforts (e.g., mediation, political pressure, and economic sanctions). As above, determining the costs and successes of different types of efforts is problematic. The hypothesis suggests that military costs will rise faster than the costs for nonmilitary strategies, so that as arms increase, military CRAs will become relatively less effective than nonmilitary CRAs. We approached this test assuming that the incidence of a third-party CRA is a function of the costs of the CRA. We coded cases with any efforts involving military troops as 1, and efforts only using other approaches as 0, using the same sources previously identified for cases of third-party involvement. Military force (to varying degrees) was used in twelve disputes, while other strategies were used as the sole form of intervention in fourteen conflicts. Tables 5.5a, 5.5b, and 5.5c relate arms to the type of CRA.

Table 5.5a   The Impact of Government Arms Imports on the Type of Conflict Resolution Attempt (CRA)

		CRA	
		Military	*Other*
Government Imports	High	2	7
	Low	12	8

$N = 29$; $\chi^2 = 3.55$; p-value = 0.06

Table 5.5b   The Impact of Group Arms Type on the Type of Conflict Resolution Attempt (CRA)

		CRA	
		Military	*Other*
Group Arms Type	Heavy	6	5
	Light	9	11

$N = 31$; $\chi^2 = 0.259$; p-value = 0.611

Table 5.5c   The Impact of Arms Access by Ethnopolitical Groups on the Type of Conflict Resolution Attempt (CRA)

		CRA	
		Military	*Other*
Group Arms Access	High (0, 1)	8	7
	Low (2, 3)	7	8

$N = 30$; $\chi^2 = 0.133$; p-value = 0.715

As table 5.5a indicates, when governmental arms are high, military CRAs are not generally employed. While arms might increase the costs of military CRAs more than nonmilitary CRAs, high government arms levels also can be an indication that the state in which the ethnopolitical conflict occurs is relatively powerful. Powerful states have greater control over their sovereignty than less well-armed governments, although there are clear exceptions, such as Iran and the USSR during their revolutionary breakdowns (states might over-arm and deplete their economic resources in the process). While many states would not usually prefer outside military intervention, more powerful states are in a better position to keep that intervention from occurring. Thus, there is unlikely to be a military deployment by third parties in Tibet/China or Spain's Basque country. For ethnic group arms, however, there does not seem to be any clear pattern between arms imports and the type of CRA employed. Again, the type of CRA appears to be a function of a variety of factors, of which one is cost as affected by arms.

We supplemented this analysis by adapting Regan's (2000) intervention success data to our arms indicators. Regan considers military and economic intervention here, and, of course, the motives can vary from peacemaking to taking advantage. Nevertheless, the data offer some indication of rated success in various interventions, so we can see whether heavier or more plentiful armament tends to retard success. For those of our forty-nine cases where Regan presented conclusions regarding success, the results are displayed in tables 5.6a, 5.6b, and 5.6c.

Table 5.6a   The Impact of Government Arms Imports on the Success of Third-Party Military Interventions

		Intervention Outcome		
		Success	*Failure*	*Mixed*[a]
Government Imports	High	0	11	0
	Low	4	15	1

N = 31; χ^2 = 3.278; p-value = 0.194
[a] According to Regan (2000), mixed outcome means that in multiple interventions in the same conflict by states or IGOs, some were successful and some failed.
Source: Intervention outcome data from Regan (2000, 153–58).

Table 5.6b   The Impact of Group Arms Type on the Success of Third-Party Military and Economic Interventions

		Intervention Outcome		
		Success	*Failure*	*Mixed*[a]
Group Arms Type	Heavy	2	9	0
	Light	3	18	1

N = 33; χ^2 = 0.600; p-value = 0.741

Table 5.6c   The Impact of Group Arms Access on the Success of Third-Party Military and Economic Interventions

		Intervention Outcome		
		Success	*Failure*	*Mixed*[a]
Group Arms Access	High (2, 3)	3	12	0
	Low (0,1)	2	13	1

N = 31; χ^2 = 1.209; p-value = 0.546

The results appear to indicate the difficulty of successful conflict resolution intervention in cases where government arms imports were high, and where group arms and access were heavy and high, respectively. This corresponds to expectations outlined above. Of course, by Regan's criteria, successes were rare in our sample under any circumstances. Failed attempts abounded (in approximately 85 percent of the cases). Most failures occurred when groups employed light weapons, perhaps reflecting the relative underdevelopment and dislocation of such states to begin with. Successes appeared when government arms imports were low, but the numbers are too small for valid conclusions. Indeed, overall, none of the relationships in tables 5.6a, 5.6b, and 5.6c were statistically significant, so there is basically no reliable or consistent impact of arms on the success of intervention attempts.[26]

CONCLUSION

This chapter has suggested that arms types and levels play an important role in the likelihood but only a limited direct role in the success of third-party efforts to resolve ethnopolitical conflict. Arms were thought to influence the probability of successful conflict resolution by facilitating hurting stalemates, by raising conflict intensity, and by raising the costs faced by actors and for different tools of conflict resolution. Preliminary tests of the hypotheses suggest that arms are a salient though indirect factor in conflict resolution mainly because as arms levels increase, evidence of hurting stalemates also rises. For all their destructiveness, then, and recognizing that the number of cases examined here was limited to fairly recent disputes and preliminary estimates, given the right timing (no mean feat) arms can have a facilitative effect on conflict resolution. Manipulating arms levels to produce hurting stalemates, however, would appear still to be problematic, and the success of outside intervention in our sample of cases was rare indeed.

There was, of course, also some support for the hypothesis linking arms to greater conflict intensity, and this is not a very salutary effect, producing as it does more disruption, casualties, and refugees. However, these consequences also lead to humanitarian interest in conflict resolution by third parties. Although arms increases are not necessary for intense conflicts, higher access to arms by ethnopolitical groups is associated with more intense conflicts, and this in turn seems to stimulate outside peacemaking initiatives. Again, though, there seems to be no consistent direct impact on humanitarian refugee crises.

It appears, then, that arms work in opposing directions and as an indirect influence both in raising and limiting violence. Arms levels create greater occasion for involvement in pursuing solutions and creating the potential stalemate on the one hand, but appear to complicate solutions and discourage peacemaking particularly when the disputant government is well armed on the other hand. Regional actors and major powers also appear to respond more when government arms are low.

Unexpectedly, in terms of cost calculations, the results also suggested that all actors were more—not less—likely to get involved as ethnopolitical group access to arms increased, a factor that groups might even attempt to manipulate.

Certain types of arms increases, therefore, appear to draw third parties more deeply into the dispute. Determining whether these parties also were arms suppliers might help sort out their interests and involvement levels more clearly. If it appears that arms transfers increase the likelihood that the supplier will later be drawn directly into the warfare, suppliers might be more reticent about the terms and circumstances of their supply commitments.

Successful peacemaking interventions are rare, whether counted as military or diplomatic (see appendix 5). If our sample is any indicator, most military interventions in ethnopolitically disrupted countries fail. It appears that well-armed governments do not generally need or welcome third-party interventions. Many military interventions fail, presumably for political reasons, even when the insurgents are lightly armed.

Our intention in this study was as much to spark interest in the impact of changes in armament as it was to assess that impact conclusively. Clearly there is room for improvement in the arms and peacemaking data. Interestingly, while the focus of many arms trade scholars today is shifting to light weapons, we also need to rethink how scholars could better measure arms employed internally by governments. Unfortunately, there are still many conflicts for which we know very little about the role of supplies and access. The ultimate goal of data collection efforts should be to obtain temporal information, specifically when arms of various types and amounts, together with related supplies and equipment, were brought in or taken out of the conflict.

A second concern is equal parts conceptual and data-oriented, that is, to better define "successful conflict resolution." Using a strict definition of success as the ending of the conflict is unlikely to produce a satisfactory mix of successful and failed cases. It also downplays the important strides third parties have taken to forge cease-fires and facilitate negotiations. Therefore, a more restricted definition of success is appropriate. However, such a definition is likely to lead to multiple cases of success and failure within a single dispute (something we have termed "mixed" outcomes in tables 5.6a, 5.6b, and 5.6c). In any case, a better measure of success and failure would allow us to test propositions that the costs facing third parties and certain conflict resolution techniques rise as a result of changes in arms and that this has an impact on success.

Finally, data could be improved for the other variables indicated in our study. This would include, for example, a measure of the costs and benefits facing different types of third parties, or a measure of the costs of different conflict resolution techniques. Hurting stalemates could be defined in terms of their duration and by some quantifiable indicator, not simply their inferred presence. Each of these improvements would facilitate further analysis into ethnopolitical conflict, conflict resolution, and the role of arms.

Data concerns aside, findings here are sufficient to draw some preliminary conclusions about the role of arms. By affecting factors thought to have an impact on
intervention probabilities and success, arms levels appear to play a role in the decision to try peacemaking and the outcome of such efforts. Since ethnopolitical conflicts are likely to continue to occur across the globe with arms continuing to flow
into these conflicts through varied networks, the complex arms-violence-peace-
making relationship will remain of primary research and policy concern, as we will
see in the next chapter.

NOTES

1. According to Gurr and Harff (1994), the beginning of the most recent phase of violence began in the following years: for Burma in 1948 (for some groups), Sudan in 1983,
in Northern Ireland since 1969, and in Israel beginning in the 1980s. Additionally, Basque
separatists have been fighting in Spain since 1968, East Timorans have had a conflict with
Indonesia since 1976, and the Chinese conflict over Tibet dates to 1951.

2. Indeed, according to media reports early in the Bosnian crisis, then U.S. Undersecre-
tary of State Lawrence Eagleberger indicated that if the Soviet Union were still in existence,
the United States would be compelled to do something about the crisis, but since it did not
exist any longer, there was no pressing reason to become involved.

3. Occasionally nonstate actors also play an intervening role in conflict resolution. One
example was the position of the World Council of Churches and the All-African Conference of Churches in the southern Sudanese civil war in 1972 (Zartman and Touval 1992,
257). Former President Jimmy Carter is a noteworthy example of a distinguished or "emi-
nent person" acting as mediator.

4. Strong obstacles make it difficult for third parties to act under the banner of humanitarian assistance. The notion of sovereignty is perhaps the most important of these. The
principle of noninterference in domestic affairs is enshrined in the United Nations Charter,
for example (Ryan 1992 and 1995). Thus, the Security Council of the United Nations, for
example, seems likelier to condemn threats to peace in situations where governmental
authority has broken down (Somalia, former Yugoslavia) than where governments have
victimized minorities (Iraq and Kurds, China and Tibet, for example; see McCoubrey and
White 1995). An additional complication is the difficulty of ascertaining the extent of
humanitarian abuses in many cases. Some abuses, or the full scope of abuses, may go unre-
ported. Additionally, coverage of ethnopolitical conflict tends to wane over time. A final
obstacle is the reluctance of third parties to develop or apply consistent international norms,
such as those codified in the United Nations Charter or Declaration of Human Rights. States
may have foreign policy goals (e.g., security or political goals, and with special reference
to such regions as the Middle East) that may take precedence over or condition the definition of humanitarian goals. IGOs, and in particular the United Nations, have to some extent
avoided making these principles concrete and definitive (Ryan 1995).

5. Of course, few decision makers exhibit the capability or inclination for a full calculus, nor have perfect information on likely outcomes readily at hand. Thus, the reality of
third-party deliberations could fall far short of this expected utility model.

6. In one bizarre report, it was rumored that Balkan disputants offered arms to Italian mafiosi

in 2000 in order to cement deals whereby females for sex and prostitution were funneled into Italy from the east from places such as Albania (National Public Radio, August 14, 2000).

7. As a final point on the definition of successful conflict resolution, however, it is worth noting that success as an empirical phenomenon can differ from success as a normative goal. Success, that is, need not be a good thing. As Cooper and Berdal (1993, 198) write: "'Success'. . . is not necessarily palatable to the international community. Ethnic conflict has been constrained in Cyprus by enforced separation, in Lebanon by the imposition of order from outside (in fairly brutal fashion) in the form of a *Pax Syriana*."

8. A number of scholars, including Regan (1996) and Posen (1993), focus on the idea that third parties, governments, and ethnopolitical groups make (or act as if they are making) cost-benefit calculations. The goals of third parties lie in altering the calculations of the disputants. For example: "The war in the Western Sahara was waged on the basis of cost-benefit calculations, with the Polisario fighting on in the expectation that the burdens of war would topple the Moroccan monarchy" (Zartman 1991, 17).

9. This idea is adapted from Bercovitch, Anagnoson, and Wille (1991). Their model is applied specifically to mediation of international conflicts, but works similarly when applied to internal conflicts and to other forms of involvement.

10. Mitchell (1991) has suggested that there are several forms of asymmetry in ethnic conflicts. For example, the parties may have legal asymmetries, where one party is officially recognized while the other is not. These asymmetries may affect conflict resolution efforts, as third parties might manipulate them to seek to end a conflict. It is important to recognize that the stalemate need not, and generally will not, be equivalent to a balance of power in a military or political sense of the term. The British, for example, are militarily much stronger than the IRA, yet the former have been unable effectively to neutralize the group. The IRA, however, does not have sufficient resources to force the British from Northern Ireland.

11. Washington's fear, however, was that the Iranians, who transferred much of the arms, would take up the third point in the triangular relationship. This balancing goal raises the point of the impartiality of mediation, since it may imply that the mediator should take sides—a circumstance that seems to cut across the grain of the notion of mediation. Thus, a "mediator" might, by taking sides, advance the peace, but at the possible expense of its own position and influence on subsequent events.

12. Thus, a third party might focus on relative military power, while the disputants focus on political clout; both the government and ethnopolitical fighters might see themselves as possessing superior long-term political leverage. In such a case, would it be surprising if the third party misperceived the potential for a hurting stalemate?

13. Intervention by states might be favored by "neorealists," who believe that outcomes are directly conditioned by the power brought to bear through the international system. Individual nation–states, especially major powers, are judged more likely to succeed in promoting, forcing or demanding settlements, and more likely to use intervention to accomplish their goals. For "neoliberals," concerned about the development of institutions and norms in the international community, international organizations can be more efficacious actors in resolving third-party conflict, in place of or along with states. (See Ganguly and Taras 1998; Stedman, 1996; Oudraat, 1996; and Lindley, 1996.)

14. Regan (1996a), however, finds that the probability of successfully resolving ethnic or religious conflicts is slightly higher (5 percent) than for interventions in conflicts over ideological issues. However, in a later analysis, Regan (2000, 141) found that interventions in quite intense conflicts (high casualties over time) had a 70-percent better chance of stop-

ping the fighting than in less-intense struggles, with interventions in intense religious disputes having a 30-percent to nearly 50-percent better chance of stopping violence than in ethnic and ideological disputes. It is, of course, possible to further subdivide ethnopolitical conflict into a variety of subsets. For example, Gurr and Harff (1994) classified the ethnopolitical groups involved in conflict as ethno-nationalists, indigenous peoples, ethno-classes, communal contenders, and religious groups. Regan (1996a) focused on the conflict issue (ethnic or religious). Other ideas concerning characteristics of parties are drawn from international conflict analysis, including such themes as regime type and relative power (Bercovitch, Anagnoson, and Wille 1991).

15. He also found that if casualties mounted toward the one-million level, there was next to no chance of outsiders successfully containing the violence, no matter what the approach.

16. One could respond by arguing that arms to government forces might in theory create greater security for the regime and thus foster de-escalation in the conflict. Empirically this does not seem to be the case. As seen in chapter 4, when governments go out of their way to acquire additional arms, it is very likely that this is to support a widening or lengthening of the war in an effort to bring closure to the fighting. We can see this occurring in Sri Lanka. The government took possession of arms prior to most of its major military offensives. Arms to the government facilitated escalation (O'Ballance 1989). The use of *heavy* arms seems to decrease the length of wars and heighten intensity, perhaps the former resulting from the latter. We would need a better account of the effect of one side versus both sides using heavy weapons to form a firm conclusion, however.

17. Hence, we focus on the impact of arms acquisitions and availability on factors that have been shown to affect the probability either of successful conflict resolution or of third-party decisions to intervene. Because we have limited cases and data, we focus on simple and basic statistical tests, such as chi-square, throughout our analysis. We are guided by two case-selection criteria: the domestic conflicts should be ethnopolitical in nature, and data on arms acquisitions and the various dependent variables should be available. Of these, the arms acquisition data remain the most problematic, since systematic attempts to quantify light armament and arms to ethnic groups have been extremely rare.

18. We use U.S. Arms Control and Disarmament Agency (ACDA) data to test the impact of arms acquisitions by governments. Since this is a rough measure, we decided to present government arms data as dichotomous (high or low), with high government arms defined as average annual arms imports of at least $50 million, and low government arms as average arms imports of less than $50 million. To determine this amount, we take the average of annual arms imported to a state for the period 1983–1993, or from the beginning of the conflict through 1993, whichever is more current (ACDA 1995). Government arms were high in nineteen cases and low in twenty-five, with five missing observations.

19. Data on ethnic groups' arms are the most difficult to obtain. Most of the data come from journalistic accounts, some from field research. The most rigorous study to date is Sislin et al. (1998), which used Gurr and Harff's list of ongoing ethnic conflicts to identify various dimensions of ethnic group armaments. However, as that analysis indicated, information on what types of weapons ethnic groups used and how they obtained those weapons remains scarce, even for conflicts in the 1990s. Available data also tend to be fairly static (episodic), rather than a dynamic portrayal of arms flows across time (see also Goldring 1997). It is substantially easier to get *some* information on the arms an ethnic group possesses, rather than to identify chronological changes in those armaments.

20. We make this distinction with importation since it might make a substantial difference in ethnic fighting. Karp (1993, 12) argues that the role of state sponsors is "decisive" in the supply of arms to internal wars since they are the "only reliable source of major weapons and advanced equipment." Multiple suppliers offer greater importation opportunities and security of transfer. One final comment with this measure is that we update the data presented in chapter 2 in one important way: by filling in missing data. Consider the China-Tibetan case: there was no evidence that the Tibetans used arms to attack Chinese, and while this case was treated as missing in the original research, we feel that we could reasonably identify this case as "light" arms and "0" for access. Our updating of Sislin et al. (1998) is listed in uppercase entries in the appendix.

21. To carry out this test, we first identified conflict resolution attempts through a variety of sources: Zartman (1995), SIPRI (various years), and a review of *Keesing's Record of World Events* (various years), *Facts on File* (various years) and the *Minorities at Risk* Web site. In all, we identified twenty-six conflicts in which one or more third-party *military or diplomatic* conflict resolution initiatives occurred and twenty-three conflicts where no effort appeared. In appendix 5, third-party Conflict Resolution Attempts (CRA) were coded as "yes" if one or more occurred, and "no" if no attempt occurred for a particular conflict. We then identified the type of actor who made the attempt. Regional state or major power efforts were coded as 1, and efforts by international IGOs, as 0. Note that in many cases, both types of actors made efforts. We code these cases as 2. For the thirty-one cases where CRAs occurred, states acted unilaterally or multilaterally in eleven disputes, international organizations acted in six conflicts, and a combination of both types of third parties acted in fourteen cases.

22. Note that government arms here represent import levels. We ran a separate test for all our hypotheses measuring government arms *arsenals,* classified as high or low, based on four classes of weapons thought appropriate for domestic ethnopolitical warfare: number of main battle tanks, armored personnel carriers, helicopters, and mortars. An index was created ranking twenty-eight governments in our sample cases (see appendix) on these weapons using data from IISS (1999) for all those conflicts that were ongoing, or otherwise for the middle year of the crisis (or the closest available data to the middle year). Burma data came from Dupuy and Blanchard (1972). Nineteen governments were rated as "low," and nine as "high" in arms levels for their conflicts. When this measure was substituted for government arms imports, findings were uniformly statistically *insignificant* for all analyses, coming the closest to significance at .10 for arms levels and human needs (refugees)—that is, higher-armed governments tended to see higher human need generated by the violence, though most cases of high human need still had low arms levels. Thus, import values appear to be a somewhat better predictor than overall arms levels of when government arms will affect the course of ethnic warring or peacemaking.

23. It might be possible to see an objective manifestation of a stalemate by observing whether one side or the other can sustain more than one military battlefield victory. If the two sides continually exchange victories—one side makes an advance that is countered by an advance of the other—this might be an indication of stalemate. Geographical positioning or confinement of forces might be another indicator.

24. Zartman's (1995b) book offers some interpretations by various scholars. We used these as a jumping-off point and followed up by judging the history of each conflict, mutually checking our conclusions, and consulting colleagues in a position to assess these disputes.

The results, presented in the appendix, should be considered our own rough-and-ready first approximation.

25. Note that states and IGOs frequently both try conflict interventions in the major cases we have studied. This tandem approach means that statistical analysis of the cases in tables 5.4a, 5.4b, and 5.4c, beyond frequencies, is not attempted here because of the coincidence of cases in more than one category (not statistically independent).

26. As a further test, we ran the same analysis using our own estimates of intervention or CRA success or failure attained from various case analyses and listed them in the appendix. The findings were remarkably similar; success again was quite rare (only two of twenty-three cases), and again the chi-square levels did not reach statistical significance.

APPENDIX: CHARACTERISTICS OF RECENT AND ONGOING ETHNOPOLITICAL CONFLICTS

Location	Ethnic Groups	Duration	Govt. Arms Imports	Govt. Arsenal	Ethnic Type of Arms	Ethnic Access (Imports)	Ethnic Access	Human. Need	Hurting Stalemate	CRA	Actor Type	CRA Type	Outcome
Abkhazia	Abkhazians	1992–98	Low	—	Heavy	Low	1	High	Yes	Yes	2	1	Failure
Afghanistan	Pashtuns	1991–	High	—	Heavy		3	—	Yes		2	0	Failure
	Tajiks					High				Yes			
	Uzbeks												
Angola	UNITA	1975–	High	Low	Heavy	High	3	High	Yes	Yes	2	1	Failure
Azerbaijan	Karabakh	1988–	Low	Low	Heavy		2		Yes	Yes	2	0	Failure (F)
	Armenians					High		High	Yes	Yes			
Bangladesh	Chittagong Hill Peoples	1982–96	High	Low	Light	Low	0	Low	No	No	—	—	—
Bhutan	Nepalese	1988–	Low	—	LIGHT	Low	0	—	No	Yes	1	0	Failure
Bosnia and Herzegovinia	Serbs Croats	1992–	Low	High	Heavy	Low	2	High	Yes	Yes	2	1	Failure (F)
Burma	Karen	1948–	High	Low	Light	High	3	High	Yes	Yes	1	0	Failure (F)
	Kachin												
	Sham												
	Mon												
	Other groups												
Burundi	Tutsi	1988–	Low	Low	Heavy	Low	1		No	Yes	2	0	Failure
	Hutu							High					

continued

APPENDIX: CHARACTERISTICS OF RECENT AND
ONGOING ETHNOPOLITICAL CONFLICTS CONTINUED

Location	Ethnic Groups	Duration	Govt. Arms Imports	Govt. Arsenal	Ethnic Type of Arms	Ethnic Access (Imports)	Ethnic Access	Human. Need	Hurting Stalemate	CRA	Actor Type	CRA Type	Outcome
Cambodia	Vietnamese	1992–95	Low	Low	LIGHT	Low	0	—	No	No	—	—	—
Chad	Bideyet	1990–94	Low		LIGHT	Low	0	Low	—	No	—	—	—(F)
Chechnya	Chechen	1994–97	—	High	Heavy	High	2	High	Yes	Yes	1	0	Failure
China	Tibetans	1951–	High	High	LIGHT	Low	0	High	No	No	—	—	—
Croatia	Serbs	1991–95	Low	Low	Heavy	Low	1	High	—	Yes	2	1	Failure
Djibouti	Afars	1991–94	Low	Low	Light	High	1	—	No	Yes	1	1	Failure (S)
Ethiopia	Oromo	1991–	Low	Low	Light	Low	1	—	No	Yes	0	0	?
Fiji	E. Indian	1987–?	Low	Low	LIGHT	Low	0	—	No	Yes	2	0	?
Georgian/ Russian Border	Ossetians	1991–93	—	Low	LIGHT	Low	0	Low	Yes	Yes	2	1	? (S)
Ghana	Konkombas Gonja Dagomba Namumba	1994–?	—	Low	Light	—	—	—	No	No	—	—	—
Guatamala	Indigenous peoples	1962–95	Low	Low	LIGHT	Low	0	High	No	Yes	0	0	Success
India	Hindus Kashmiris Sikhs Bodos Tripuras Nagas	1990– 1981– 1988–	High	High	Light	High	3	High	No	No	—	—	? (F)

Indonesia (East Timor)	E. Timorans	1976–	High	Low^b	Light	Low	1	—	No	Yes	0	1	Failure (F)
Indonesia (West Papua)	Papuan	1963–	High	Low	Light	Low	1	—	No	No	—	—	—
Indonesia (North Sumatra)	Aceh	1989–	High	Low	Light	Low	1	Low	No	No	—	—	—
Iran	Kurds Baha'i	1979–	High	High	LIGHT	Low	1	High	No	No	—	—	—
Iraq	Kurds Shiites	1991–	Low	High	Heavy	Low	2	High	Yes	Yes	1	1	Success (S)
Kenya	Kalenjin Rift Valley Peoples	1991–?	Low	Low	Light	Low	2	Low	—	No	—	—	—
Liberia	Various factions	1989–97	Low	Low	Light	High	2	High	Yes	Yes	2	1	?(S)
Mali/Niger	Tuareg	1990–96	Low	Low	Light	Low	2	—	—	Yes	1	0	Failure (F)
Mexico	Chiapas Mayans	1994–	—	High	Light	Low	1	—	No	No	—	—	—
Moldova	Slavic Minority	1992–92	Low	Low	Heavy	Low	2	Low	No	Yes	2	1	?(S)
Morocco	Polisario	1975–	High	High	Heavy	High	1	—	Yes	Yes	0	0	?(F)
Nigeria	Muslims Christians	1980s–	High	Low	LIGHT	—	—	—	No	No	—	—	—
N. Ireland	IRA	1969–	High	High	Light	Low	2	—	Yes	Yes	1	0	Failure

continued

APPENDIX: CHARACTERISTICS OF RECENT AND ONGOING ETHNOPOLITICAL CONFLICTS CONTINUED

Location	Ethnic Groups	Duration	Govt. Arms Imports	Govt. Arsenal	Ethnic Type of Arms	Ethnic Access (Imports)	Ethnic Access	Human. Need	Hurting Stalemate	CRA	Actor Type	CRA Type	Outcome
Papua-New Guinea (Bougainville Island)	BRA	1990–98	Low	Low	Light	Low	1	——	No	Yes	1	1	Failure
Peru	Indigenous Peoples Shining Path	1981–	High	Low	Light	——	1	High	No	No	——	——	——(F)
Philippines	Moros	1972–	High	Low[b]	Light	Low	2	——	No	Yes	2	0	Failure
Rwanda	Hutu Tutsi	1990–	Low	Low	Light	High	2	High	No	Yes	0	1	Failure (F)
Senegal (Casamance Region)	MFDC	1982–	Low	Low	Light	Low	1	Low	——	Yes	1	0	Failure
Serbia (Kosovo)	Albanians	1990–	Low	High	Light	Low	1	——	No	Yes	2	1	Failure
Somalia	Isaaq Various clans	1988–	Low	——	Light	High	2	High	Yes	Yes	0	1	Failure (F)
South Africa	Zulu ANC	1990–94	Low	High	Light	——	1	High	Yes	No	——	——	——(M)

Location	Ethnic Groups	Duration	Government Arms Imports	Government Arsenal	Humanitarian Need	Ethnic Type of Arms	Ethnic Access Import	Ethnic Arms Access	CRA	Hurting Stalemate	CRA Type	Actor Type	Outcome
Spain	Basques	1968–	High	High	High	Light	Low	0	No	No	—	—	—
Sri Lanka	Tamils	1983–	Low	Low	Low	Light	High	3	Yes	Yes	1	1	Failure (F)
Sudan	Christians Animists	1983–	High	Low	High	Light	High	1	Yes	Yes	2	0	Failure (F)
Turkey	Kurds	1984–	High	High	High	Light	Low	—	No	No	—	—	(F)
Uganda	Acholi Landi	1987–	Low	Low	Low	LIGHT	Low	—	No	No	—	—	—
West Bank and Gaza	Palestinians	1987–	High	High	High	Light	High	—	Yes	Yes	1	0	Failure
Zaire	Kasaians	?–1996	—	—	Low	LIGHT	—	—	No	No	—	—	—

Note: Location and Ethnic Groups are from Gurr and Harff (1994). Duration is from Gurr and Harff (1994), Sivard (1996), SIPRI (various years). "?" indicates uncertainty over the start or stop date. Government Arms Imports is the average arms imports to the country that was the primary location of the ethnic conflict, SIPRI (1996), Wallensteen and Sollenberg (1995), and Regan (1996). Government Arms Imports is the average arms imports to the country that was the primary location of the ethnic conflict for the period 1983–93 or from the initiation of the conflict, whichever came later (ACDA, 1995). "High" indicates the amount was over 50 million. Government Arsenal is based on quantities of main battle tanks, armored personnel carriers, helicopters, and mortars possessed by a country (see chapter 5, note 22). (Indonesia and the Philippines ranked at the borderline of high on three of four arms type categories (the IISS did not list their battle tank totals), but were rated "low" because they did not qualify at the cutoff. They should nevertheless be considered relatively well armed in relation to the others in the "low" category.) Ethnic Type of Arms describes whether the arms possessed by the group are light arms or major conventional arms, and is drawn from data in chapter 2. Entries in all capitals, (e.g., LIGHT), indicate that no information on weapons was found for this group, and we assume that only light weapons were present. Ethnic Access Import, also drawn from chapter 2, refers to imports only, and is rated as "low" if the group(s) involved in the dispute had no or only one source of arms from abroad, and "high" if there were two or more arms sources (regardless of the quantities or values of shipments). An additional scaled variable (Ethnic Arms Access) was calculated awarding one point for indigenous production or domestic procurement, one additional point for having one or two foreign arms sources, or two additional points for having more than two foreign sources. Humanitarian Need, based on number of refugees, is drawn from Gurr and Harff (1994) and Brown (1996). Hurting Stalemate is the presence or absence of a hurting stalemate at any time during the conflict. CRA indicates whether there was a conflict resolution attempt. Actor Type identifies the type of third party that intervened (0 = an IGO, 1 = a state, 2 = both). CRA Type is the type of intervention (0 = nonmilitary, 1 = military or both military and nonmilitary). Military CRAs include military interventions and peacekeeping missions. Other CRAs include political pressure and mediation attempts. Outcome is the outcome of the intervention (success or failure). Data for presence of a CRA, CRA Type, Actor Type, and Outcome are drawn from SIPRI (various years), *Keesings Record of World Events*, *Facts on File*, and Zartman (1996). Outcome data in parentheses are Regan's (2000) rating of intervention success and failure (mixed success/failure is any case with more than one attempt resulting in some successes and some failures).

Chapter 6

Reducing the Negative Impact of Arms

As NATO and Russian troops raced into Kosovo in 1999 to impose a peacekeeping arrangement on the violence-torn Yugoslav province, the disarming of ethnic fighters emerged as a particularly difficult challenge. The West had insisted all along on the disbanding of the KLA, composed of nationalist Albanians, as part of any peace settlement. Formally denying Albanian independence demands, NATO continued to recognize Serbia's sovereignty and imposed a settlement ostensibly designed to let Serbs and Albanians coexist in the province. The long-term question of who rules in Kosovo, however, remained unclear. As Albanian refugees flocked back to their villages under NATO protection, many Serbs fled. At that point ethnic violence continued, particularly in the form of revenge killings of Serbs and Roma Gypsies. Killings per day peaked at about sixteen before tapering off to about one over the next few months (Gall 1999).

Hoping to style itself as a constabulary, the KLA was not anxious to honor the disarmament pledge or to abandon demands for Kosovar independence. Extended negotiations with the United States and NATO resulted in a vague understanding that the KLA would instead convert to a lightly armed local civilian guard and political organization. Compliance with these terms was predictably slow, although in October of 1999, peacekeepers reportedly seized two submachine guns, five AK-47s, three rifles, seven pistols, three grenade launchers, twelve hand grenades, and ammunition from two towns alone (Ruppe 1999).

Indeed, the expectation that strongly armed militia will simply melt away, convert immediately to civilian status, or hand over the bulk of their weapons contradicts both political realities and the psychology of violence. This is particularly true of organizations, such as the IRA, that are long established, with well-organized cellular units of hardened fighters, and a long history of grievances. Even the less-entrenched KLA and the Indonesian militia that ravaged East Timor in 1999 before retreating to West Timor in the face of UN-sanctioned forces, retained its capability to attack ethnic minorities and raid across the border as much as a year later.

In the stalled Northern Irish power-sharing accords of 1997, disarmament remained a prominent sore point, with high-pressure negotiations under the auspices of U.S. mediator George Mitchell in the autumn of 1999. The Ulster Unionist side refused to join the Northern Irish executive (cabinet) until the IRA complied with supposed commitments to begin disarming. Sinn Fein, the IRA's political arm, and Irish nationalists, on the other hand, denied any such promise beyond compliance with the cease-fire until the power sharing was proven workable and satisfactory. Ultimately, wording was artfully framed by which the IRA agreed to open disarmament discussions in return for the start of power sharing. When the Ulster Unionists, who remarkably were left immune from disarmament requirements, approved the plan, they stipulated an evaluation of disarmament progress within three months. Analysts continued to doubt that significant arms would be handed over in the foreseeable future.

The psychological and symbolic political importance of armament is seldom fully appreciated. For ethno-nationalists, arms often become a symbol of organizational efficacy and the viability of political struggle. For the IRA to renounce them at the outset of power sharing would in effect signify the group's emasculation in the face of Anglo-Irish and Ulster unionist pressure. Thus, as in Kosovo, the agreement reached in effect was politically symbolic: to entertain the *possibility* of disarmament but forestall practical moves in that direction. When the dispute was renewed three months later, we will see below that Mitchell had to scramble to facilitate a new diplomatic solution that would again hinge largely on symbolism.

Our analysis has shown that arms competition and balance sometimes produce stalemates, paving the way to meaningful peace negotiations. One prominent feature of such negotiations in the context of ethnopolitical violence is the (re-)establishment of civil society. This entails substituting rule of law for resort to arms. Thus, weapons might have to be removed from the previously warring sides. That very demand, however, itself can undermine confidence building and mutual security by seeming to threaten one side with loss of its security blanket. As more numerous ethnopolitical and identity conflicts are negotiated, a central question will, therefore, concern the wisdom, practicality, and timing of disarmament or arms control measures and recognition that political interests, as much as disarmament, are responsible for keeping the peace.

In the last chapter we noted the complications of promoting conflict resolution amid armed violence. Increased arms flows and the stimulation of destructive violence, as in Kosovo, Indonesia, and Ulster, tend to increase the benefits of third-party peacemaking intervention, though government opposition represents a formidable obstacle. Intervening states and IGOs might reduce death and suffering, stop migration, and improve political stability. Yet, the consequences also can include stimulation of further violence, as seen in the aftermath of NATO's Kosovo bombing. Arms flows also raise the costs of intervention. Particularly with casualty-minimization as a guiding principle of cost-conscious and politically sensitive decision makers, the risk to intervening peacekeepers and soldiers, as well as the risk to domestic political support can seem too high.

Thus, the premium is on agreements to silence, if not eliminate, the guns. Increasingly, policies and means will be sought to blunt or reduce threats from accumulated weapons in conflict zones as international peacekeeping or peace-making strategies are contemplated or launched. What then can be done to deal with these arms? Three possibilities appear to exist. First, guns might be reduced in *potential* future conflicts, before the violence begins. This entails the linkage of early warning with arms reduction strategies. We saw in chapter 3 that arms are generally acquired before rebellions are launched, and that governments sup-ply arms with increasing frequency to repressive ethnic militia forces. Thus, arms flows and accumulations, if they can be discovered, are an excellent early warning indicator. The goal of conflict prevention would involve precluding some of the impetus to arm as well as increasing the transparency (i.e., report-ing) of arms transfers. Part of the task involves confidence and security-building measures, to improve security and reduce fear for individuals and communities living in close proximity. Improved security, in all its political, economic, cul-tural, and psychological manifestations, would in turn reduce grievances and ten-sion and avert violence. Reducing the fuel for violence, in the form of arms and ammunition, might reduce fear and anxiety, though as in Rwanda, not preclude threat and insecurity.

Means to arms reduction in such pre-violence situations would entail regulating arms traffic to minimize general accumulation in the region, as well as promoting norms to regulate permissible arms technologies, and effective embargoes on arms shipments to specific recipients. As light weaponry or small arms remain the hall-mark of most ethnopolitical fighting, mechanisms must be devised to better link reporting of such arms accumulations to other facets of early warning (O'Prey 1995, 39). Governments have been relatively cooperative in reporting their major international arms transactions through the *UN Register of Conventional Arms*; pre-sumably they could be convinced to report on lighter arms (the United States and Canada have begun to lead the way) and on regional accumulation.[1]

On the demand side of the equation, some regions or subregions, seeing the wanton destruction in local wars, have begun to move toward joint limits or sus-pensions of arms imports. Mali led the way toward articulation of such principles for the Economic Community of West African States (ECOWAS) in 1998—a three-year moratorium on import, export, and manufacture of small arms and light weapons. Other African regions, the Southern African Development Community (SADC) and east African states, have begun similar discussions. The Organiza-tion of American States (OAS) has taken steps toward controlling the elusive black market arms trade, recognizing its links to organized crime and drug traffic. In a 1997 convention, they required member states to outlaw this trade system and to cooperate in policing it (Boutwell and Klare 2000, 51–53).

A second way to diminish destabilizing armament would entail measures in the early stages of warfare, once violence is under way. The goals here would be to track arms and reduce their flow, particularly in the form of vital replenishments such as spare parts, ammunition, and reserve supplies. Additional efforts might be aimed at freezing or limiting arms technology levels, precluding escalation to new and heightened arms levels or the introduction of more sophisticated weapons, as well as steps to constrain or slow arms races between the warring sides. Of course, since stalemates can be constructive, as seen in chapters 4 and 5, arms control technically might also involve steps to arm and empower weaker parties in order to impede losses, genocide, and ethnic cleansing. This task requires the establishment of norms and oversight for the type and level of permissible arms acquisition and employment, better enforcement of bans on reexport of arms once a conflict ends, as well as supplier discretion and restraint and the closure of arms smuggling routes. Providing arms infusions might be made conditional on recipients' opening peace talks and agreeing to greater transparency and weapon "decommissioning" once the fighting ends.

Among the principal methods to reduce the number or types of arms entering a violent conflict are embargoes or other arms control measures, such as more uniform and tougher supplier export restrictions, accurate reporting of small-arms flows, international norms relating to particular types of weapons (e.g., land mines) or transfers under particular conditions (e.g., to countries with obvious human rights violations), and more coordinated law enforcement (Klare 1997).[2] However, the effectiveness of such approaches can vary by situation.

A third strategy, also quite complicated diplomatically, is to pull arms out of war zones as the fighting winds down, as part of the endgame we described in Kosovo, East Timor, and Northern Ireland. Here the goal is to restabilize the country and potentially promote long-term political reform and settlement. This means significantly reducing the kindling for a reignition of the fighting or renewal of fear and tension at a later date, the kind of assurance upon which successful peace negotiations can depend. This is the emerging area of "micro-disarmament," defined by UN secretary-general Boutros-Ghali in 1995 as "practical disarmament in the context of the conflicts the United Nations is actually dealing with and of the weapons, most of them light weapons, that are actually killing people in the hundreds of thousands" (quoted by Laurance and Meek 1996, 5; the concept has been applied to all three stages of conflict control, but most often to the process of demobilizing combatants).

Of course, arms tend to be reduced in the midst of fighting itself as a natural consequence of attrition, as ammunition is used up and weapons break down. The process can be artificially stimulated by disarmament accords such as those tried with varying results in Northern Ireland and Kosovo or through military sweeps and confiscation. For example, an abortive clause of the 1987 Indo-Sri Lanka Accords "called for all Tamil guerrilla groups to turn their weapons over to the Indian troops" (Oberst 1992, 129).

We examine each of these options and their prospects in light of global political developments and our earlier findings. However, one final set of complications is to distinguish strategies for removing arms from ethnopolitical groups versus removal or reduction of government arms. At least one study (Craft and Smaldone 2001) has shown that government arms imports as well as government military expenditures join other factors such as partial democratization in spurring both cross-border and domestic warfare in sub-Sahara Africa. Most of the disarmament efforts in ethnic fighting have so far been directed at groups and militia, either in the form of voluntary or negotiated agreements to hand over weapons, or in devising incentives or payoffs to buy such concessions (so-called buyback provisions for reclaiming arms). It would appear, though, that for certain disputes, especially in places such as Sri Lanka or Cyprus where autonomous enclaves might be one solution, there should also be agreed levels and perhaps restricted deployment of government arms so that relative balances and reassurances can be maintained. Negotiations in the Philippines between the government and Muslim Moro insurgents in 2000 appeared to hinge, and come apart, on whether government forces would allow a Muslim encampment and enclave to go unchallenged. Even in Chiapas there might be government agreement not to build up armed forces in the region beyond certain levels and not to supply ethnic militia. This is complicated by having to distinguish arms acceptable for internal and external security, but at least the parties themselves or arms inspectors conceivably could readily monitor the agreements.

PREVENTIVE MEASURES

The end of the Cold War has greatly complicated the task of reducing arms accumulations in hopes of preventing violent outbreaks.

> Since the end of the Cold War, tens of millions of powerful military-style weapons have been sold or given away worldwide, as former Warsaw Pact and NATO countries scaled back their military forces, and Cold War-era conflicts, such as that in Afghanistan, simmered down.
>
> More of the weapons are produced and sold every day. UN studies have estimated some 300 manufacturers in 74 countries are adding new weapons to more than 500 million already in circulation around the globe.
>
> Experts say such weapons—pistols, rifles, assault weapons, light artillery, and hand grenades—increasingly end up in the hands of belligerents . . . often through circuitous routes. . . . A UN study . . . concludes that "virtually every part of the United Nations system is dealing in one way or another with the consequences of the armed conflicts, insecurity, violence, crime, social disruption, displaced peoples and human suffering that are directly or indirectly associated with the wide availability of these weapons. (Ruppe 1999, 2)

A combination of economic and political incentives continue to drive light arms transfers, some of which are masked by governments using third parties, private dealers, and agents. In addition, in justifying arms acquisitions, states' "sovereign right to arm" can be extended by ethno-nationalists to a "national right of self-defense." Most governments and many NGOs believe that small arms have important purposes. "We're dealing with weapons that under international law have legitimacy." (Ruppe 1999, 4, quoting Peter Hanby of the International Red Cross).

In a sense, the world is still digesting the massive arms sales of the early 1990s. Some $37 billion in sales were recorded in 1993 alone, driven by the former Soviet Union and the aftermath of the Gulf War. While much of these were new and used major or heavy arms, they included substantial tallies of small arms and light weapons, now circulating among regional wars in the developing world. One estimate for the Horn of Africa typifies the situation in many regions:

> While it is impossible to quantify the number of weapons circulating in one country, let alone a region or continent, examples may illustrate the point. It is estimated that the Mengistu government in Ethiopia inherited thousands of weapons that flooded into Somalia. These same weapons, and additional ones from the war in Sudan, are now in Kenya and other parts of East Africa. Now, renewed fighting between Eritrea and Ethiopia, and its spill-over effects on Somalia, have prompted fears of another arms race in the Horn . . . a region of unstable peace with hardly enough money to feed its people. ("Overview: Weapons Proliferation in East Africa and the Horn" 1999, 2)

It was not until the year 2000, amid intense negotiations to bring a halt to Eritrean-Ethiopian fighting, that the United States finally joined other Western powers in establishing an embargo on arms shipments to the area. Then after a peace agreement was reached, Washington almost immediately began to call for lifting the ban.

IGOs at both the regional and global level have responded to this proliferation challenge by holding discussions and formulating proposed arms transfer restrictions. The 35th Assembly of OAU Heads of State and Government renewed a commitment to limit small-arms proliferation, promoting the 1998 moratorium on import, export, and manufacture of light weapons among ECOWAS. The group also lauded the destruction of surplus and obsolete small arms in South Africa and Mozambique ("Overview: Weapons Proliferation in East Africa and the Horn," 1999, 1).

Mexico, a state facing internal ethnopolitical disruption, pushed "fast-track" OAS negotiations for a convention to restrict the illicit manufacture and trade of firearms, ammunition, and related materials, resulting in a U.S.-backed hemispheric treaty signed in Washington in November 1997. Fearing increased demands for and threats to its peacekeepers in heavily armed zones, the United Nations itself planned a global conventional arms control conference for 2001.

Since 1995, the UN Department for Disarmament Affairs (DDA) has promoted discussions on a global response to small-arms proliferation, proposing in 1998 to consolidate efforts in a single office.[3] Key impediments to multilateral cooperation remain, however, as member states have disagreed about defining light weapons and about rights of self-defense (Wurst, 1998, 4–6). The task was more complicated than developing the successful Ottawa Conference on the Global Ban on Land Mines in December 1997, at least partly because the topic is larger and humanitarian concerns are less focused than they are for land mines. Still, the same campaign approach was adopted, expanding the agenda to include not just light weapons themselves but also their humanitarian, social, and economic effects. Related agencies, such as the UN Department of Peacekeeping Operations (DPKO), the Office for the Coordination of Humanitarian Affairs (OCHA), and the Commission on Crime Prevention and Criminal Justice were linked to the DDA effort.

In July 1998, delegates of twenty-one nations concerned with international arms traffic met in Oslo and drafted an initial statement on "Elements of a Common Understanding." Though disagreements persisted and little action resulted, and while key arms suppliers such as Russia, China, and Israel were absent, the draft nevertheless touches on issues that will characterize international negotiations regarding small-arms traffic for years to come. Among these are:

- coordination regarding illicit trade, legal sales, and existing stocks of weapons
- tightened border controls and enhanced laws and enforcement, information sharing, and weapons marking or coding
- improved controls at the points of arms manufacture, transit, and transfer, including licenses and notification of country of origin and shipments
- codes of conduct related to acceptable transfers and humanitarian law
- weapon collection and destruction initiatives to reduce stockpiles
- efforts written into peace accords to demobilize and reintegrate combatants at the end of armed conflicts, including alternate economic opportunities
- measures to reverse "cultures of violence" and excessive societal militarization.

Other proposed provisions, such as a Canadian effort to ban arms transfers to non-state actors, were not adopted.

The Oslo meeting was part of a growing set of diplomatic gatherings to consider small-arms proliferation, including the April 1998 meeting, also in Oslo, of thirty countries that led to the moratorium on the production and trade of light arms in West Africa (Joseph 1998, 1–3). One factor appearing to spur such efforts is the growing concern among major powers, and particularly the United States, that arms transfers, spreading uncontrolled from state to state and group to group, are dogging efforts to maintain regional stability, influence, and control.

Paradoxically, of course, Washington has remained the world's prime exporter of arms, including vast supplies of small arms to countries undergoing significant ethnopolitical conflict, involved in the drug traffic, or facing strategic challenges — including Mexico, Latvia, Taiwan, Colombia, Bosnia, Israel, the Philippines, and Thailand. U.S. embassy personnel often have acted as agents for these sales and transfers, particularly in the Western Hemisphere. In addition, the State Department has authorized hundreds of millions of dollars in light weapons exports ($470 million in 1996 alone) negotiated by arms manufacturers or private agents, and the Commerce Department has added approvals of additional long guns and police equipment. "Although these dollar figures are small in the context of the overall arms trade (estimated at some $30 billion annually), at $100–500 per gun these transactions represent enormous quantities of weapons" (Lumpe 1998, 2).[4]

Because U.S. military assistance has been directed increasingly at unstable and hard-pressed client states such as Colombia, it has become apparent that rogue groups, such as drug traffickers and guerrillas, are sometimes better prepared for battle than local governments and also benefit from weapons captured or obtained from those governments. Therefore, while stepping up arms shipments and training for favored regimes, Washington also seeks greater global coordination of restrictions that could keep arms out of the hands of terrorists, rebels, and criminal syndicates. At the fiftieth anniversary of the UN General Assembly in 1995, President Clinton called for states "to shut down the gray markets that outfit terrorists and criminals with firearms" (Lumpe 1998, 1).

Since we have determined that much armament is derived from sources within countries or taken from government forces and armories, any serious effort to stem proliferation would have to entertain more effective restrictions on exports to governments themselves as well as those via black and gray markets. Acquired or locally manufactured arms also have been crucial in state-sponsored terrorism and repression of the type that led to deadly conflict and the rise of ethno-nationalists and resistance groups in places such as East Timor, Kosovo, and Mexico (Lumpe 1998, 1).

Major powers seriously interested in preventing ethnopolitical wars would be well advised to bring combinations of diplomatic and political pressure to bear on recipient governments much earlier than in the past. Under congressional pressure in 1994, the Clinton administration stopped small-arms sales to Indonesia after government forces massacred civilians in the Timorese capital, Dili, with U.S.-supplied M-16 assault rifles. However, between 1993 and 1998, the administration also approved some $140 million in other arms shipments to Jakarta, much of it suited to internal repression, "including equipment and raw materials for manufacturing ammunition, explosives, missiles, military communications equipment, and spare parts for the Indonesian military's aircraft" ("U.S. Complicity in East Timor" 1999, 1). Indonesian forces also continued to receive American military training under the Joint Combined Exchange Training program even after regular U.S. training programs were suspended for human rights concerns. Thus, when Washington finally imposed a comprehensive arms embargo and strong economic pressure on the vulnerable and shaky Indonesian government after the Timor violence erupted in September 1999, which also targeted UN election monitors, it had missed numerous previous opportunities to limit Indonesia's repressive capability and to signal its serious displeasure at Jakarta's human rights policies. Washington's interests in supporting the Indonesian military and in promoting economic stability during the Asian economic crisis of the late 1990s evidently discouraged the Clinton administration from doing so.

It is easier, though still politically controversial, to bring strong measures against a renegade regional power such as Milosevic's Serbia than to discipline a regionally pivotal client state such as Indonesia, Israel, or Turkey in the interest of human rights or domestic violence prevention. To prevent ethnic violence, embargoes such as that in 1994 efforts regarding Indonesian small arms, would have had to be accompanied by more decisive diplomatic and economic pressure for political reform. As seen in chapter 3 and as learned in South Africa's long-term domestic ethnic repression in the face of an official international arms embargo, the mere withholding of certain arms by international sources far from the battle scene hardly precludes violence, though in the long term and given other sorts of collective sanctions it might help choke off and limit the spread of fighting. Governments and some rebel groups can either manufacture or find requisite equipment to launch offensives. Sterner accompanying measures would appear to be required, and even then, the effectiveness of the sanctions depends on target governments' vulnerability to the form of restrictions and denials employed.

Two approaches appear to underlie the latest global efforts to restrict conventional weapons transfers and acquisitions. One is to reduce the total of small arms circulating in regions of conflict. Hence, in 1999 Secretary of State Madeleine Albright articulated a somewhat vague policy of refusing U.S. arms transfers to "regions of conflict" not already covered by arms embargoes. The State Department was given the power to restrict sales of communications satellites, and Congress moved to require better reporting of incentives in arms sales contracts. The second approach is to deny particular arms to particularly troublesome states or groups. In 1999 as well, the Clinton administration applied quiet pressure on Israel to drop its proposed sale of a sophisticated airborne radar system to China, halted handgun sales to Venezuela, and toughened terms of arms sales to Canada citing "retransfers" to third countries such as Iran.

Much of Washington's effort in limiting small-arms trade has been related to weakening "rogue states" such as Iran and North Korea (i.e., states willing to act against American interests), and preventing regional threats by foreign policy rivals such as China. The idea of restraining *domestic* political violence abroad is newer and has not necessarily been thoroughly thought out. Washington, along with the major European arms dealing states, appears more interested in stemming the illegal transfer of firearms (as embodied in a 1998 UN resolution) and other weapons likely to fall to terrorists than in curtailing the overall legal trade in light weapons.[5]

Approaches aimed at reducing regional arms supplies might diminish the confidence of ethnopolitical disputants in their reliance on external arms sources, but given the resourcefulness of international agents, dealers, and arms customers, it would appear that they could still prepare for war. Focused efforts to deny arms to particular targets also would appear insufficient if the states with requisite leverage on those target states or groups were not heavily engaged in the sanctions. It is not clear that Israel or Canada would have much chance of restraining arms recipients, but the United States, in combination with Russia, Britain, France, and smaller arms suppliers, might potentially convince vulnerable leaders to modify their ethnic policies. Prospects for such pressure are of course complicated by political realities, such as Russia's own severe economic needs, internal ethnic conflict difficulties, cross-border ethnic affinities, and clashes with Washington and the European Union over places such as Chechnya. In addition, targets of diplomatic pressure might resist in any case if territorial or security issues are seen as severe enough. Broader international security guarantees might have to be devised for hard-pressed governments and groups, augmenting any arms sanctions.[6]

Despite the growth of diplomacy on the subject, the global record of response to "early warning" of ethnopolitical violence remains poor. There was ample long-term warning about the violence potential in Kosovo and East Timor long before they exploded into bloodbaths. The 1991 massacres in Dili alone should have alerted the international community to the Timorese dangers. The Bosnian war brought global attention to Kosovo, but it was difficult to determine whether the relative arms accumulations of ethnic rebels or the Serbian government meant that warfare was imminent. As is often the case, the United Nations, regional organizations, big power alliances, and major powers themselves did little to address the violence potential early on, and few observers reported accurately on the weapons stockpiles. Indeed, U.S. policy toward Indonesia was inconsistent along these lines, and few other states even bothered to respond to the unfolding Timorese human rights concerns during the 1990s. The best the "international community" seemed able to come up with for Kosovo before the ethnic cleansing of 1999 was the dispatch of token troops to nearby areas such as Macedonia to keep regional violence from spreading across borders and involving powers such as Greece and Turkey. Because of the need for Serb cooperation in the Bosnian peace accords next door, there was little latitude for pressing President Milosevic on the domestic issue of Albanian rights in Kosovo.

The complications of diverse outside interests, therefore, frequently come into play. Major powers and regional actors were cross-pressured in both the East Timorese case and the less-publicized independence struggle in the Indonesian province of Aceh, where some tallies claimed casualties of up to 5,000 in the 1990s ("Indonesian General," 1999). Both regions are deemed to be oil rich, and therefore of significant international economic consequence. Since UN election monitors were attacked after the Timorese independence vote in Dili, Security Council members were compelled to respond. Australia was greatly concerned about the disorder in a geographically close neighbor, especially one with important commercial ties and natural resources. Australia also had a strong historical attachment to the area; Timorese had been helpful in Australian resistance to the Japanese during the Second World War. Yet, from Indonesia's perspective as a state that pioneered the nonaligned and anticolonial movement, Australia and other UN powers were indulging in neocolonial dictation and interference in sovereign rights.

Thus, it is seldom clear what should be done once the potential for ethnopolitical violence has been recognized. Should major powers cut relations with repressive and potentially violent governments? Cutting relations forestalls potential negotiation leverage through continued trade and other ties, and the government involved probably will argue that it was provoked by acts of the ethnopolitical militants. Do the disputants' identities or particular strategic circumstances matter?

What are the limits of sovereignty in such situations? At what points should diplomatic pressure be backed with the threat or reality of military force? How should interests in one conflict or set of issues, such as the need for economic recovery in a large, diverse state such as Indonesia, be related to human rights and arms shipments? Does it matter which states propose to undertake "peacemaking" intervention? What if these states are traditional enemies or allies of the government in question? Should arms embargoes be employed, against whom, and with what degree of enforcement or coordination?

Clearly the arms embargo is a visible and discrete form of pressure, rather easily coupled with early warning reports. Yet with the large array of available arms sources, the possibility of disguising shipments through third parties, and the general lack of border enforcement against trade and smuggling, often these are more rhetorical than real steps. Because it is diplomatically necessary to appear evenhanded, embargoes generally are indiscriminate in targeting, supposedly penalizing all local arms recipients regardless of the "justness" of their cause. Still, if influential decision makers such as those in the Clinton administration who promised to refrain from arms shipments to conflict zones, are serious about their commitment to starve conflicts of arms early, and if they consult with their allies and adversaries, the major arms sources would be dealt with.

Aside from black and gray markets, the problem with embargoes and other sanctions is the temptation to defect from multilateral arms control commitments. States are tempted to arm the favored client, match the arms shipments of rival powers, respond to export inducements, look the other way while arms get through, or balk at the costs involved in patrolling and enforcing embargoes. The very act of "getting serious" about arms limitations sometimes can be enough to jar a repressive government into rethinking its domestic priorities or shake the confidence of an ethnopolitical militia or liberation force. However, threats also can cement the resolve of extremist leaders to resist outside pressure. Thus, the disputants themselves must be engaged in the dialogue, but this may mean negotiating with quite unsavory characters.

Several types of guidelines have been proposed for U.S. and major power small-arms exporters. These include factors such as the recipient government's reliability and arms control capability as well as its past responsible handling and use of small arms shipments. Careful end-user certification, documentation, and enforcement should be sought so that arms are not reexported, misused, or diverted without approval. Realistic governmental needs assessments should be derived, backed by agreements for spot inspections and reporting, and not exceeded. Satisfactory controls should be established before licensing of overseas weapons production. These proposals also include the enactment of an "arms sales code of conduct" in legislation to integrate human rights, democratic reform, and nonaggression criteria. One of the key guiding principles and challenges, as in the UN major arms *Register,* is to enact a workable system to promote greater transparency in small arms shipments, so that discrepancies in the supplier/recipient reports can be identified for greater reassurance. In the U.S. case, for example, this would also mean a greater U.S. State Department willingness to disclose information on commercially negotiated agreements—up to now the department has been highly responsive to manufacturer worries over trade secrets—and more stringent U.S. domestic gun legislation to set qualitative if not quantitative restrictions, accounting for weapons and keeping them out of criminal and terrorist hands. Given the thriving arms bazaars in zones of prior covert arms shipments, such as Pakistan, Afghanistan, Angola, and West Africa, bans on covert supplies to insurgent forces also would be necessary, including those by Washington (Lumpe 1998, 3).

These recommendations stress greater supplier oversight and responsibility for anticipating the long-term effects and dangers inherent in arms shipments. They stress the past record and responsible behavior of recipients. The international small-arms traffic, like a runaway locomotive, cannot be stopped immediately if crisis looms. Rather, the hope is that arms will not accumulate in the hands of vicious and unstable parties or recipients likely to retransfer them to such parties. The general traffic can only be gradually slowed through restrictions at the source combined with pressure on resupply and retransfer points and negotiations with recipients to lessen the demand.

ARMS AND WAR

Many of the arms control problems and approaches related to prevention apply as well *during* ethnopolitical wars. The quest for transparency of shipments, negotiations about arms levels and technologies, and the potential for sanctions to choke off supply relate to resupplies during warfare as well as to generally reducing regional weapons flow. Indeed, depending upon the gravity of the situation, the international community might pay more attention to the need for restraint once violence is under way.

However, political and military issues are just as complex, if not more so, once the passions of war are unleashed. We saw in chapter 4 that arms infusions tend to accompany escalations of domestic fighting and that the policies of major power patrons can, as in Angola, greatly prolong wars.

One troubling example comes from the Chiapas case in Mexico, where the United States adopted policies designed to bolster the government. These involved not simply arms shipments but personnel training as well, with a decidedly negative impact on both human rights and the conflict resolution process. Despite Church-mediated negotiations between the government and EZLN rebels, leading to the San Andreas accords in 1995 on indigenous rights and autonomy, Mexican President Ernesto Zedillo rejected the text.

> Understanding that they could not win a political battle against the widely popular Zapatista movement, the Mexican government decided instead to seek a military vic-

tory. It stationed about one-third of its military forces in Chiapas to systematically harass and intimidate the indigenous peasant population. . . . The Mexican military created, armed, and trained paramilitary groups aligned with the ruling PRI party, militarizing existing tensions and exacerbating disputes by—for example—giving both sides unique rights to the same land or natural resources. Mexico's shift in strategy paralleled a significant rise in participation in U.S. military training courses. The number of Mexican soldiers trained at the infamous School of the Americas (SOA) more than doubled from 1996 to 1997, to 305 students, or a third of all those enrolled in the SOA. . . . The government's tacit support for this approach along with impunity for their violent tactics culminated in a massacre of 45 unarmed men, women, and children in Acteal in December 1997. (Gabelnik 1999, 9–10)

While it can be argued that U.S. training programs also stress consideration of human rights and democracy, the bulk of the courses deal with strategy and tactics, reportedly ranging from counterinsurgency and torture to narcotics interdiction, and the overall effect, especially in the midst of delicate peace negotiations, has seldom been to develop civil societies abroad.

It is one thing to arm or train forces suffering severe one-sided losses, as the United States did in Bosnia; it is quite another to further empower the dominant local power. While Washington's counsel in Mexico's internal affairs is always a political dilemma given Latin sensitivities to "Yankee imperialism," it would seem that offering assistance to the peace process, as in Northern Ireland, is a far better approach than military resupply and training if winding down violence is the goal. If the interest lies merely in cementing relations with Mexico City, of course, arms supplies are seen as a symbol of solidarity. Certainly there are temptations to arm the government in such ethnopolitical conflicts to preserve order, discipline marauding militia, and cement future relations on a variety of issues, including, in Mexico's case, trade, investment, oil, narcotics, the environment, security, and migration. But military assistance is quite often the wrong medicine for a malady of violence, and governments may benefit more by counseling restraint, providing requisite economic aid, and assistance in negotiations.

At least as applied to the perspective of state repression in ethnopolitical disputes, it appears that productive strategies are coming to stress devolution of power and autonomy provisions at subregional levels. The 1998 bombing of Omagh in Northern Ireland, which caused the worst damage since the 1960s and was a profound psychological shock to the peace process, nevertheless did not lead to further escalation. There appeared to be a growing belief that nonviolent strategies, including negotiations about local power sharing and addressing the provocative "marching season" for rival nationalist organizations, could produce both orderly change and security guarantees. It is uncertain how far into the "grass roots" these hopes or beliefs extended; grass-roots public support is indeed crucial for lasting peace (Byrne 2001). Nevertheless, though the threat of renewed violence is likely to linger until a workable formula such as the Northern Irish power-sharing accords is proven feasible, weapons stockpiles and their political effects can be isolated from peace processes. As we have tried to demonstrate, this depends on groups' belief that the benefits of restraint outweigh those of war.

While it might be relatively late to propose local autonomy once fighting has erupted (ethno-nationalists, as in Sri Lanka, by this time frequently demand full independence), the autonomy concept has clearly been gaining adherents in many troubled areas, even including the fairly desperate proposals of Sri Lanka's hard-pressed government. Sometimes warring parties can be urged to accept less than full demands in order to end the war on basically acceptable terms. Older states and advanced economies increasingly appear to prefer autonomy experiments to the horrifying prospect of prolonged civil wars and terrorism; Britain, Canada, Russia, Israel, and others have experimented with such proposals (also at times employing repressive measures). Bigger states might assume that small autonomous regions would have to continue relations with the central power for economic and social reasons. Newer states and those with troubled economies dependent on rich provinces, such as Indonesia, India, Congo, Nigeria, and Mexico have appeared more hesitant about such experiments, but in some cases also have tried them.[7]

If local autonomy arrangements or other political reforms designed to allow room for ethnic diversity in multicultural societies proliferate in the future, as they appear likely to do, their linkage to negotiated security arrangements and arms balances also appears feasible. Whenever formal legislation is passed, as was the case regarding Mexico's Chiapas state despite setbacks in 1995, it opens the way toward formal confidence-building measures, the development of norms, and greater transparency regarding arms and arms technology levels. These might include periodic inspections by local, national, or international agencies, regular reporting of arms transactions, and other reassurance measures by both central and local governments and mobilized identity groups. Any break with these agreements would set off alarms about possibly renewed warfare, and hopefully those alarms would ring in the halls of IGOs or major power capitals in time for intervention and remedies.

One interesting example of a bilaterally negotiated *international* armament freeze offers a possible model for civil wars as well. In early 1999, "the Presidents of Ecuador and Peru pledged to halt new weapons acquisitions in a move designed to bolster the long-term prospects for peace between the two nations. The two governments initiated a peace process in October 1998 when they signed a treaty ending a 183-year border dispute that had erupted into war in early 1995" ("Ecuador/Peru Pledge Arms Freeze" 1999, 1). Entailed in this agreement were pledges not to buy arms for the next four years, to reduce the military draft by some 60 percent, and to transfer military personnel to police functions. Of course, both states reportedly had stocked up on aircraft and other equipment after the 1995 clash, with the United States acting as both mediator and "guarantor" of the peace treaty and arms dealer to both states. (Ecuador/Peru Pledge Arms Freeze 1999, 3).

It is probably easier to obtain short-term arms freezes when the parties are confident of their arsenals.

Verifiable provisions for downsizing forces, transferring personnel, decommissioning or storing weapons, ending arms imports, and freezing arms technology levels all could be included in ethnopolitical bargains containing larger social reform elements. Governments, of course, would not be anxious to formally recognize the military status and legitimacy of ethno-nationalist rebels; diplomatic language has to be artfully designed, as in promises to "begin discussions" of disarmament. But for a state such as Sri Lanka, a lasting cease-fire opening the way for effective political reform could be worth the de facto recognition that the Tamil Tigers were not a disappearing force. It appears that the vague disarmament and mutual recognition rhetoric of the Northern Irish cease-fire and peace accords is a way forward.

While we have discovered an unexpected prevalence of weapons obtained domestically in ethnopolitical fighting, external supply is still very important because it tends to link suppliers to the insurgents' or governments' cause, both practically and symbolically. Sometimes this linkage involves supplier pressure for restraint by the recipient parties, but arms shipments also signal external backing. The development of at least one reliable external source can be seen as a major political achievement, though one potentially diminishing the recipient's own autonomy of action.

Finally, in the mid-war picture one must deal with clandestine arms sources. It has been estimated that low-cost, easy-to-use, low-technology small and light weapons, in the hands of determined fighters, have wreaked the most damage and up to 90 percent of the deaths (increasingly inflicted on civilians) in violent political conflicts worldwide (Mandel 1999, 40, citing figures from Brown et al. 1998, 131). We have seen that these readily portable weapons are highly subject to black market theft and smuggling and semi-legal gray market transfers even including the complicity of major arms manufacturers. The black market revolves heavily around international criminal and terror syndicates, often bartering arms for goods such as natural resources, gems, drugs, animal products, and so on. The gray market can include legal transfers of "dual-use" technology or equipment convertible to weapons, as well as "laundered" transactions through third parties.

It is estimated that up to a third of the $3 billion in annual traffic in small and light weapons is illegal. Spare parts, which are crucial to the continuation of wars, are most readily obtained through illegal sources. Add to this the sometimes massive infusion of government arms in covert operations such as those in Central America, Afghanistan, and Southern Africa during the 1980s, and it is clear that the control spigot for downsizing ethnic wars can be difficult to find or engage (Mandel 1999, 40–41).

With the Cold War's passing, there is presumably less need for major covert governmental armament programs of the type seen in Angola, and there have even been congressional proposals in Washington to ban them. However, it is unlikely that major powers will forego this tactic completely, especially in the face of provocation by leaders such as Yugoslavia's Milosevic. Minor powers bent on promoting their own interests abroad also will occasionally contribute to the arms flow, as Libya did in its clandestine 1985–86 arms and explosives shipments to the IRA during a period of intense British-American pressure on the North African state (Mandel 1999, 43).

Illicitly obtained weapons also appear more likely to be employed in battle than legally derived or locally manufactured equipment. Their acquisition is often driven by immediate war needs, particularly those of the insurgent groups (Pearson 1994, 60–61). Therefore, despite the difficulties, it is worth attempting to restrain this trade if one wants to increase the pressure for peace negotiations by creating more pessimism about the long-term chances for combat success. Of course, from the point of view of ethnic nationalists, such arms can represent a lifeline in their liberation struggles and hope of some kind of stalemate that would force the government into concessions.

The very fact that NATO has now joined the United Nations as a locus for peacekeeping operations means that the major powers, indeed including Russia, if not China, will have to become more aware and undertake more regular consultation about the flow of small arms into war zones. At a Netherlands conference of thirty nations in 1996, the so-called Wassenaar Arrangement was drafted, including a code of conduct to increase transparency and national responsibility for arms sales and technology transfers. However, little has been done subsequently to generate common code enforcement. Indeed, in 1999, the Clinton administration opposed congressional (largely Democratic) revisions to the Security Assistance Act "that would require the President to begin negotiations with U.S. allies that could lead to blocking weapons transfers to undemocratic governments, those that abuse human rights or those that engage in illegal acts of aggression" (White House Weighs in on Code 1999).

In June of that year, American and European Union representatives met in Brussels to discuss possible joint efforts to restrain the proliferation of small and light arms. They agreed to speed negotiations on the UN protocol on the illicit manufacture and transfer of arms and ammunition, and the voluntary arms moratorium for the African Great Lakes region. Again, this represents the minimalist approach familiar in the dealings of major arms-exporting states. However, coming in the context of new NATO undertakings, and possible Organizational of European Security and Cooperation (OESC) activity in places like Chechnya, it appears to represent a likely continuing dialogue to increase reporting and transparency to forestall the "destabilizing accumulation and spread of military small arms and light weapons beyond those required for legitimate security needs" (EU–U.S. Meet to Discuss Small Weapons 1999). Added to this is the mounting pressure by networks of some two hundred NGOs and individuals from more than thirty countries, the so-called International Action Network on Small Arms, "to tranfer the momentum of the International Campaign to Ban Land Mines to small and light weapons control in general" (Grillot 2001; see also Brem 2001).

ARMS REMOVAL AND PEACEMAKING

Any hopes for effective removal of arms from domestic war zones depend on the form of overall peace settlements and the parties' readiness for implementation. If, as in some parts of Central America, the settlement includes the reintegration of former rebels into society or into the state armed forces and constabulary, the prospect for the orderly decommissioning of arms can be reasonably good. This might at first involve more obsolete and dysfunctional weapons, but would in time come to include most arms caches. If, on the other hand, the agreements are confined basically to the cease-fire level or are seen as temporary expedients, it is unreasonable to expect more than token disarmament. Since armament relates both to prestige and security guarantees, in order for parties to disarm, their political legitimacy and viability must be insured, their grievances reduced, and their fears allayed. These are all trust-building challenges that take time and must be painstakingly nurtured. As seen in Israel and the Palestinian territories in 2000, armed uprising and massive repression can seriously impair and threaten ongoing peace talks even right up to the point of possible agreement. Killing each other's civilians and children has a chilling effect on the possibilities of reconciliation.

Beginning with the UN peacekeeping effort in Namibia in 1989, a number of UN-brokered or peacekeeping operations have come to involve disarmament measures, with varying degrees of successful implementation. These include Central America (1989), Cambodia, Bosnia, and Somalia (all beginning around 1992), and Haiti (organized around September 1994). The United Nations has been asked to help troubleshoot and facilitate, inspect, monitor, and safeguard the processes whereby forces are demobilized and arms collected (Cox 1996, 83–85).

Not all of these wars involved primarily ethnic issues, but they do illustrate the type of situations more or less amenable to effective micro-disarmament. Namibia and Nicaragua were judged to be relative successes, especially by the UN Secretariat. Problems nevertheless persisted, for example, when Contra and Sandanista forces retained some weapons after turning in equipment such as heavy machine guns and surface-to-air missiles. Individuals reportedly then engaged in gunrunning for profit after land reforms and resettlement assistance did not materialize. Thus, it appears that social reconstruction has to accompany demobilization in order to solidify disarmament.[8] The fact that the peacekeepers lacked "baseline data" from which to judge the completion of arms submissions was not an impediment in this case, since the parties were ready to accept that sufficient arms reductions were present. Such political flexibility and readiness might not be present in other cases (Cox 1996, 90–93).

Under dominant U.S. influence, the multinational force deployed to Haiti sought to "establish and maintain a secure and stable environment" (Mendiburu and Meek 1996, 15, citing UN Security Council Resolution 940). The mandate for disarmament here was less specific than in Nicaragua and other cases. Nevertheless, the occupying forces undertook takeover of the heavy weapons company of the Haitian army, seizure of arms found in vehicles, disarmament of the feared attaché militia, and "initiation of a weapons control program that included a buyback program designed to rid the streets of as many illegally-held weapons as possible" (Mendiburu and Meek 1996, 19, 21). The gun buyback effort was similar to previous ones conducted by the United States, as in Panama during the 1980s. Cash was paid only for weapons deemed functional. The Americans invested nearly $2 million in the program, which ended in mid-1995 with 13,281 weapons and munitions pieces collected, much of them in poor condition. Prices paid, which ranged from $100 for a handgun to $600 for heavy and large-caliber weapons, were initially below the black market level, which restricted customers. Prices were soon raised, however, nearly doubling by early 1995. Some additional 2,000 weapons were seized from police stations and prisons, and more through roadside checkpoints. Haitians were allowed to keep arms in their homes, however, according to the constitution. All of this came in the context of a relatively effective UN arms embargo as well (Mendiburu and Meek 1996, 25–32). The isolation of the island country (despite the shared border with the Dominican Republic) and the heavy U.S. military presence basically allowed the fulfillment of the evolving mission in this case, although some significant arms probably were unaccounted for.

The Cambodian operation was one of unprecedented size and challenge, involving the withdrawal of foreign forces and equipment as well as domestic reconciliation (more than 200,000 forces had to be reintegrated into society). The UN Transitional Authority in Cambodia (UNTAC) was charged with such formidable missions as finding and destroying arms caches and de-mining the countryside. In 1992, the Khmer Rouge simply refused to comply with the disarmament provisions, and therefore the other parties refused as well. While efforts to force their disarmament were discussed, the United Nations backed off from such an undertaking at that time. It was argued that had UNTAC deployed more promptly, it might have calmed the situation so the provisions could have been met, but this is not at all clear. Logistical concerns abounded, such as demands for staffing the many "regroupment sites" since the various forces were scattered so widely. Dry and rainy seasons were concerns, as was the popular fear of reintegrating former soldiers into society with possibly resultant crime and banditry (Cox 1996, 97–107).

The challenge for two United Nations Protection Force (UNPROFOR) missions in Bosnia and Croatia in the early 1990s was about as complicated and diverse as in Cambodia. Again it ranged from supervising withdrawal of outside forces to demobilization of combat units, border patrol, and de-mining.

UNPROFOR's methods included checkpoints on roads and paths for inspection of vehicles and individuals. The results here were mixed, with success coming mostly in the West (in or near Croatia), especially in initial demobilization provisions and the removal or relocation of heavy weapons (in some cases to be reaccessed later by fighters). Failures mainly came in subsequent violations by the parties. The most serious of these was the reconstitution of Serb militia as self-styled local police units armed with armored personnel carriers, mortars, and machine guns. One of the markers of success was the presence in some cases of well-armed and well-prepared UN forces in some sectors, as in a Canadian deployment, concentrating forces to achieve "tactical disarmament objectives" (Cox 1996, 114). In line with attempts to rescue endangered ethnic enclaves, local UN commanders brokered and initially implemented an agreement for the surrender and demilitarization of Srebrenica in 1993, but this was not sufficient to prevent the ultimate disaster that befell that town and others even as UN forces watched.

The mission of the United Nations Operation in Somalia II (UNOSOM II) seemed relatively straightforward in the Addis Ababa peace agreement of early 1993. It involved reclaiming all heavy weapons from the rival political movements (storing them in special secured cantonments), creating encampments for disarming (small arms) and demobilizing militia, and disarming and rehabilitating bandits and other armed elements. As governmental reconstitution developed, a joint UN–Somali council would determine which arms would be destroyed and which would be handed over to the new government forces (Cox 1996, 123–26). Obviously, the simplicity was deceptive. Unlike Cambodia, UNOSOM II was conceived with an enforcement mandate, with forces entitled to seize and destroy arms from noncooperating factions. The mission began, though, with the prior United Task Force (UNITAF) negotiating voluntary weapon turn-ins at camps guarded by the militia themselves but subject to inspection.

As UNOSOM's deployment neared, its greater mandate frightened the militia leaders enough about losing control that they reclaimed their guns. NGO aid organizations also often hired for protection the very armed elements the United Nations was trying to disarm, thus creating friction between the United Nations and relief workers. Peacekeepers toyed with an incentive gun buyback program (guns for food), but backed off, concluding that there were so many arms in the country that to provide food incentives would merely fuel the corruption and the weapons trade. UNOSOM's own efforts were derailed in 1993 when Pakistan's inspection team was ambushed by Somali General Hussein Aideed's militia, suffering severe losses. The United Nations reverted to locally negotiated efforts, some involving "weapon-free zones" or arrangements for carrying and storing small arms. In other areas, the inspectors backed off disarmament attempts in order to cement better local relations with various militia. Peacekeepers did get more serious and aggressive with the Aideed forces in 1993, destroying some 400 machine guns, 50 armored vehicles, and 400 artillery pieces. This weakened but did not eliminate the resistance, however. Growing strains, conflicts, and misunderstandings among governments and commanders on the UN side clearly hampered and ultimately doomed the disarmament process alongside all the other enforcement mandates (Cox 1996, 127–29).

Basic consensus on the disarmament mandate did facilitate successes in Central America, and to a degree, Cambodia, at least in such tasks as sealing cross-border weapons traffic. Cooperation of the supplying countries helped in these cases. In Haiti, forces led by the United States, with a massive advantage in firepower, evolved a disarmament mandate and an effective strategy as they went. With the porous borders surrounding Bosnia and Somalia, on the other hand, and with militia arms advantages, weapons trafficking and stockpiling continued. Delayed deployment along with insufficient UN forces and preparation bedeviled micro-disarmament efforts in several cases. Expecting successful coercive disarmament through UN or IGO forces also can be expecting too much, as the cases of Somalia and, to an extent, Bosnia show. Motives on the spot can be mixed as various peacekeepers or relief workers negotiate directly with armed groups, sometimes for protection or security. The Security Council and member governments must be more willing to undertake joint offensive military enforcement on the ground (Cox 1996, 132–33).

External peacekeepers, generally, are likely to favor hastening arms decommissioning processes, since they face dangers daily from armed gangs, roving bands, extremist militia, and youthful fighters. Indeed, in many ethnopolitical wars, particularly in Africa, youths have come to play a predominant combat role. Such soldiers are usually tragically ill prepared for peacetime life, often having known only warfare since childhood. The effective pacification of conflicts requires that these individuals, as well as their adult counterparts and bosses, are not only disarmed and prosecuted for crimes, but also offered some hope of a useful civilian life and livelihood. This is especially difficult in war-torn and already backward economies.

Turning to other forms of multilateral disarmament efforts, in September 1999, NATO and the KLA leadership held extended negotiations over the issue of demilitarization. The plan under discussion was to transform the guerrilla organization into a 5,000-strong civilian "Kosovo Corps" to perform humanitarian and rescue missions in the context of an evolving peace. The group would be only lightly armed. The KLA, however, objected to various points reportedly including the name "Kosovo Corps," its administration, and the low limit on arms. NATO also had to contend with strong Russian and Serb objections to the KLA remaining a viable fighting force and independence movement.

Some KLA disarmament initially took place with the handover of AK-47 rifles to NATO troops and with the return of some rebels to civilian life. However, the KLA by no means reverted to a civilian corps status. Serbia charged that guerrillas mounted incursions into Serbia in November 1999 across the border patrolled by NATO, two months after the decommissioning agreement (KLA Demilitarization Delayed 1999). Subsequently in 2000 and 2001, such raids persisted, as Serbs contended that the NATO buffer zone provided the KLA with staging areas to attack inside Serbia. The issue threatened to reignite the war.

Aside from micro-disarmament involving military operations, there have been important diplomatic initiatives as well. Primary among these was Ambassador Mitchell's Northern Ireland mediation effort. This often involved artful political and diplomatic negotiation and the careful drafting of agreements to allow the peace process to continue even amid disagreement on its terms. One variation to get past the refusal of disputants to turn over or "decommission" arms, for example, ultimately in 1999 was the agreement to store weapons visible "beyond use" at certain sites remote from the major battlegrounds or away from cities. This would enhance inspection prospects (carried out initially in 2000 by international monitors: former government and party officials from South Africa and Finland [see Stohl 2000]) and put some distance between ethnic fighters and their arms and ammunition stores.

Commenting on the difficulties of Northern Irish negotiations among parties that, despite two-year-old peace accords, still were barely willing even to speak to each other, Mitchell described a hastily devised tactic. As the parties faced a deadlock over IRA weapon decommissioning in 1999, he asked the negotiators to drop discussion of interests and demands, and instead merely exchange their own hopes and fears for the coming years. Through this listening process, he felt that he allowed a modicum of cooperation to seep into the discussions, as the parties came for the first time to at least a minimal understanding of each other's deeply felt ideals, insecurities, and distrust (Mitchell 1999).

Skeptics might say that such tenuous demilitarization terms are a thinly veiled permit for continued military presence. Nevertheless, if peace negotiators and peacekeepers are serious about limiting violence through arms control, despite personnel and funding shortages, sufficient inspection machinery can be built into agreements at least to politically satisfy the constituents. Arms confiscation and inspection need not account for every single weapon, but as with weapons of mass destruction at the international level, parties must strive for a satisfactory level of reassurance, balance, and early warning whereby they can at least rest easy at night. If official agreements clearly spell out the limits of armament, there are grounds to monitor and to report on the arms, as in Iraq. Certainly, much was learned about Iraqi disruptive capabilities and intentions from such an inspection regime. However, the inspection machinery can itself become a point of contention depending upon its composition and degree of intrusiveness.[9] Diplomatic pressure might be necessary to broaden internal arms inspection and decommissioning regimes. Diligence similar to that displayed against Saddam Hussein's regime would have to accompany all ethnic peacekeeping operations. This takes requisite funding, organization, cohesion, and political will. The task is not impossible, but it clearly represents a prime challenge for future world order.

CONCLUSION

Western powers have spent a great deal of money since 1990 subsidizing the decommissioning of nuclear arms and the alternate use of weapon designers in Russia and the former Soviet Union. This investment was considered imperative for stabilizing global security in the face of great financial pressures and temptations to release sensitive technologies. Likewise, there have been major diplomatic attempts to convince arms exporting states, ranging from Russia to Israel, India, and China to refrain from sending advanced technologies to certain distrusted recipients. It would seem that this level of concern should now extend to the small-arms trade, to the black and gray markets, to weapon smuggling, and to recalcitrant local militia. Despite the rationale and zeal that ethno-nationalists feel for their causes, if the international community sees intervention in such disputes as imperative in regard to standards of law and if the entry of peacekeepers is duly authorized or negotiated, then those charged with finding and eliminating the armed threats to the peace must be adequately supported.

In this study we have seen the urgent need for greater global transparency in reporting on small-arms transactions. In addition to early warning, this is related to the necessity of providing arms baselines from which micro-disarmament efforts can verifiably proceed. We have seen that arms acquisitions before and during wars often lead to enlarged violence and frequently to hurting stalemates as well. We have seen that combatant-group arms acquisitions tend to attract outside intervention and conflict resolution attempts, while those of governments tend to preclude them. We have seen that arms meant for one dispute often wind up fueling violence in subsequent disputes throughout the region and the world. With due recognition to the limits of available data, and hopefully with the intent of increasing open reporting on legal, illegal, and covert transactions, policy makers can wisely use these and other findings presented here in deciding whom to arm, to what extent, and when and whom to disarm by what means and under what terms.

As noted in the preface, the severe violence in Israel and the Palestinian territories in 2000 and 2001 should be a prod to arms control as a key element in peace negotiations. In one of the archetypal ethnic conflicts of the past century, mounting arms availability appeared to carry away political decision makers on both sides. Palestinians could shoot guns and mortars as well as throw stones, Israelis could readily respond with what many would label disproportionate force—helicopter gun ships, antitank weapons, battle tanks, F-16s—against protesters, Palestinian police, and armed Fatah and Hamas factions. The preferred Israeli approach appeared to be to shoot from a distance when possible rather than attempting close-quarter crowd control. Therefore, the casualties mounted lopsidedly on the Palestinian side, and came to include Israeli Arab citizens for the first time as well, but the pain, trauma, and anger spread to both sides. While the decision to take to the streets and respond with live ammunition were not direct products of arms availability alone, it seems that they were conditioned by advancing arms technologies and availability as well as by strategic planning and foreign military assistance and sales.

Therefore, it can be argued that governments can be over-armed, especially in domestic settings, with catastrophic consequences, or they can be armed mainly for international warfare when better-developed antiriot and nonlethal technologies might be available for domestic insurrections. Ironically, even well-armed governments, such as those in Belgrade, Tehran, Johannesburg, and Moscow cannot stem the tide of domestic resistance if it goes beyond a certain point. This is a serious dilemma that must be faced by the international community and in bilateral and multilateral peace negotiations. People kill people, but guns make it easier and high armament levels provoke as well as retard entrenched resistance. This was the case when armed Rwandan forces compelled one ethnic community to chop up its counterparts with primitive implements. It is the case when well-armed governments such as those in Indonesia, Mexico, and Serbia unleash ad hoc ethnic militia to wreak havoc on opposition groups, and when decision makers can too easily and recklessly revert to heavy-handed military solutions in the face of unresolved ethnopolitical grievances and uprisings.

This chapter has shown that arms control and micro-disarmament are possible but exceedingly difficult in intense conflict situations. They require commitment, innovation, persistence, sage judgment, and considerable third-party support. Nevertheless, agreement and effective acts to limit and remove arms from the fray, including international assistance in doing so, can pay extensive dividends in peace processes.

NOTES

1. See Boutwell and Klare 2000. They also call for major military suppliers—the United States, Russia, China, the United Kingdom, and France—along with other European, Asian, and Latin American exporting states to adopt stricter laws and export standards especially regarding exports to "areas of instability."

2. As noted, arms are acquired not just through importation, but also domestically. Embargoes, export controls, and similar actions speak little to domestic procurement, although if successful, they might prevent resupply and thus indirectly affect the amount of arms in a war. For example, if ammunition and spare parts are successfully blocked, domestic weapon procurement loses appeal.

3. Among the varied UN provisions related to micro-disarmament are General Assembly Resolution 40/151H (1985) providing for advisory services to member states; General Assembly Resolution 46/36 H (1991) on the illicit trade in small arms; UN Disarmament Commission Working Group (after 1995) for guidelines on arms transfers; General Assembly Resolution 49/75 G (1994) welcoming Mali's initiatives for Saharan Africa; Security Council Resolution 1013 (September 1995) for an International Commission of Inquiry regarding arms supplies to Rwanda; UN Center for Disarmament Affairs micro-disarmament workshop (November 1995); Ninth UN Congress on the Prevention of Crime and the

Treatment of Offenders (April–May 1995), a resolution on regular intergovernmental exchange of information on illicit firearms trafficking; General Assembly Resolution A/RES/50/70 B (1995) requesting the establishment of a group of experts to report on small arms; and the UN Institute for Disarmament Research (UNIDIR) Disarmament and Conflict Resolution Project (1996) (see Laurance and Meek 1996, 7–9).

4. Lumpe also notes that much of this flood of small arms entered into illegal circulation, with large numbers of U.S.-originated firearms unlawfully acquired, particularly in Mexico, after retransfer from initial legal sales.

5. See Mandel (1999, 44). Indeed, given a combination of military pressure, security, and commercial interests, the United States did not even sign the global land mine convention in the early 1990s.

6. It is, of course, difficult to grapple with the sovereignty issue in devising such guarantees. The example of U.S. and British planes flying protection over Kurdish enclaves in Iraq is unique and unusual, devised at a time when these powers had direct military control over large segments of Iraq in the early 1990s. Normally protective provisions would have to be negotiated at length with the host government involved.

7. Unfortunately, population mixes are sometimes complex and also complicated by class hierarchies so that reversion to one group's increased autonomy can be seen to threaten others. Such has been the case in the Indian state of Assam, for example, where Assamese prominence tends to be seen as hegemonic by the local hill tribes. See, for example, Phukon (2000, 6). Therefore, one does not know quite whom to empower with local autonomy and how much that might entail the right of armament.

8. Cox (1996, 91) also notes that the Nicaraguan success depended on somewhat special circumstances in that the Sandanistas were defeated at the polls, thus removing the Contra's raison d'être. The Contra's main arms supplier, the United States, also quit the war effort and reverted to supporting the peace process. Craft and Smaldone (2001) also found that economic vitality acted as an antidote to the outbreak of violence in Africa.

9. One of the points of contention surrounding these inspections of course was the Iraqi charge that American intelligence officers were part of the inspection team. This appears to have been the case, but the United States argued that weapons inspection often involves skills best handled by intelligence experts. Clearly, the mistrust engendered by such a contingent can be detrimental to the political prospects of inspection regimes.

Bibliography

Abrams, Jason. 1995. Burundi: Anatomy of an Ethnic Conflict. *Survival* 37:144–64.

Abrashi, Fisnik. 2001. Albanians Lay Aside Weapons in Southern Serbia. Associated Press. May 22.

ACDA (U.S. Arms Control and Disarmament Agency). 1996. *World Military Expenditures and Arms Transfers, 1995*. Washington, D.C.: U.S. Government Printing Office.

Afghanistan's Neighbors Carry On Playing the Great Game. 1995. *Jane's Defence Weekly* 24 (December 9): 14.

Africa Research Bulletin. 1998. (July 1–31): 13184.

———. 1997. (July 1–31):12757–58.

———. 1995. (March 1–31):11789–90.

———. 1994a. (December 1–31):11667–69.

———. 1994b. (April 1–30):11406.

Africa Watch. 1993. *Divide and Rule: State-Sponsored Ethnic Violence in Kenya.* New York: Human Rights Watch.

Algeria Accuses bin Laden of Financing Islamic Terrorists. 1998. *Deutsche Press-Agentur*, October 8.

Anderson, Marion. 1978. *The Empty Pork Barrel: Unemployment and the Pentagon Budget*. Lansing, Mich.: PIRGIM.

Arming the IRA. 1990. *Economist* 314 (March 31):19–22.

Arms to Bosnia: Serbs Still Win. 1994. *Economist* 332 (August 6): 41.

Asia Watch. 1993. *The Human Rights Crisis in Kashmir*. New York: Human Rights Watch.

Assefa, Hizkias. 1987. *Mediation of Civil Wars: Approaches and Strategies—the Sudan Conflict*. Boulder: Westview.

Associated Press. More than 25 Bombs Dropped on Southern Sudan During the Last Week. March 27, 2000.

Austin, Dennis, and Anirudha Gupta. 1988. *Lions and Tigers: The Crisis in Sri Lanka*. Conflict Studies No. 211. London: Centre for Security and Conflict Studies, Institute for the Study of Conflict.

Avery, William. 1978. Domestic Influences on Latin American Importation of U.S. Armaments. *International Studies Quarterly* 22:121–42.

Bandit Country. 1988. *Economist* 307 (May 7): 38, 42.

Barber, Tony. 1994. Romania Rejects Special Status for Its Hungarians. *The Independent.* August 11, p. 11.

Barnes, John. 1987. Kurds Locked in One More Losing War? *U.S. News & World Report* 103 (November 9): 55.

Baruah, Sanjib. 1994. The State and Separatist Militancy in Assam. *Asian Survey* 34:863–77.

Baugh, William, and Michael Squires. 1983. Arms Transfers and the Onset of War Part I: Scalogram Analysis of Transfer Patterns. *International Interactions* 10:39–63.

Beaver, Paul. 1994. Flashpoints. *Jane's Defence Weekly* 22 (September 10).

Bedi, Rahul. 1995. Casualties Rise in Kashmir. *Jane's Defence Weekly* 23 (January 28): 18.

———. 1994. India Says It Is Winning against Separatists. *Jane's Defence Weekly* 22 (December 10):12.

Beecher, William. 1991. Vigilante Rumblings in Russia Raise Fears of Warfare. *Minneapolis–St. Paul Star Tribune,* November 24, p. 3.

Bell, J. Bowyer. 1978. Arms Transfers, Conflict, and Violence at the Substate Level. In *Arms Transfers to the Third World,* edited by Uri Ra'anan, Robert Pfaltzgraff, and Geoffrey Kemp. Boulder: Westview, 309–23.

Benjamin, Robert. 1995. Mediator as Trickster: The Folkoric Figure as Professional Role Model. *Mediation Quarterly* 113, no. 2 (Winter 1995): 131–64.

Bercovitch, Jacob, J., Theodore Anagnoson, and Donnette Wille. 1991. Some Conceptual Issues and Empirical Trends in the Study of Successful Mediation in International Relations. *Journal of Peace Research* 28, no. 1:7–17.

Berenson, Douglas. 1992. Weapons Monitors, No-Fly Zone Fail to Stem Bosnian Violence. *Arms Control Today* 22 (October): 35, 41.

Berkeley, Bill. 1993. An African Horror Story. *Atlantic* 272 (August): 20–28.

Bespalov, Yury, and Valery Yakov. 1995. Who Armed Dzhokhar Dudayev? *Current Digest of the Post-Soviet Press* 47 (February 8): 8. Translation. Originally published in *Izvestia,* January 10, pp. 1–2.

Blaustein, Susan. 1990. The Insurgents. *Nation* 250:600.

Blechman, Barry, and Stephen Kaplan. 1978. *Force without War.* Washington, D.C.: Brookings Institution.

Bloodbath. 1994. *Economist* 331 (April 2): 41.

Blood in the Square. 1990. *Time* 135, no. 14 (April 2): 33.

Bohlen, Celestine, 1997. On Divided Isle of Cyprus, Missile Deal Widens Rift. *New York Times,* January 18, p. 2.

Bonner, Raymond. 1998a. Tamil Guerrillas in Sri Lanka: Deadly and Armed to the Teeth. *New York Times,* March 7, pp. 1, 3.

———. 1998b. The Murky Life of an International Gun Dealer. *New York Times,* July 14, p. 3.

———. 1998c. Bulgaria Becomes a Weapons Bazaar. *New York Times,* August 3, p. 3.

Boutwell, Jeffrey, and Michael Klare. 2000. A Scourge of Small Arms. *Scientific American* 282 (June 2000): 48–53.

———. 1999. *Light Weapons and Civil Conflict.* Lanham, Md.: Rowman & Littlefield.

Boutwell, Jeffrey, Michael Klare, and Laura Reed, eds. 1995. *Lethal Commerce: The Global Trade in Small Arms and Light Weapons.* Cambridge, Mass.: American Academy of Arts and Sciences.

Brem, Stefan. 2001. Restricting the Illicit Trade in and the Misuse of Small Arms and Light Weapons: What Can We Learn from Ottawa. Paper presented at the annual meeting of the International Studies Association, Chicago, February.

Brown, James. 1995. The Turkish Imbroglio: Its Kurds. *Annals of the American Academy of Political and Social Science* 541:116–29.

Brown, Justin. 1998. KLA's Blind One Speaks Candidly about the Kosovo War. *Christian Science Monitor,* September 3, p. 6.

Brown, Lester R. et. al. 1998. State of the World 1998: A Worldwatch Institute Report on Progress Toward a Sustainable Society. New York: Norton.

Brown, Michael E., ed. 1996. *The International Dimensions of Internal Conflict.* Cambridge, Mass.: MIT Press.

———. 1993. Causes and Implications of Ethnic Conflict. In *Ethnic Conflict and International Security.* Edited by Michael Brown. Princeton, N.J.: Princeton University Press, 3–26.

Brown, Michael E., et al., eds. 1997. *Nationalism and Ethnic Conflict.* Cambridge, Mass.: MIT Press.

Brown, Michael E., Sean M. Lynn-Jones, and Steven E. Miller, eds. 1996. *Debating the Democratic Peace.* Cambridge, Mass.: MIT Press.

Brzoska, Michael, and Thomas Ohlson. 1987. *Arms Transfers to the Third World, 1971–1985.* Oxford: Oxford University Press.

Brzoska, Michael, and Frederic S. Pearson. 1994. *Arms and Warfare: Escalation, De-escalation, Negotiation.* Columbia: University of South Carolina Press.

Buchan, David. 1998. Radical Groups Arming Kosovo Albanians. *Financial Times,* May 8, p. 3.

Bugajski, Janusz. 1997. Containing a Kosovo Crisis. *Christian Science Monitor,* June 30, p. 19.

Burke, Jason. 1992. Moldova Calls on Russia To End Aid to Separatists. *Christian Science Monitor,* May 27, 1992, p. 3.

Burns, John. 1995. In Sri Lanka, Glimmer of Peace After Years of War. *New York Times,* April 16, p. 8.

———. 1994. Sri Lankan Rebels and New Government Agree to Talks. *New York Times,* September 5, p. 5.

Byrne, Sean. 2001. The Role for Complementarity: Consociational and Civic Society Approaches to Peacebuilding in Northern Ireland. *Journal of Peace Research* 36, no. 2, forthcoming.

Campbell, Kurt M. 1988. Soviet Policy in Southern Africa: Angola and Mozambique. In *Regional Conflict and U.S. Policy,* edited by Richard J. Bloomfield. Algonac, Mich.: Reference Publications, 89–119.

Capturing Kabul: Afghan Civil War Set to Enter New Phase. 1995. *Jane's Defence Weekly* 23 (April 22): 19–20.

Carlson, Lisa. 1995. A Theory of Escalation and International Conflict. *Journal of Conflict Resolution* 39 (September): 511–34.

Carment, David. 1994. The Ethnic Dimension in World Politics: Theory, Policy, and Early Warning. *Third World Quarterly* 15, no. 4:551–82.

Carment, David, and Patrick James. 1996. Two-Level Games and Third-Party Intervention: Evidence from Ethnic Conflict in Balkans and South Asia. *Canadian Journal of Political Science* 29, no. 3:21–554.

Castle, Robert, and Abdel Faau Musah. 1998. *Eastern Europe's Arsenal on the Loose: Managing Light Weapons Flow to Conflict Zones.* London & New York: BASIC Papers, Occasional Papers on International Security, No. 26, May.

Catrina, Christian. 1994. Main Directions of Research in the Arms Trade. *Annals of the American Academy of Political and Social Science* 35 (September): 190–205.

Chalmers, Malcolm, and Owen Greene. 1995. *Taking Stock: The UN Register after Two Years.* Boulder, Colo.: Westview.

Chossudovsky, Michel. 1999. Kosovo Freedom Fighters Financed by Organized Crime. *World Socialist* Web site, published by the International Committee of the Fourth International, April. <http://www.wsws.org/articles/1999/apr1999/kla-a10.shtml>.

Claiborne, William. 1983. Sri Lanka's Tamil Stronghold Is Tense Under Tight Security. *Washington Post,* August 5, p. A1.

Clinton, William. 1995. Policy Statement on American Arms Exports. *Presidential Directive* 34. Washington, D.C.: National Security Council.

Colarusso, John. 1995. Chechnya: The War without Winners. *Current History* 94 (October): 329–36.

Conflict in Kashmir Continues. 1993. *Jane's Defence Weekly* 20 (July 3): 21.

Cooper, Robert, and Mats Berdal. 1993. Outside Intervention in Ethnic Conflicts. In *Ethnic Conflict and International Security,* edited by Michael Brown. Princeton, N.J.: Princeton University Press, 181–205.

Costly Campaign. 1987. *Economist* 305 (November 28): 36.

Cox, David. 1996. Peacekeeping and Disarmament: Peace Argreements, Security Council Mandates, and the Disarmament Experience. In *Managing Arms in Peace Processes: The Issues.* Geneva: United Nations Institute for Disarmament Research, 83–133.

Craft, Cassady. 1999. *Weapons for Peace, Weapons for War: The Effect of Arms Transfers on War Outbreak, Involvement, and Outcomes.* New York: Routledge.

Craft, Cassady, and Joseph Smaldone. 2001. The Arms Trade and Conflict Incidence in Sub-Saharan Africa, 1967–1997. Paper presented at the annual meeting of the International Studies Association, Chicago, February.

Crosette, Barbara. 1999. U.N. Details Its Failure to Stop '95 Bosnia Massacre. *New York Times.* November 16, p. A3.

———. 1998. U.N. Chief Reports Little Help in Monitoring Balkan Arms Ban. *New York Times,* August 11, p. 3.

Curbing Small Arms. 2001. *New York Times.* April 10, p. 20.

Czech Weapons for Islamic Extremists in Algeria. 1996. Czech News Agency National News Wire, September 8.

Da Costa, Peter. 1993. Talking Tough. *Africa Report* 38 (January/February): 18–21.

———. 1991. Peace for a Province. *Africa Report* 36 (September/October): 52–54.

Darby, John, and Roger MacGinity, eds. 2000. *The Management of Peace Processes.* Houndmills, Hampshire, U.K.: MacMillan.

Davies, Derek. 1989. Four Rays of Hope. *Far Eastern Economic Review* 143 (March 23): 20–22.

Deadlier Intifadah: Palestinians. 1992. *Economist* 323 (April 11): 43.

De Silva, Manik. 1995a. Back to War. *Far Eastern Economic Review* 158 (May 25): 21.

———. 1995b. Tigers and Tanks. *Far Eastern Economic Review* 158, no. 30:24, 26.

Death Toll in Ethnic Violence in Sri Lanka Revised to 362. 1983. *New York Times,* August 11, p. 6.

Deng, Francis, Sadikiel Kimaro, Terrence Lyons, Donald Rothchild, and I. William Zartman. 1996. *Sovereignty as Responsibility: Conflict Management in Africa.* Washington, D.C.: Brookings Institution.

Desmond, Edward. 1991. Sri Lanka's Tamil Tigers. *Time* 138 (September 16): 41.

Dinmore, Guy. 1997. Kosovo's Albanian Rebels Take Up Arms. *Financial Times,* December 20, p. 2.

Dixon, William. 1996. Third-Party Techniques for Preventing Conflict Escalation and Promoting Peaceful Settlement. *International Organization* 50 (Autumn): 653–81.

Dobbs, Michael. 1992. Russian Troops Caught In Growing Ethnic Strife; Pullouts Spark Controversy in Karabakh, Moldova. *Washington Post,* March 4, p. 16.

Doherty, Carroll. 1995. The Arms Embargo Dilemma: Questions and Answers. *Congressional Quarterly Weekly* 53:2008–10.

Donnelly, Jack.1995. The Past, Present, and the Future Prospects. In *International Organizations and Ethnic Conflict,* edited by Milton Esman and Shibley Telhami. Ithaca, N.Y.: Cornell University Press, 48–71.

Don't Feed the Tigers. 1987. *Economist* 303 (June 13): 14.

Doyle, Michael. 1995. Liberalism and World Politics Revisited. In *Controversies in International Relations Theory: Realism and the Neoliberal Challenge,* edited by Charles Kegley. New York: St. Martin's, 83–106.

Drying Up. 1991. *The Economist* 321 (November 2): 41–42.

Dupuy, Trevor Nevitt, and Wendell Blanchard. 1972. The Almanac of World Military Power, 2d. ed. New York: R. R. Bowker.

Ecuador/Peru Pledge Arms Freeze. 1999. *Arms Trade News* (February): 1, 3. 80 Per Cent of Islamic Fighters Lay Down Arms. 2000. *Montreal Gazette,* January 20, p. 18.

Ellingsen, Tanja. 2000. Colorful Community or Ethnic Witches' Brew? *Journal of Conflict Resolution* 44 (April): 28–249.

Empire Falls to Bits. 1992. *Economist* 323 (April 11): 44, 48.

Ethnic Purification Taking Place in North Ossetia: Official. 1992. Agence France Presse, November 28, 1992.

EU–U.S. Meet to Discuss Small Weapons. 1999. *Arms Trade News* (July): 1.

Erwin, Sandra. 1998. U.S. Interests Undermined by Unlawful Firearms Trade. *National Defense* 82 (May/June): 32.

Evangelista, Matthew. 1996. Historical Legacies and the Politics of Intervention in the Former Soviet Union. In *The International Dimensions of Internal Conflict,* edited by Michael Brown. Cambridge, Mass.: MIT Press, 107–40.

Fearon, James, and David Laitin. 1996. Explaining Interethnic Cooperation. *American Political Science Review* 90 (December): 715–35.

Feinstein, Lee. 1992. Relief Forces in Somalia Facing Country Awash in Small Arms. *Arms Control Today* 22 (December): 20, 25.

Financial Times. 1999. November 27, p. 5.

Freed, Kenneth. 1988. Shift Seen in Palestinian Unrest Tactics. *Los Angeles Times,* February 25, p. 1.

From Dream to Nightmare. 1991. *Economist* 320 (June 29): 36–37.

Fukuyama, Francis. 1992. *The End of History and the Last Man.* New York: Free Press.

Gabelnik, Tamar. 1999. U.S. Training: Impact on Chiapas. *Arms Sales Monitor* no. 40 (May).

Gall, Carlotta. 1999. Albanians in Kosovo Grateful U.S. Army Is There. *New York Times,* November 24, p. A12.

Ganguly, Rajat, and Ray Taras. 1998. *Understanding Ethnic Conflict: The International Dimension.* New York: Longman.

Gargan, Edward. 1993. Sri Lanka is Choking Off Long Ethnic Revolt. *New York Times,* March 20, pp. 1, 5.

German Court Convicts Four Algerian Smugglers. 1997. *New York Times,* June 24, p. 8.

Gerner, Deborah. 1983. Arms Transfers to the Third World: Research on Patterns, Causes and Effects. *International Interactions* 10 (August): 5–37.

God Helps, So Does Iran. 1991. *Economist* 318 (April 27): 46–47.

Goldring, Natalie. 1997. Bridging the Gap: Light and Major Conventional Weapons in Recent Conflicts. Paper presented at the 1997 annual meeting of the International Studies Association, Toronto.

Goose, Stephen, and Frank Smyth. 1994. Arming Genocide in Rwanda. *Foreign Affairs* 73 (September/October): 86–96.

Grillot, Suzette R. 2001. Small Arms, Big Problems: IANSDA and the Making of a Transnational Advocacy Network. Paper presented at the annual meeting of the International Studies Association, Chicago, February.

Grobar, Lisa Morris, and Shiranthi Gnanaselvam. 1993. The Economic Effects of the Sri Lankan Civil War. *Economic Development and Social Change* 41 (January): 396–405.

Gunasekera, Rohan. 1996. Arms Pour in as Sri Lanka Prepares for Long War. *Reuters.* January 12.

Gonchar, Ksenia and Peter Lock. 1995. Small Arms and Light Weapons: Russia and the Former Soviet Union. In *Lethal Commerce,* edited by Jeffrey Boutwell, Michael Klare, and Laura Reed. Cambridge, Mass.: American Academy of Arts and Sciences, 116–23.

Gurr, Ted Robert. 2000a. Ethnic Warfare on the Wane. *Foreign Affairs* 79 (May/June): 52–64.

———. 2000b. *Peoples Versus States: Minorities at Risk in the New Century.* Washington, D.C.: U.S. Institute of Peace Press.

———. 1998. A Risk Assessment Model of Ethnopolitical Rebellion. *Preventive Measures: Building Risk Assessment and Crisis Early Warning Systems,* edited by John Davies and Ted Gurr. Lanham, Md.: Rowman & Littlefield, 15–26.

———. 1994. Peoples Against States: Ethnopolitical Conflict and the Changing World System. *International Studies Quarterly* 38 (September): 347–77.

———. 1993. *Minorities at Risk.* Washington, D.C.: United States Institute of Peace Press.

Gurr, Ted Robert, and Barbara Harff. 1994. *Ethnic Conflict and World Politics.* Boulder, Colo.: Westview.

Gurr, Ted Robert, and Will Moore. 1997. Ethnopolitical Rebellion: A Cross-Sectional Analysis of the 1980s with Risk Assessments for the 1990s. *American Journal of Political Science* 41 (October): 1079–1103.

Gurr, Ted Robert, Monty Marshall, and Deepa Khosla. 2000. Peace and Conflict 2001: A Global Survey of Armed Conflicts, Self-Determination Movements, and Democracy. College Park, Md.: Center for International Development and Conflict Management.

Hammer, Joshua. 1995. Fears of "Another Rwanda." *Newsweek* 125 (April 10): 38–39.

Harff, Barbara, and Ted Gurr. 1998. Systematic Early Warning of Humanitarian Emergencies. *Journal of Peace Research* 35, no. 5:551–79.

Harkavy, Robert. 1979. Arms Transfers in the Modern World. New York: Praeger.

Hartung, William. 1995a. Nixon's Children: Bill Clinton and the Permanent Arms Bazaar. *World Policy Journal* 12 (Summer): 25–35.

———. 1995b. *U.S. Weapons at War.* New York: Arms Trade Resource Center, World Policy Institute.

Hazarika, Sanjoy. 1987. India Says Delay in Sri Lanka is Result of Tamils' Rivalries. *New York Times,* August 15, p. 3.

Hermida, Alfred. 1993. The Forgotten Front. *Africa Report* 38 (May/June): 41–43.

Hey, Anybody Want a Gun? 1998. *Economist* 347 (May 16): 47–48.

Holloway, Robert. 2001. NGOs Call for Tough Action by UN to Ban Fire-arms Trafficking. *Agence France Press.* March 20.

Howe, Russell Warren. 1981. *Weapons: The International Game of Arms, Money, and Diplomacy.* London: Abacus.

Hufbauer, Gary, Jeffrey Schott, and Kimberly Elliot. 1990. *Economic Sanctions Reconsidered.* 2d ed. Washington, D.C.: Institute for International Economics.

Human Rights Watch. 1999. *Angola Unravels.* New York: Human Rights Watch.

———. 1994a. *Arming Rwanda: The Arms Trade and Human Rights Abuses in the Rwandan War.* New York: Human Rights Watch, January.

———. 1994b. *Azerbaijan: Seven Years of Conflict in Nagorno-Karabakh.* New York: Human Rights Watch.

Human Rights Watch Arms Project. 1994. *Angola: Arms Trade and Violations of the Laws of War Since the 1992 Elections.* New York: Human Rights Watch.

Hundreds Flee Ethnic Battles That Killed Dozens in Nigeria. 1999. *New York Times,* November 29, p. 5.

Husbands, Jo. 1995. Controlling Transfers of Light Arms: Linkages to Conflict Processes and Conflict Resolution Strategies. In *Lethal Commerce,* edited by Jeffrey Boutwell, Michael Klare, and Laura Reed. Cambridge, Mass.: American Academy of Arts and Sciences, 127–39.

ICRC (International Committee of the Red Cross). 1999. *Arms Availability and the Situation of Citizens in Armed Conflict.* Geneva: International Committee of the Red Cross. International Peacekeeping News. 1996. no. 12 (January 21).

IISS (International Institute for Strategic Studies). (1999). The Military Balance, 1999–2000. London: International Institute for Strategic Studies.

Illarionov, Andrei. 1996. Chechen War Wrecks Economic Stabilization. *Moscow News,* February 2, p. 7.

India Troops Attack ULFA Guerrilla Camp in Bhutan. 1996. *Jane's Defence Weekly* 25 (February 28): 15.

Indonesian General Denies Ordering Atrocities in Aceh Conflict. 1999. *New York Times,* November 26, p. A8.

Ionescu, Dan. 1992. Romanian Concern over the Conflict in Moldova. *RFE/RL Research Report* 1:46–51.

Isaac, Kalpana. 1996. Sri Lanka's Ethnic Divide. *Current History* 95, no. 600:177–81.

Islamic Militants Face Up to Eight Years in Jail. 1999. *Associated Press,* April 21.

Iyad, Abu. 1990. Lowering the Sword. *Foreign Policy* 78 (Spring): 91–112.

Jane's Defence Weekly. 1994. December.

Jane's International Review.

Jayamaha, Dilshika (2000). Rebels Claim Gains in Sri Lanka. *Washington Post,* April 23, p. 27.

Jensen, Holger. 1998. New Killing Field Is Called Kosovo: Ethnic Warfare Flares Up in Another Balkan Region. *Denver Rocky Mountain News,* March 10, p. 3.

Jongman, A. J. 1999/2000. Downward Trend in Armed Conflicts Reversed. *PIOOM Newsletter* 9, no. 1:1.

Joseph, Kate. 1998. More Talk, Little Action on Light Weapons in Oslo. *Basic Reports. Newsletter of British American Security Information Council,* no. 65 (August 14).

Kalashnikovs for Chickens: Small Arms Boom in East Africa. 2001. *Africa News.* May 7.

Kalpana, Isaac. 1996. Sri Lanka's Ethnic Divide, *Current History* 95, no. 600:177–81.

Karadjis, Michael. 1999. Chossudovsky's Frame-Up of the KLA. *Green Left Weekly,* no. 360 (May 12). <http://www3.silas.unsw.edu.au/greenlft/1999/360/360p21.htm>.

Karp, Aaron. 1995. Small Arms—The New Major Weapons. In *Lethal Commerce,* edited by Jeffrey Boutwell, Michael Klare, and Laura Reed. Cambridge, Mass.: American Academy of Arts and Sciences, 17–30.

———. 1993. Arming Ethnic Conflict. *Arms Control Today* 23 (September): 9–13.

Kaufman, Stuart. 1996. Spiraling to Ethnic War: Elites, Masses, and Moscow in Moldova's Civil War. *International Security* 21 (Fall): 108–38.

Keerawella, Gamini, and Rohan Samarajiva. 1994. Sri Lanka in 1993. *Asian Survey* 34:168–74.

Keesings Record of World Events. 1994–1995.

Keller, William, and Janne Nolan. 1997/1998. The Arms Trade: Business as Usual? *Foreign Policy,* no. 109 (Winter): 113–25.

Kemp, Geoffrey. 1971. The International Arms Trade: Supplier, Recipient and Arms Control Perspectives. *Political Quarterly* 42:376–89.

Khripunov, Igor. 1999. Russia's Weapons Trade. *Problems of Post-Communism* 46 (March/April): 39–48.

Kinsella, David. 1998. Arms Transfer Dependence and Foreign Policy Conflict. *Journal of Peace Research* 35, no. 1:7–23.

———. 1995. Nested Rivalries: Superpower Competition, Arms Transfers, and Regional Conflict, 1950–1990. *International Interactions* 21, no. 2:109–25.

———. 1994a. The Impact of Superpower Arms Transfers on Conflict in the Middle East. *Defence and Peace Economics* 5 (February): 19–36.

———. 1994b. Conflict in Context: Arms Transfers and Third World Rivalry During the Cold War. *American Journal of Political Science* 38 (August): 557–81.

KLA Demilitarization Delayed. 1999. <http://www.ABCNews.com>. September 20.

Klare, Michael. 1999a. The International Trade in Light Weapons: What Have We Learned? In *Light Weapons and Civil Conflict.* Edited by Jeffrey Boutwell and Michael Klare. Lanham, Md.: Rowman and Littlefield, 9–27.

———. 1999b. The Kalashnikov Age. *Bulletin of the Atomic Scientists* 55 (January/February): 19–21.

———. 1997. The New Arms Race: Light Weapons and International Security. *Current History* 96, no. 609:173–78.

———. 1996. The Guns of Bosnia. *Nation* 262 (January 22): 23–24.

———. 1995. The Global Trade in Light Weapons and the International System in the Post–Cold War Era. In *Lethal Commerce,* edited by Jeffrey Boutwell, Michael Klare, and Laura Reed. Cambridge, Mass.: American Academy of Arts and Sciences, 31–43.

✓ Klare, Michael, and David Andersen. 1996. *A Scourge of Guns.* Washington, D.C.: Federation of American Scientists.

Kleiboer, Marieke. 1996. Understanding Success and Failure of International Mediation. *Journal of Conflict Resolution* 40, no. 2: 360–89 (June).

———. 1994. Ripeness of Conflict: A Fruitful Notion? *Journal of Peace Research* 31, no. 1:109–16.

Klepak, Hall. 1994. Rebellion Spoils Mexico's Aim for New Respectability. *Jane's Defence Weekly* 21 (January 29): 17.

Kosovo Liberation Army (KLA), Intelligence Resource Program, May 1999. Federation of American Scientists. <http://www.fas.org/irp/world/para/kla.htm>.

Krause, Keith. 1992. *Arms and the State: Patterns of Military Production and Trade*. Cambridge, U.K.: Cambridge University Press.

Kurds Bid for Freedom. 1991. *Economist* 318 (March 30): 37.

Lake, David, and Donald Rothchild. 1996. Containing Fear: The Origins and Management of Ethnic Conflict. *International Security* 21, no. 2:41–75.

Landay, Jonathan. 1998. Inside a Rebellion: Banking on War. *Christian Science Monitor*, April 15, p. 1.

Lanpher, E. Gibson. 1995. *Sri Lanka in Turmoil: Implications of Intensified Conflict*. Report prepared for Questions for the Record, Subcommittee on Asian and Pacific Affairs, Committee on International Relations, House of Representatives, 104th Cong., November 14.

Laurance, Edward J. 1999. *Light Weapons and Intrastate Conflict: Early Warning Factors and Preventative Action*. A report prepared for the Carnegie Commission on Preventing Deadly Conflict. New York, July.

———. 1992. *The International Arms Trade*. New York: Lexington.

Laurance, Edward J., and Sara Meek. 1996. The New Field of Micro-Disarmament. *Brief* 7 (September). Bonn: BICC.

Laurance, Edward J., Siemon T. Wezeman, and Herbert Wulf. 1993. *Arms Watch: SIPRI Report on the First Year of the UN Register of Conventional Arms*. Oxford: Oxford University Press.

Led by a Saint. 1993. *Economist* 329 (October 9): 36, 41.

Leontyeva, Lyudmilla. 1991. Avars Leaving Georgia. Moskovskiye Novosti, No. 21. *Russian Press Digest* (May 26): 4.

Licklider, Roy. 1995. The Consequences of Negotiated Settlements in Civil Wars, 1945–1993. *American Political Science Review* 89 (September): 681–90.

———. ed. 1993. *Stop the Killing: How Civil Wars End*. New York: New York University Press.

Lindley, Dan. 1996. Collective Security Organizations and Internal Conflict. In *The International Dimensions of Internal Conflict*, edited by Michael Brown. Cambridge, Mass.: MIT Press, 537–68.

Lintner, Bertil. 1995. The Chinese Connection. *Far Eastern Economic Review* 158 (October 18): 30.

———. 1993. One More to Go. *Far Eastern Economic Review* 156 (October 21): 32.

Lock, Peter. 1999. *Pervasive Illicit Small Arms Availability: A Global Threat*. No. 14. Helsinki: HEUNI.

Lumpe, Lora. 1999. The Leader of the Pack. Special Issue, Small Arms, Big Problems. *Bulletin of the Atomic Scientists* 55 (January/February): 27–33.

———. 1998. Small Arms Trade. *Foreign Policy in Focus* 3 (May). Albuquerque: Interhemispheric Resource Center and Institute for Policy Studies.

Lumpe, Lora, ed. 2000. *Running Guns: The Global Black Market in Small Arms*. New York: St. Martin's.

MacFarquhar, Emily. 1990. The Kashmir Question. *U.S. News & World Report* 108 (June 11): 42–44.

Malik, Michael. 1989. Island Insurrection. *Far Eastern Economic Review* 145 (August 3): 20–22.

Mandel, Robert. 1999. *Deadly Transfers and the Global Playground: Transnational Security Threats in a Disorderly World*. Westport, Conn.: Praeger.

Marsh, Virginia. 1994. Flag Law Angers Hungarians, *Financial Times*, November 11, p. 2.

✓ Mathiak, Lucy. 1995. Light Weapons and Internal Conflict in Angola. In *Lethal Commerce,* edited by Jeffrey Boutwell, Michael Klare, and Laura Reed. Cambridge, Mass.: American Academy of Arts and Sciences, 81–97.

McCoubrey, Hilaire, and Nigel White. 1995. *International Organizations and Civil Wars.* Brookfield, U.K.: Dartmouth.

McKinley, James. 1998. Fueled by Drought and War, Starvation Returns to Sudan. *New York Times,* July 24, 1, 8.

McLaughlin Mitchell, Sara, Scott Gates, and Havard Hegre. 1999. Evolution in Democracy–War Dynamics. *Journal of Conflict Resolution* 43 (December): 771–92.

McMillan, Susan. 1997. Interdependence and Conflict. *Mershon International Studies Review* 41 (May): 33–58.

Meldrum, Andrew. 1987. At War with South Africa. *Africa Report* 32 (January/February): 28.

Melman, Seymour. 1970. *Pentagon Capitalism: the Political Economy of War.* New York: McGraw-Hill.

Mendiburu, Marcus, and Sarah Meek. 1996. *Managing Arms in Peace Processes: Haiti.* Geneva: United Nations Institute for Disarmament Research.

Minneapolis–St. Paul Star Tribune. 1991. November 24, p. 3A.

Minorities at Risk Web site. <http://www.bsos.umd.edu:80/cidcm/mar/>.

Military and Arms Trade News. 1994–1995.

Mishal, Shaul, and Re'uven Aharoni, eds. 1994. *Speaking Stones: Communiqués from the Intifada Underground.* Syracuse, N.Y.: Syracuse University Press.

Mitchell, C. R. 1991. Classifying Conflicts: Asymmetry and Resolution. *The Annals of the American Academy of Political and Social Science* 518:23–38.

Mitchell, George. 1999. 12th annual lecture of the Cranbrook Peace Foundation, December 14, Bloomfield Hills, Michigan.

Moldavian Militants Threaten Sentries. 1990. *Toronto Star,* October 31, p. A16.

Montalbano, William. 1988. Israeli Officials Worry: Palestinian Uprising May Change but Endure. *Los Angeles Times.* June 5, p. 1.

Moscow Unable to End Chechen Conflict. 1995. *Asian Defense Journal* (May): 14–19.

Most, Benjamin, and Harvey Starr. 1989. *Inquiry, Logic and International Relations.* Columbia: University of South Carolina Press.

Mueller, John. 1989. *Retreat from Doomsday: The Obsolescence of Major War.* New York: Basic.

Muller, Edward N., and Erich Weede. 1990. Cross-National Variation in Political Violence: A Rational Action Approach. *Journal of Conflict Resolution* 34 (December): 624–51.

Multiplicity and Complementarity in Conflict Resolution. 2001. Panel presented at the annual meeting of the International Studies Association, Chicago, February.

Mydans, Seth. 1987. Tamil Surrender: Painful Compromise. *New York Times,* August 6, p. 3.

Myers, Steven Lee. 1999. Arms Sales Sink Globally but the U.S. Still Leads. *New York Times,* August 6.

Mystery of the Russian Arms. 1988. *Economist* 307 (June 11): 38.

✓ Naylor, R. T. 1995. The Structure and Operation of the Modern Arms Black Market. In *Lethal Commerce,* edited by Jeffrey Boutwell, Michael Klare, and Laura Reed. Cambridge, Mass.: American Academy of Arts and Sciences, 44–57.

Nemenzo, Francisco. 2000. Speech at Wayne State University, Detroit, Mich., November.

Neuffer, Elizabeth. Albania is Suddenly Awash with Guns. *Boston Globe,* March 19, 1997, p. 1.

Neuman, Stephanie. 1995. The Arms Trade, Military Assistance, and Recent Wars: Change and Continuity. *The Annals of the American Academy of Political and Social Science* 541:47–74.

New Boat People. 1991. *Economist* 319 (May 11): 31.

No Sign of KLA Action in Serbia, NATO Says. <http://www.ABCNews.com>. November 24.

O'Ballance, Edgar. 1989. *The Cyanide War*. London: Brassey's.

Oberst, Robert. 1992. A War without Winners in Sri Lanka. *Current History* 91, no. 563:128–31.

On the Dilemmas of a Horn. 1989. *Economist* 311 (June 10): 37–38.

On the Kashmir Beat. 1994. *Jane's Defence Weekly* 21 (May 21):19–20.

O'Neill, Kathryn, and Barry Munslow. 1995. Angola: Ending the Cold War in Southern Africa. In *Conflict in Africa,* edited by Oliver Furley. New York: I. B. Tauris.

O'Neill, William. 1993. Liberia: An Avoidable Tragedy. *Current History* 92:213–17.

O'Prey, Kevin P. 1995. *The Arms Export Challenge: Cooperative Approaches to Export Management and Defence Conversion.* Washington, D.C.: Brookings Institution.

Oudraat, Chantal de Jonge. 1996. The United Nations and Internal Conflict. In *The International Dimensions of Internal Conflict.* Edited by Michael Brown. Cambridge, Mass.: MIT Press, 489–536.

Out of the Bush. 1995. *Economist* 335 (May 6): 41–42.

Overview: Weapons Proliferation in East Africa and the Horn. 1999. *Small Arms Proliferation and Africa.* Addis Ababa, Ethiopia: Newsletter of the Organization of African Unity in collaboration with Institute for Security Studies, no. 3 (April/June).

Peace of a Kind. 1999. *Economist* 351 (June 19): 41–42.

Pearson, Frederic S. 1994. *The Global Spread of Arms: Political Economy of International Security.* Boulder, Colo.: Westview.

Pearson, Frederic S., Robert Baumann, and Gordon Bardos. 1989. Arms Transfers: Effects on African Interstate Wars and Interventions. *Conflict Quarterly* 9 (Winter): 36–62.

Pearson, Frederic S., Robert Baumann, and Jeffrey Pickering. 1994. Military Interventions and Realpolitik. In *Reconstructing Realpolitik.* Edited by Frank Wayman and Paul Diehl. Ann Arbor: University of Michigan Press.

Pfaffenberger, Bryan. 1988. Sri Lanka in 1987. *Asian Survey* 28, no. 2:137–47.

Phukon, Girin. 2000. Ethnic Politics in Northeast India: Understanding Elite Conflict and Political Mobilization. Paper presented at the international conference, Perspectives on Ethnicity, Identity, and State in South Asia, of the Indo-American Centre for International Studies, June 15–17, in Hyderabad, India.

Physicians for Human Rights. 1994. *Mexico: Waiting for Justice in Chiapas.* Boston: Physicians for Human Rights.

Pierre, Andrew. 1982. *The Global Politics of Arms Sales.* Princeton, N.J.: Princeton University Press.

Pierre, Andrew, and William Quandt. 1996. *The Algerian Crisis: Policy Options for the West.* Washington D.C.: Carnegie Endowment for International Peace.

Polisario Reportedly Selling Arms to Algerian FIS. 1997. MENA News Agency, 1410 GMT, February 3, in *BBC Summary of World Broadcasts,* February 5.

Posen, Barry. 1993. The Security Dilemma and Ethnic Conflict. In *Ethnic Conflict and International Security.* Edited by Michael Brown. Princeton, N.J.: Princeton University Press, 103–24. Originally published in *Survival* 35 (Spring): 27–47.

Pressberg, Gail. 1988. The Uprising: Causes and Consequences. *Journal of Palestine Studies* 17 (Spring): 38–50.

Quandt, William. 1998. *Between Ballots and Bullets.* Washington, D.C.: Brookings Institution.

Rana, Swadesh. 1995. *Small Arms and Intrastate Conflicts.* Research paper no. 34. Geneva: United Nations Institute for Disarmament Research.

Ray, James Lee. 1989. The Abolition of Slavery and the End of International War. *International Organization* 43 (Summer): 405–39.

Rahman, Reaz. 1997. Small Arms and Transparency: The Illicit Flow of Small Arms in South Asia. *Disarmament* 20, no. 2–3:79–102.

Refugee Situation Worsens in Continuing Afghan Stalemate. 1994. *Jane's Defence Weekly* 22 (December 3): 15.

Regan, Patrick. 2000. *Civil Wars and Foreign Powers: Outside Intervention in Intrastate Conflict.* Ann Arbor: University of Michigan Press.

———. 1996a. Conditions of Successful Third-Party Intervention in Intrastate Conflicts. *Journal of Conflict Resolution* 40 (June): 336–59.

———. 1996b. Decisions by Outside Actors to Intervene in Internal Conflicts. Paper presented at the annual meeting of the American Political Science Association, in San Francisco.

Rempel, William, and Sebastian Rotella. 2000. Arms Dealer Implicates Peru Spy Chief in Smuggling Ring Weapons. *Los Angeles Times,* November 1, p. A1.

Renner, Michael. 1999. Arms Control Orphans. Special Issue, Small Arms, Big Problems. *Bulletin of the Atomic Scientists* 55 (January/February): 25.

Ring, Wilson. 1987. Indians Move on Self-Rule in Honduras: Miskitos at Border Voicing Discontent. *Washington Post,* June 11, p. 33.

Risks of Getting Noticed. 1989. *Economist* 313 (October 14): 52.

Roth, Brad R. 1999. *Governmental Illegitimacy in International Law.* New York: Oxford University Press.

Rothchild, Donald. 1997. *Managing Ethnic Conflict in Africa.* Washington D.C.: Brookings Institution.

Rothchild, Donald, and Caroline Hartzell. 1995. Interstate and Intrastate Negotiations in Angola. In *Elusive Peace,* edited by I. William Zartman. Washington D.C.: Brookings Institution, 175–203.

Rothman, Jay. 1997. *Resolving Identity-Based Conflict in Nations, Organizations, and Communities.* San Francisco: Jossey-Bass.

Rudolph, Joseph. 1995. Intervention in Communal Conflicts. *Orbis* 39, no. 2:259–73.

Ruppe, David. 1999. Movement Grows to Fight Small Arms. <http://www.ABCNews.com>, October 7.

Russell, Philip L. 1995. The Chiapas rebellion. Austin, Tex.: Mexico Resource Center.

Russian Army Admits Fighting in Moldova Civil War; Romania Says It Has Assisted the Ex-Republic. 1992. *Minneapolis–St. Paul Star Tribune,* June 23, p. 1.

Russian Forces Fighting Alongside Ossetian Volunteers. 1992. *United Press International,* November 3, 1992.

Russians Take Up Their Burden. 1993. *Economist* 328 (July 24): 38–39.

Ryan, Stephen. 1995. *Ethnic Conflict and International Relations.* 2d ed. Aldershot, U.K.: Dartmouth.

———. 1992. The United Nations and the Resolution of Ethnic Conflict. In *Early Warning and Conflict Resolution,* edited by Kumar Rupesinghe and Michiko Kuroda. New York: St. Martin's, 105–35.

Salla, Michael. 1997. Creating the "Ripe Moment" in the East Timor Conflict. *Journal of Peace Research* 34, no. 4:449–66.

Salpeter, Eliahu. 1988. Israel Assesses the Damage. *The New Leader* 71 (June 13): 6–7.

Sample, Susan. 1997. Arms Races and Dispute Escalation: Resolving the Debate. *Journal of Peace Research* 34 (February): 7–22.

Sanjian, Gregory S. 1999. Promoting Stability of Instability? Arms Transfers and Regional Rivalries, 1950–91. *International Studies Quarterly* 43, no. 4 (December): 641–70.

———. 1995. A Fuzzy Systems Model of Arms Transfer Outcomes. *Conflict Management and Peace Science* 14:1–24.

Schraeder, Peter J. 1993. Ethnic Politics in Djibouti: From "Eye of the Hurricane" to "Boiling Cauldron." *African Affairs* 92:203–21.

———. 1992. Paramilitary Intervention. In *Intervention into the 1990s: U.S. Foreign Policy in the Third World*. 2d ed., edited by Peter J. Schraeder. Boulder, Colo.: Lynne Rienner, 131–51.

Seabury, Paul, and Angelo Codevilla. 1989. *War: Ends and Means*. New York: Basic.

Serbs Ad-Lib with MiG-21 Rockets. 1995. *Jane's Defence Weekly* 23 (May 13): 12.

Shalev, Aryeh. 1991. *The Intifadah: Causes and Effects*. Boulder, Colo.: Westview.

Shapiro, Margaret. 1992. Moldova Accuses Russia of Waging "Undeclared War." *Washington Post,* June 23, p. 1.

Sherwin, Ronald. 1983. Controlling Instability and Conflict through Arms Transfers: Testing a Policy Assumption. *International Interactions* 10:65–99.

Sherwin, Ronald and Edward Laurance. 1979. Arms Transfers and Military Capability. *International Studies Quarterly* 23 (June): 360–89.

Showdown in Punjab. 1988. *Economist* 307 (May 7): 27–28.

Sierra Leone: 1,200 Combatants Disarmed. 2001. *Africa News*. May 24.

Singer, Marshall. 1996. Sri Lanka's Ethnic Conflict. *Asian Survey* 36, no. 11:1146–55.

Singh, Jasjit, ed. 1995. *Light Weapons and International Security*. Delhi: Indian Pugwash Society and BASIC.

Siniora, Hanna. 1988. An Analysis of the Current Revolt. *Journal of Palestine Studies* 17 (Spring): 3–13.

SIPRI (Stockholm International Peace Research Institute). 1995 and 1991. *SIPRI Yearbook: World Armaments and Disarmament*. Oxford: Oxford University Press.

Sislin, John. 1994. Arms as Influence: The Determinants of Successful Influence. *Journal of Conflict Resolution* 38 (December): 665–89.

Sislin, John, Frederic S. Pearson, Jocelyn Boryczka, and Jeffrey Weigand. 1998. Patterns in Arms Acquisitions by Ethnic Groups in Conflict. *Security Dialogue* 29, no. 4:393–408.

Sislin, John, and Frederic S. Pearson. 1996. Arms, Mediation and Ethnopolitical Disputes. *Peace Review* 8, no. 4 (December): 541–46.

Sivard, Ruth. 1996. *World Military and Social Expenditures 1996*. 16th ed. Washington, D.C.: World Priorities.

Small, Melvin, and J. David Singer. 1985. Patterns in International Warfare, 1816–1980. In *International War,* edited by Melvin Small and J. David Singer. Homewood, Ill.: Dorsey Press, 7–19.

Smith, Anthony. 1993. The Ethnic Sources of Nationalism. In *Ethnic Conflict and International Security,* edited by Michael Brown. Princeton, N.J.: Princeton University Press, 27–41.

Smith, Chris. 2000. *The Conflict, Security and Development Group Bulletin*. Center for Defense Studies, King's College, University of London, no. 6 (June/July).

————. 1995. Light Weapons and Ethnic Conflict in South Asia. In Lethal Commerce. Edited by Jeffrey Boutwell, Michael Klare, and Laura Reed. Cambridge, Mass.: American Academy of Arts and Sciences.

Smucker, Philip. 1998. Ethnic Albanian Students Trade Books for Weapons. *(Pittsburgh) Post-Gazette*. December 27, p. 7.

Smyth, Frank. 1994. Arms for Rwanda: Blood Money and Geopolitics. *Nation* 258:585–88.

Sollenberg, Margareta, Peter Wallensteen, and Adres Jato. Major Armed Conflicts. In *SIPRI Yearbook 1999: Armaments, Disarmament and International Security*. Oxford: Oxford University Press, 15–25.

Spear, Joanna. 1996. Arms Limitations, Confidence-Building Measures, and Internal Conflict. In *The International Dimensions of Internal Conflict,* edited by Michael Brown. Cambridge, Mass.: MIT Press, 377–410.

Spriggs, Matthew. 1990. Bougainville, December 1989–January 1990: A Personal History. In *The Bougainville Crisis,* edited by R. J. May and Matthew Spriggs. Bathurst, Australia: Crawford House.

Sri Lanka Delays Lifting Emergency Decree in Tamil Areas. 1987. *New York Times.* August 16, p. 21.

Sri Lanka Introduces Crisis Measures. 2000. *Washington Post,* May 5, p. 22.

Sri Lanka: The War without End. 1994. *Asian Defence Journal* (October): 60–64.

Sri Lanka Wants Peace, Perhaps. 1999. *Economist* 353 (December 18): 35–36.

Stalinist Repressions Trigger Ossetian-Ingushi Conflict. 1992. *Itar-Tass,* November 2.

Stavenhagen, Rodolfo. 1996. *Ethnic Conflicts and the Nation–State*. New York: St. Martin's.

————. 1993. *The Ethnic Question: Conflicts, Development, and Human Rights*. Tokyo: United Nations University Press.

Stedman, Stephen John. 1996. Negotiation and Mediation in Internal Conflict. In *The International Dimensions of Internal Conflict,* edited by Michael Brown. Cambridge, Mass.: MIT Press, 341–76.

Stockwell, John. 1978. *In Search of Enemies: A CIA Story*. New York: Norton.

Stohl, Rachel. 2000. IRA Arms Inspected. *Weekly Defense Monitor* 4, no. 26 (June 29).

Stone, Martin. 1997. *The Agony of Algeria*. New York: Columbia University Press.

Sylvan, Donald. 1976. Consequences of Sharp Military Assistance Increases for International Conflict and Cooperation. *Journal of Conflict Resolution* 20 (September): 609–36.

Tambiah, S. J. 1986. *Sri Lanka: Ethnic Fratricide and the Dismantling of Democracy.* Chicago: University of Chicago Press.

Tamil Tigers' Bloody Assault Investigated. 1995. *Jane's Defence Weekly* 24 (July 15): 15.

Telephone interview by authors with Australian government official. 1995.

Tiglao, Rigoberto. 1995. Hidden Strength. *Far Eastern Economic Review* 158 (February 23): 22–26.

Touval, Saadia and I. William Zartman. 1985. *International Mediation in Theory and Practice*. Boulder, Colo.: Westview.

Tuareg Return. 1990. *Economist* 317 (October 13): 47–48.

21 Slain in Fierce Moldovan Clashes. 1992. *Toronto Star,* March 16, p. 12.

Unhappy Birthday. 1989. *Economist* 313 (December 2): 46–47.

United Nations General Assembly. 1992. Report of the Secretary General. General and Complete Disarmament: Transparency in Armaments. Report on the Register of Conventional Arms. A/47/342.

United Nations High Commissioner for Refugees. *Refworld.* <http://www.unhcr.ch/refworld/welcome.htm>.

Urigashvili, Besik. 1993. Abkhaz Troops Storm Sukhumi. E. Shevardnadze Accuses Russia of Aggression. *Current Digest of the Post-Soviet Press* 45 (April 14): 14–15. Translation. Originally published in *Izvestia,* March 17, p. 1.

————. 1995. *World Military Expenditures and Arms Transfers, 1993–1994.* Washington, D.C.: U.S. Government Printing Office.

U.S. Complicity in East Timor. 1999. *Arms Sales Monitor.* Federation of American Scientists Fund, no. 41, October. Washington, D.C.: Federation of American Scientists Fund.

U.S. House. 1995. Committee on International Relations. Subcommittee on Asian and Pacific Affairs. *What is the Most Effective Way for the United States Government to Help in Resolving the Sri Lankan Ethnic Conflict?* Report prepared by Marshall Singer. 104th Cong. *Sri Lanka in Turmoil: Implications of Intensified Conflict.* November 14.

Vachudova, Milada Anna. 1996. Peaceful Transformations in East-Central Europe. In *The International Dimensions of Internal Conflict,* edited by Michael Brown. Cambridge, Mass.: MIT Press, 69–105.

Van Evera, Stephen (1994). Hypotheses on Nationalism and War, *International Security* 18 (Spring): 5–39.

Vatikiotis, Michael. 1991. Troubled Province. *Far Eastern Economic Review* 151 (January 24): 20–21.

————. 1990. Ancient Enmities. *Far Eastern Economic Review* 148 (June 28): 12–13.

Volman, Daniel. 1993. The Role of Foreign Military Assistance in the Western Sahara War. In *International Dimensions of the Western Sahara Conflict.* Edited by Yahia Zoubir and Daniel Volman. Westport, Conn.: Praege, 151–68.

Von Gruber, Pamela. 1994. *Defence and Foreign Affairs Handbook.* London: International Media Corporation.

Walker, Jenonne. 1993. International Mediation of Ethnic Conflicts. In *Ethnic Conflict and International Security,* edited by Michael Brown. Princeton, N.J.: Princeton University Press, 165–80.

Wallensteen, Peter, and Margareta Sollenberg. 1997. Armed Conflicts, Conflict Termination, and Peace Agreements, 1989–96. *Journal of Peace Research* 34, no. 3:339–58.

————. 1995 After the Cold War: Emerging Patterns of Armed Conflict 1989–1994. *Journal of Peace Research* 32, no. 3: 345–60.

War Battered. 1994. *Economist* 332 (September 3): 44–45.

Weaver, Mary Ann. 1983. Terrorists Gain Support among Sri Lanka's Troubled Tamils. *Christian Science Monitor,* August 19, p. 5.

Weede, Erich, and Edward N. Muller. 1998. Rebellion, Violence, and Revolution: A Rational Choice Perspective. *Journal of Peace Research* 35, no. 1:43–59.

Weisman, Steven. 1987. Weapon Issue Stirs Doubt in Sri Lanka. *New York Times,* August 30, p. 11.

White House Weighs in on Code. 1999. *Arms Trade News* (July): 1.

With the Rebels. 1995. *Economist* 337 (October 14): 39–44.

Wood, Brian, and Johan Peleman. 1999. *The Arms Fixers: Controlling the Brokers and Shipping Agents.* Oslo: PRIO.

Woodward, Colin. 1998. Good Neighbors. *Bulletin of the Atomic Scientists* 54 (July/August): 13–15.

Wriggins, Howard. 1995. Sri Lanka: Negotiations in a Secessionist Conflict. In *Elusive Peace: Negotiating an End to Civil Wars,* edited by I. William Zartman. Washington, D.C.: Brookings Institution, 35–58.

Wurst, Jim. 1998. UN Lobbies for Coordination on Small Arms. *Basic Reports. Newsletter of British American Security Information Council,* no. 65 (August 14).

Year of Living Dangerously. 1988. *Economist* 309 (December 10): 50.

Zartman, I. William. 1995a. Dynamics and Constraints in Negotiations in Internal Conflicts. In *Elusive Peace: Negotiating an End to Civil Wars,* edited by I. William Zartman. Washington, D.C.: Brookings Institution, 3–29.

———, ed. 1995b. *Elusive Peace: Negotiating an End to Civil Wars.* Washington, D.C.: Brookings Institution.

———. 1995c. Conclusion: The Last Mile. In *Elusive Peace,* edited by I. William Zartman. Washington, D.C.: Brookings Institution, 332–46.

———. 1991. Conflict and Resolution: Contest, Cost, and Change. *The Annals of the American Academy of Political and Social Science* 518:11–22.

Zartman, I. William, and Saadia Touval. 1992. Mediation: The Role of Third-Party Diplomacy and Informal Peacemaking. In *Resolving Third World Conflict: Challenges for a New Era,* edited by Sheryl Brown and Kimber Schraub. Washington, D.C.: United States Institute of Peace Press, 241–61.

Index

Abkhazia, 37t, 145t
Abkhazians, 35t, 80, 145t
ACDA. *See* Arms Control and
Disarmament Agency
Aceh, 35t
Acholi, 36t, 149t
acquisitions calculations, 43–56; groups
in conflict, 43–52; states in conflict,
52–56
Afars, 35t, 146t
Afghan Freedom Fighters 5
Afghanistan, 1, 11, 37t; arms flow in, 165;
ethnopolitical conflicts, characteristics
of, 145t; violence, degree of, in, 36
Afghan weapons network, 73
African conflicts, 86
African Great Lakes region, 166
African National Congress, 36t
African regions, 153
aircraft, combat, 28t
AIS. *See* Islamic Salvation Army
AK-47 rifles, 2, 89, 99, 151, 170
Albania, 1, 89, 101–5, 140n6
Albanians, Kosovar 35t, 59, 63, 101–5,
114n15, 115n17, 160
Albanian Socialist Party, 103
Albright, Madeleine: on arms trade,
human costs of, 1, 11 on arms transfer
policy, 159
Algeria, 72–74

All-African Conference of Churches,
140n3
American Champion. *See* USN American
Champion
Anagnoson, Theodore: conflict analysis,
141n14; mediation, 123, 125, 141n9
Anglo-Irish, 152
Angola, 105–11; arms, financing of, 95;
arms movements, 37t, 38, 53t, 54t,
58n12, 95, 111, 115n21, 162; Cuban
intervention in, 18; violence, degree
of, in, 36, 89. *See also* National Union
for the Total Independence of Angola
(UNITA)
Animists, 149t
Annon, Kofi: on UN peacekeeping, 127
Arabization law, 73
Arab League States, 69
armament availability, impact of changes
in, 88–112, 136t; case studies, 98–111,
143n20; duration, 89–93; escalation,
95–98; intensity, 93–94; volatility,
111–12
armament effects, benefits of examining,
19–21
Armed Berber Movement (MAB), 73
armed conflicts: self-determination for, 8f
Armed Islamic Group (GIA), 72
Armenians, 145t
arms, diffusion of, 23–58

191

Index

About the Authors

John Sislin is Research Associate at the Center for International Development and Conflict Management at University of Maryland. He received his Ph.D. in 1993 from Indiana University. His research interests focus on the international arms trade and ethnic conflict. He has published several articles on the arms trade in the *Journal of Conflict Resolution, Peace Review*, and *Jane's Intelligence Review*. Dr. Sislin was a visiting assistant professor of Political Science at Bowling Green State University, Penn State University, and Southwest State University before joining the Center of International Development and Conflict Management in February 2000.

Frederic S. Pearson is Director of the Center for Peace and Conflict Studies and Program on Mediating Theory and Democratic Systems and Professor of Political Science at Wayne State University. Dr. Pearson received his Ph.D. in 1971 from the University of Michigan and has become a recognized authority in the fields of international military intervention, arms transfer effects on wars, and ethnic conflict analysis. Among his six books are *Arms and Warfare: Escalation, De-escalation, Negotiation* (1994 with Michael Brzoska) and *The Global Spread of Arms: Political Economy of International Security* (1994). In 2000 Dr. Pearson was designated a conflict resolution consultant to the U.S. Commission on National Security/21st Century in Washington. He lives in Detroit with his wife, Melvadean M. Pearson, and has three children.